R0021816979

CHICAGO PUBLIC LIBRARY
HAROLD WASHINGTON LIBRARY CENTER

R0021816979

```
TL
215
.R38    Chilton's repair &
C47       tune-up guide,
1982      Aries, Reliant,
          1981-82
```

DATE			

Business/Science/Technology
Division

© THE BAKER & TAYLOR CO.

CHILTON'S
REPAIR & TUNE-UP GUIDE
ARIES RELIANT 1981-82
Covers all Aries and Reliant models

Managing Editor KERRY A. FREEMAN, S.A.E.
Senior Editor RICHARD J. RIVELE, S.A.E.
Editor CARL CANFIELD

President WILLIAM J. BARBOUR
Executive Vice President JAMES A. MAIDES
Vice President and General Manager JOHN P. KUSHNERICK

CHILTON BOOK COMPANY
Radnor, Pennsylvania
19089

SAFETY NOTICE

Proper service and repair procedures are vital to the safe, reliable operation of all motor vehicles, as well as the personal safety of those performing repairs. This book outlines procedures for servicing and repairing vehicles using safe, effective methods. The procedures contain many NOTES, CAUTIONS and WARNINGS which should be followed along with standard safety procedures to eliminate the possibility of personal injury or improper service which could damage the vehicle or compromise its safety.

It is important to note that repair procedures and techniques, tools and parts for servicing motor vehicles, as well as the skill and experience of the individual performing the work vary widely. It is not possible to anticipate all of the conceivable ways or conditions under which vehicles may be serviced, or to provide cautions as to all of the possible hazards that may result. Standard and accepted safety precautions and equipment should be used when handling toxic or flammable fluids, and safety goggles or other protection should be used during cutting, grinding, chiseling, prying, or any other process that can cause material removal or projectiles.

Some procedures require the use of tools specially designed for a specific purpose. Before substituting another tool or procedure, you must be completely satisfied that neither your personal safety, nor the performance of the vehicle will be endangered.

Although information in this guide is based on industry sources and is as complete as possible at the time of publication, the possibility exists that the manufacturer made later changes which could not be included here. While striving for total accuracy, Chilton Book Company cannot assume responsibility for any errors, changes, or omissions that may occur in the compilation of this data.

PART NUMBERS

Part numbers listed in this reference are not recommendations by Chilton for any product by brand name. They are references that can be used with interchange manuals and aftermarket supplier catalogs to locate each brand supplier's discrete part number.

ACKNOWLEDGMENTS

Chilton Book Company wishes to express appreciation to the Chrysler Plymouth Division, Chrysler Motor Corporation, Detroit, Michigan, and the Dodge Division, Chrysler Motors Corporation, Detroit, Michigan for their generous assistance in the preparation of this book.

Copyright © 1982 by Chilton Book Company
All Rights Reserved
Published in Radnor, Pa., by Chilton Book Company
and simultaneously in Ontario, Canada
by Nelson Canada, Limited

TL
215
.R38
C47
1982

Manufactured in the United States of America
1234567890   1098765432

Chilton's Repair & Tune-Up Guide: Aries and Reliant 1981–82
ISBN 0-8019-7163-2 pbk
Library of Congress Catalog Card No. 81-70223

CONTENTS

1 General Information and Maintenance
- 1 How to Use this Book
- 1 Tools and Equipment
- 4 Routine Maintenance and Lubrication
- 17 How to buy a used car

2 Tune-Up
- 20 Tune-Up Procedures
- 23 Tune-Up Specifications

3 Engine and Engine Rebuilding
- 28 Engine Electrical System
- 30 Engine Service and Specifications
- 42 Engine Rebuilding

4 Emission Controls and Fuel System
- 61 Emission Control System and Service
- 66 Fuel System Service

5 Chassis Electrical
- 72 Accessory Service
- 77 Instrument Panel Service
- 78 Lights, Fuses and Flashers

58 Chilton's Fuel Economy and Tune-Up Tips

6 Clutch and Transaxle
- 80 Manual Transaxle
- 84 Clutch
- 86 Automatic Transaxle

7 Suspension and Steering
- 89 Front Suspension
- 93 Rear Suspension
- 95 Steering

8 Brakes
- 102 Front Brakes
- 104 Rear Brakes
- 108 Brake Specifications

9 Body
- 114 Repairing Scratches and Small Dents
- 118 Repairing Rust
- 124 Body Care

10 Troubleshooting
- 129 Problem Diagnosis

161 Appendix
165 Index

Quick Reference Specifications For Your Vehicle

Fill in this chart with the most commonly used specifications for your vehicle. Specifications can be found in Chapters 1 through 3 or on the tune-up decal under the hood of the vehicle.

Tune-Up

Firing Order_____

Spark Plugs:

    Type_____

    Gap (in.)_____

Point Gap (in.)_____

Dwell Angle (°)_____

Ignition Timing (°)_____

    Vacuum (Connected/Disconnected)_____

Valve Clearance (in.)

    Intake_____ Exhaust_____

Capacities

Engine Oil (qts)

    With Filter Change_____

    Without Filter Change_____

Cooling System (qts)_____

Manual Transmission (pts)_____

    Type_____

Automatic Transmission (pts)_____

    Type_____

Front Differential (pts)_____

    Type_____

Rear Differential (pts)_____

    Type_____

Transfer Case (pts)_____

    Type_____

FREQUENTLY REPLACED PARTS

Use these spaces to record the part numbers of frequently replaced parts.

PCV VALVE	OIL FILTER	AIR FILTER
Manufacturer_____	Manufacturer_____	Manufacturer_____
Part No._____	Part No._____	Part No._____

General Information and Maintenance

HOW TO USE THIS BOOK

This book is written to help the Aries/Reliant owner in performing maintenance, tune-ups and repairs on his vehicle. It will be helpful to both the amateur and experienced mechanic. Information on simple operations and more complex ones is given, allowing the user to try procedures which he or she feels confident in doing and graduating to the more difficult task as more experience is gained.

In addition to this book, a willingness to do your own work, and the time to do it right, there are a few other items you will have to be aware that you will need. A basic but complete set of metric and SAE hand tools is a must. For many repair operations the factory recommends special tools be used. A conventional tool can be substituted for the special tool in a lot of cases. For those operations requiring a special tool for which no substitution can be made, this fact is called to your attention in the text. Remember that whenever the left-side of the vehicle is referred to, it is the driver's side of the car and vice versa. Also, most screws and bolts are removed by turning them counterclockwise and tightened by turning them clockwise. Left-handed threads (the opposite of above) will be brought to your attention in the text.

Before you start any project, read the entire section in the book that deals with the particular job you wish to perform. Many times a description of the system and its operation is given. This will enable you to understand the function of the system you will be working on and what must be done to fix it. Reading the procedures beforehand will help you avoid problems and to learn about your Aries/Reliant while you are working on it.

TOOLS AND EQUIPMENT

It would be impossible to catalog each and every tool that you may need to perform all the operations included in this book. It would also not be wise for the amateur to rush out and buy an expensive set of tools on the theory that he may need one of them at some time. The best approach is to proceed slowly, gathering together a good quality set of those tools that are used most frequently. Don't be misled by the low cost of bargain tools. It is far better to spend a little more for quality, name brand tools. Forged wrenches, 10 or 12 point sockets and fine-tooth ratchets are by far preferable to their less expensive counterparts. As any good mechanic can tell you, there are a few worse experiences than trying to work on a car or truck with bad tools. Your

GENERAL INFORMATION AND MAINTENANCE

monetary savings will be far outweighed by frustration and mangled knuckles.

Begin accumulating those tools that are used most frequently; those associated with routine maintenance and tune-up. In addition to the normal assortment of screwdrivers and pliers, you should have the following tools for routine maintenance jobs:

1. SAE and Metric wrenches, sockets and combination open end/box end wrenches;
2. Jackstands—for support;
3. Oil filter wrench;
4. Oil filler spout or funnel;
5. Grease gun—for chassis lubrication;
6. Hydrometer—for checking the battery;
7. A low flat pan for draining oil;
8. Lots of rags for wiping up the inevitable mess.

In addition to the above items, there are several others that are not absolutely necessary, but are handy to have around. These include oil drying compound, a transmission funnel, and the usual supply of lubricants, antifreeze and fluids, although these can be purchased as needed. This is a basic list for routine maintenance, but only your personal needs can accurately determine your list of tools.

The second list of tools is for tune-ups. While the tools involved here are slightly more sophisticated, they need not be outrageously expensive. There are several inexpensive tach/dwell meters on the market that are every bit as good for the average mechanic as a $100.00 professional model. Just be sure that it goes to at least 1200–1500 rpm on the tach scale, and that it works on 4, 6, and 8-cylinder engines. A basic list of tune-up equipment could include:

1. Tach/dwell meter;
2. Spark plug wrench;
3. Timing light (preferably a DC light that works from the battery);
4. A set of flat feeler gauges;
5. A set of round wire spark plug gauges.

In addition to these basic tools, there are several other tools and gauges you may find useful. These include:

1. A compression gauge. The screw-in type is slower to use, but eliminates the possibility of a faulty reading due to escaping pressure;
2. A manifold vacuum gauge;
3. A test light;
4. An induction meter. This is used for determining whether or not there is current in a wire. These are handy for use if a wire is broken somewhere in a wiring harness. As a final note, you will probably find a torque wrench necessary for all but the most basic work. The beam type models are perfectly adequate, although the newer click type are more precise.

Special Tools

Normally, the use of special factory tools is avoided for repair procedures, since these are not readily available for the do-it-yourself mechanic. When it is possible to perform the job with more commonly available tools, it will be pointed out, but occasionally, a special tool was designed to perform a specific function and should be used. Before substituting another tool, you should be convinced that neither your safety nor the performance of the vehicle will be compromised.

Some special tools are available commercially from major tool manufacturers. Others for your Aries/Reliant can be purchased from your dealer or from Owatonna Tool Co., Owatonna, Minnesota 55060.

SERVICING YOUR VEHICLE SAFELY

It is virtually impossible to anticipate all of the hazards involved with maintenance and service but care and common sense will prevent most accidents.

The rules of safety for mechanics range from "don't smoke around gasoline," to "use the proper tool for the job." The trick to avoiding injuries is to develop safe work habits and take every possible precaution.

Dos

• Do keep a fire extinguisher and first aid kit within easy reach.
• Do wear safety glasses or goggles when cutting, drilling, grinding or prying. If you wear glasses for the sake of vision, they should be made of hardened glass that can serve also as safety glasses, or wear safety goggles over your regular glasses.
• Do shield your eyes whenever you work around the battery. Batteries contain sulphuric acid. In case of contact with the eyes or skin, flush the area with water or a mixture of water and baking soda and get medical attention immediately.
• Do use jackstands for any undercar service. Jacks are for raising vehicles; jackstands

GENERAL INFORMATION AND MAINTENANCE

are for making sure the vehicle stays raised until you want it to come down. Whenever your vehicle is raised, block the wheels remaining on the ground and set the parking brake.

• Do use adequate ventilation when working with any chemicals or hazardous materials.

• Do disconnect the negative battery cable when working on the electrical system. The secondary ignition system can contain up to 40,000 volts.

• Do follow manufacturer's directions whenever working with potentially hazardous materials. Both brake fluid and antifreeze are poisonous if taken internally.

• Do properly maintain your tools. Loose hammerheads, mushroomed punches and chisels, frayed or poorly grounded electrical cords, excessively worn screwdrivers, spread wrenches, cracked sockets, slipping ratchets, or faulty droplight sockets can cause accidents.

• Do use the proper size and type of tool for the job being done.

• Do when possible, pull on a wrench handle rather than push on it, and adjust your stance to prevent a fall.

• Do be sure that adjustable wrenches are tightly closed on the nut or bolt and pulled so that the face is on the side of the fixed jaw.

• Do select a wrench or socket that fits the nut or bolt. The wrench or socket should sit straight, not cocked.

• Do strike squarely with a hammer; avoid glancing blows.

• Do set the parking brake and block the drive wheels if the work requires the engine running.

Don'ts

• Don't run an engine in a garage or anywhere else without proper ventilation—EVER! Carbon monoxide is poisonous; it takes a long time to leave the human body and you can build up a deadly supply of it in your system by simply breathing in a little every day. You may not realize you are slowly poisoning yourself. Always use power vents, windows, fans or open the garage doors.

• Don't work around moving parts while wearing a necktie or other loose clothing. Short sleeves are much safer than long, loose sleeves; hard-toed shoes with neoprene soles protect your toes and give a better grip on slippery surfaces. Jewelry such as watches, fancy belt buckles, beads or body adornment of any kind is not safe working around a truck. Long hair should be hidden under a hat or cap.

• Don't use pockets for toolboxes. A fall or bump can drive a screwdriver deep into your body. Even a wiping cloth hanging from the back pocket can wrap around a spinning shaft or fan.

• Don't smoke when working around gasoline, cleaning solvent or other flammable material.

• Don't smoke when working around the battery. When the battery is being charged, it gives off explosive hydrogen gas.

• Don't use gasoline to wash your hands; there are excellent soaps available. Gasoline may contain lead, and lead can enter the body through a cut, accumulating in the body until you are very ill. Gasoline also removes all the natural oils from the skin so that bone dry hands will absorb oil and grease.

• Don't service the air conditioning system unless you are equipped with the necessary tools and training. The refrigerent, R-12, is extremely cold when compressed, and when released into the air will instantly freeze any surface it contacts, including your eyes. Although the refrigerant is normally non-tox R-12 becomes a deadly poisonous gas in the presence of an open flame. One good whiff of the vapors from burning refrigerant can be fatal.

SERIAL NUMBER IDENTIFICATION

Vehicle

The vehicle serial number is located on a plate on the top left side of the instrument panel and is visible through the windshield.

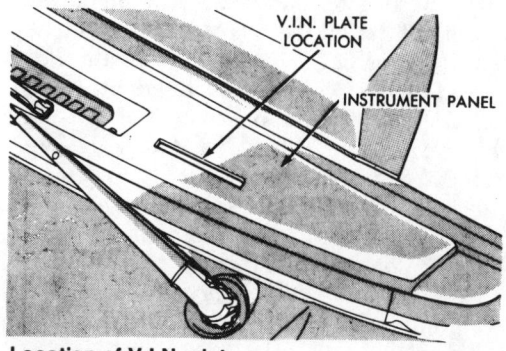

Location of V.I.N. plate

4 GENERAL INFORMATION AND MAINTENANCE

Engine Identification Number

All engine assemblies carry an engine identification number. The 135 cu. in. (2.2 Liter) engine identification number is located on the left rear face of the block directly under the head. The 156 cu. in. (2.6 Liter) identification number is located on the left side of the block between the core plug and the rear of the block.

Engine Serial Number

In addition to the EIN, each number has a serial number, which must be referred to when ordering engine replacement parts. The serial number on the 135 cu. in. (2.2 Liter) engine is located on the rear face of the block directly below the head. On the 156 cu. in. (2.6 Liter) engine it is located on the right front side of the engine block, adjacent to the exhaust manifold.

Transaxle Serial Number

All transaxles have a serial number that must be used when ordering replacement parts. Model A-412 manual transaxle serial number is located on the top of the housing between the timing window and the differential.

NOTE: *The model A-412 manual transaxle was discontinued in January 1981.*

Model A-460 manual transaxle serial number is indicated on a metal tag attached to the front side of the transaxle. On the automatic transaxle the serial number is on the pad just above the oil pan at the rear of the transaxle.

ROUTINE MAINTENANCE

Air Cleaner

The air cleaner consists of a metal housing with a paper filter on the 2.2 liter engine and a carbon filter on the 2.6 Mitsubishi engine. If your Aries/Reliant is eqiupped with a paper filter it should be replaced at 15,000 miles. Vehicles equipped with the Mitsubishi 2.6L engine should have the air filter changed at 30,000 miles.

NOTE: *If your vehicle is used under severe conditions, such as stop and go driving in dusty conditions, extensive idling, short trips, or sustained high speed driving during hot weather, these intervals should be halved.*

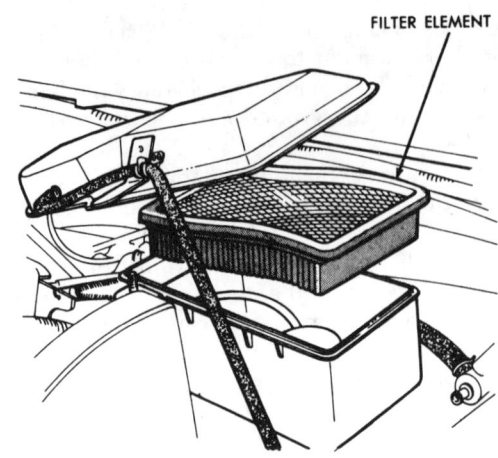

2.2L engine air cleaner filter

2.6L engine air cleaner filter

Clean the inside of the air cleaner housing before installing the air filter. A clogged air filter will decrease gas mileage, engine efficiency, and increase exhaust emissions.

PCV Valve

The PVC valve regulates the amount of air flowing through the engine crankcase to the carburetor by increasing or restricting the flow as determined by engine speed and manifold vacuum. It is recommended that the PCV valve be cleaned and inspected every 15,000 miles or 1 year.

Evaporative Control System

The function of the Evaporative Control System is to prevent gasoline vapors from the

GENERAL INFORMATION AND MAINTENANCE

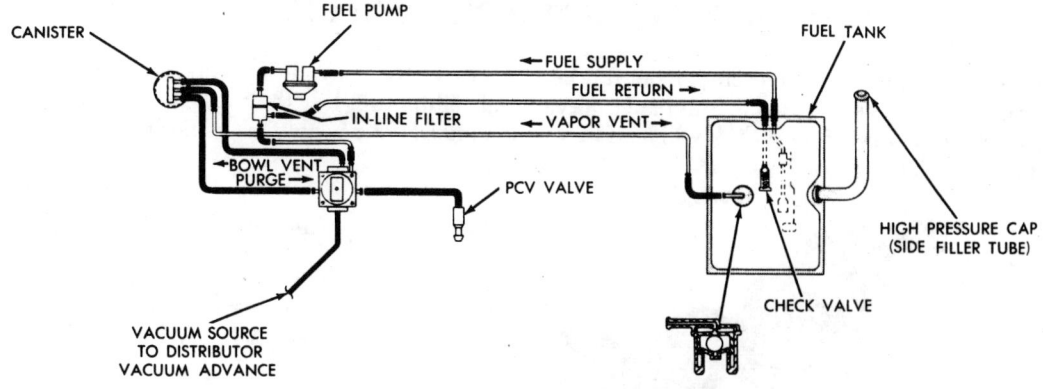

Evaporation control system—2.2L engine

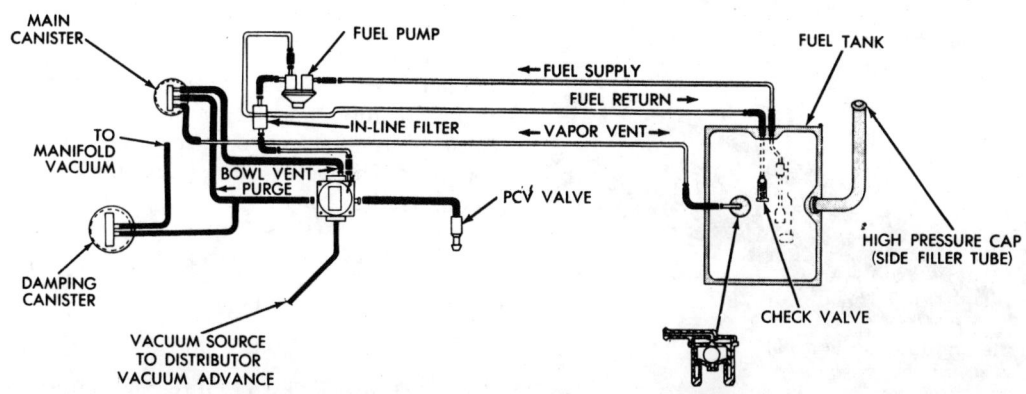

Evaporation control system—2.6L engine

fuel tank to escape into the atmosphere. The only periodic maintenance required is the replacement of the fiberglass filter in the bottom of the canister. This need only be done in extremely dusty conditions otherwise no maintenance is required.

Drive Belts

Check the drive belts every 15,000 miles for evidence of wear such as cracking, fraying, and incorrect tension.

Determine the belt tension at a point halfway between the pulleys by pressing on the belt with moderate thumb pressure. The belt should deflect about ¼–½ in. at this point. If the deflection is found to be too much or too little, loosen the accessory's slotted adjusting bracket bolt. If the hinge bolt is very tight, it too may have to be loosened. Use a wooden hammer handle or a broomstick to lever the accessory closer to or farther away from the engine to provide the correct tension. Do not use a metal prybar, which may damage the component. When the belt adjustment is correct, tighten the bolts and recheck the adjustment. Although it is better to have the belt too loose than too tight, a loose belt may place a high impact load on a bearing due to the whipping or snapping action of the belt.

CAUTION: *Be careful not to overtighten the drive belts, as this will damage the driven component's bearings.*

Hose Replacement
ALL MODELS

CAUTION: *Do not perform this procedure on a hot or warm engine, otherwise serious injury could result.*

1. Drain the cooling system.
2. Remove the top hose from the radiator neck and the thermostat housing.
3. Remove the bottom hose from the water pump and the bottom of the radiator.
4. Check the hoses for damage. Replace them as necessary.
5. Installation is the reverse of removal.

6 GENERAL INFORMATION AND MAINTENANCE

HOW TO SPOT WORN V-BELTS

V-Belts are vital to efficient engine operation—they drive the fan, water pump and other accessories. They require little maintenance (occasional tightening) but they will not last forever. Slipping or failure of the V-belt will lead to overheating. If your V-belt looks like any of these, it should be replaced.

Cracking or weathering

This belt has deep cracks, which cause it to flex. Too much flexing leads to heat build-up and premature failure. These cracks can be caused by using the belt on a pulley that is too small. Notched belts are available for small diameter pulleys.

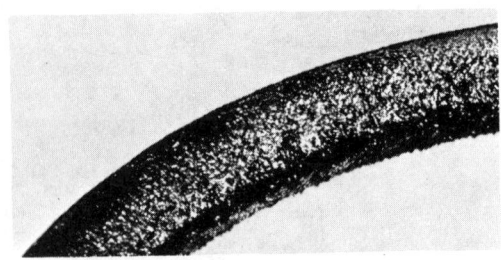

Softening (grease and oil)

Oil and grease on a belt can cause the belt's rubber compounds to soften and separate from the reinforcing cords that hold the belt together. The belt will first slip, then finally fail altogether.

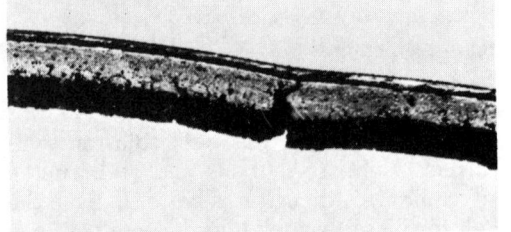

Glazing

Glazing is caused by a belt that is slipping. A slipping belt can cause a run-down battery, erratic power steering, overheating or poor accessory performance. The more the belt slips, the more glazing will be built up on the surface of the belt. The more the belt is glazed, the more it will slip. If the glazing is light, tighten the belt.

Worn cover

The cover of this belt is worn off and is peeling away. The reinforcing cords will begin to wear and the belt will shortly break. When the belt cover wears in spots or has a rough jagged appearance, check the pulley grooves for roughness.

Separation

This belt is on the verge of breaking and leaving you stranded. The layers of the belt are separating and the reinforcing cords are exposed. It's just a matter of time before it breaks completely.

GENERAL INFORMATION AND MAINTENANCE

HOW TO SPOT BAD HOSES

Both the upper and lower radiator hoses are called upon to perform difficult jobs in an inhospitable environment. They are subject to nearly 18 psi at under hood temperatures often over 280°F., and must circulate nearly 7500 gallons of coolant an hour—3 good reasons to have good hoses.

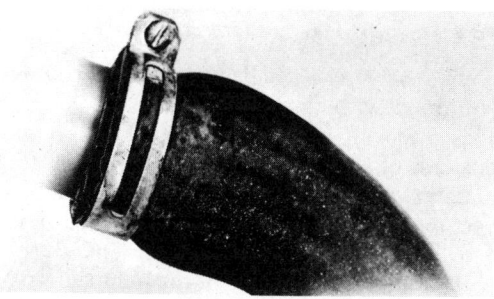

Swollen hose

A good test for any hose is to feel it for soft or spongy spots. Frequently these will appear as swollen areas of the hose. The most likely cause is oil soaking. This hose could burst at any time, when hot or under pressure.

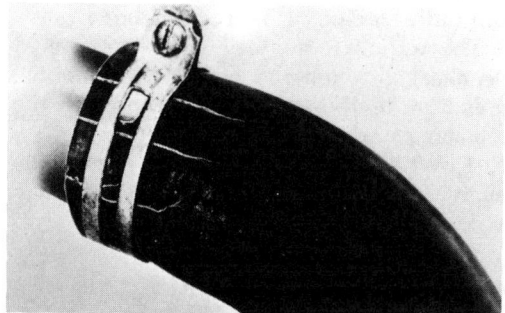

Cracked hose

Cracked hoses can usually be seen but feel the hoses to be sure they have not hardened; a prime cause of cracking. This hose has cracked down to the reinforcing cords and could split at any of the cracks.

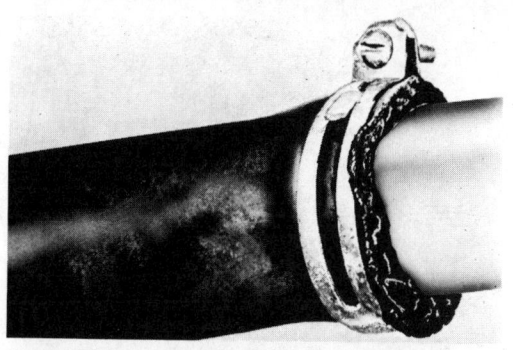

Frayed hose end (due to weak clamp)

Weakened clamps frequently are the cause of hose and cooling system failure. The connection between the pipe and hose has deteriorated enough to allow coolant to escape when the engine is hot.

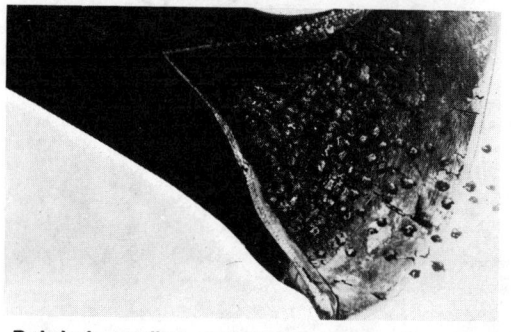

Debris in cooling system

Debris, rust and scale in the cooling system can cause the inside of a hose to weaken. This can usually be felt on the outside of the hose as soft or thinner areas.

8 GENERAL INFORMATION AND MAINTENANCE

Air Conditioning

This book contains no repair or maintenance procedures for the air conditioning system. It is recommended that any such repairs be left to the experts, whose personnel are well aware of the hazards and who have the proper equipment.

CAUTION: *The compressed refrigerant used in the air conditioning system expands into the atmosphere at a temperature of −21.7°F or lower. This will freeze any surface, including your eyes, that it contacts. In addition, the refrigerant decomposes into a poisonous gas in the presence of flame. Do not open or disconnect any part of the air conditioning system.*

NOTE: *Run the air conditioner for a few minutes, every two weeks or so, during the cold months. This avoids the possibility of the compressor seals drying out from lack of lubrication.*

You can safely determine if your car's air conditioning system needs service. The following system checks apply only to the factory-installed units. If your car has an aftermarket air conditioner, you will have to consult the manufacturer of the unit for the correct procedure to use.

Fluid Level Checks

ENGINE OIL

The engine oil level is checked with the dipstick which is located on the radiator side of the engine.

NOTE: *The oil should be checked before the engine is started or five minutes after the engine has shut off. This gives the oil time to drain back to the oil pan and prevents an inaccurate oil level reading.*

Remove the dipstick from the tube, wipe it clean, and insert it back into the tube. Remove it again and observe the oil level. It should be maintained within the full range on the dipstick.

CAUTION: *Do not overfill the crankcase. This will cause oil aeration and loss of oil pressure.*

Be sure to use only oil with an SE rating.

TRANSMISSION

Some early Aries/Reliant vehicles may be eqiupped with the A-412 manual transaxle. This unit can be identified by locating the position of the starter which is found on the radiator side of the engine compartment. If it becomes recessary to add fluid to this unit, SAE 80W-90 gear lube is recommended.

If your vehicle has the A-460 manual transaxle, the starter will be next to the firewall. When it becomes necessary to add fluid to this unit, Dexron® II is recommended.

The automatic transaxle fluid level should be checked when the engine is at normal operating temperature. It is checked in the following manner:

(1) With the parking brake engaged and the engine idling shift the transmission through

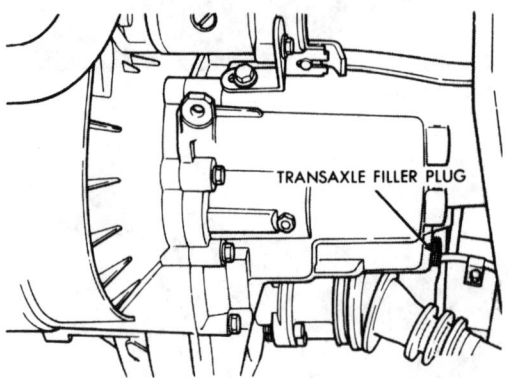

A-412 manual transaxle filler plug

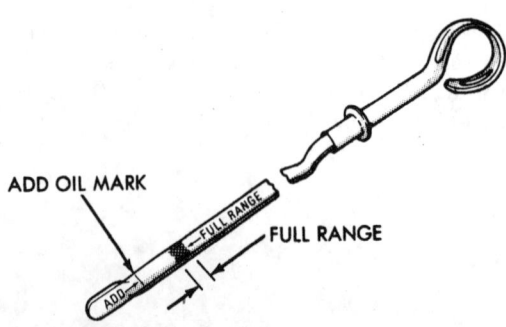

Oil dipstick

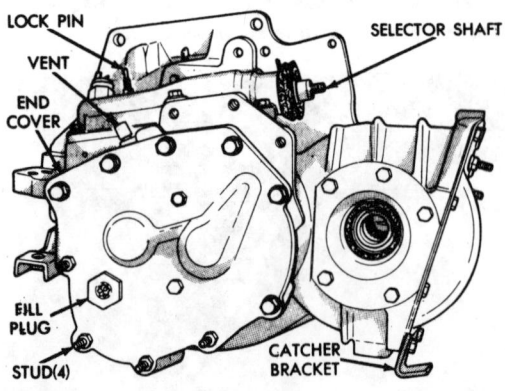

A-460 manual transaxle filler plug

GENERAL INFORMATION AND MAINTENANCE

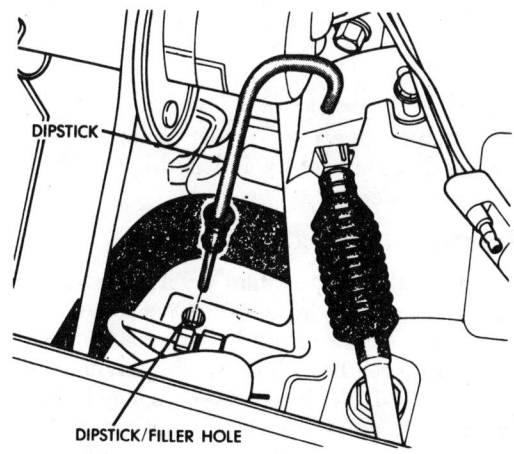

Dipstick filler hole

the shift pattern and return it to the Park position.

(2) Remove the dipstick. The fluid level should be between the ADD and Full mark, but never above the Full mark.

BRAKE MASTER CYLINDER

Once every 7500 miles or 12 months check the brake fluid level in the master cylinder. The master cylinder is mounted either on the firewall or the brake booster, and is divided into two reservoirs. The fluid must be maintained at the bottom of the split ring.

Remove the two master cylinder caps and fill to the bottom of the split rings using DOT 3 brake fluid. If the brake fluid is chronically low there may be a leak in the system which should be investigated immediately.

NOTE: *Brake fluid absorbs moisture from the air, which reduces its effectiveness and causes corrosion. Never leave the brake fluid can or master cylinder uncovered any longer than necessary. Brake fluid also damages paint. If any is spilled, it should be washed off immediately with clear, cold water.*

COOLANT

The coolant should be checked at each fuel stop, to prevent the possibility of overheating and serious engine damage. If not, it should at least be checked once each month.

The cooling system was filled at the factory with a high quality coolant solution that is good for year around operation and protects the system from freezing. To check the coolant level simply look into the expansion tank.

CAUTION: *The radiator coolant is under pressure when hot. To avoid the danger of physical injury, coolant level should be checked or replenished only when cool. To remove the cap, slowly rotate it counterclockwise to the stop, but do not press down. Wait until all pressure is released (indicated when the hissing sound stops) then press down on the cap while continuing to rotate it counterclockwise. Wear a glove or use a thick rag for protection.*

If coolant is needed, a 50/50 mix of ethylene glycol antifreeze and water should be used. Alcohol or methanol base coolants are specifically not recommended. Antifreeze solution should be used all year, even in summer, to prevent rust and to take advantage of the solution's higher boiling point compared to plain water. This is imperative on air conditioned models; the heater core can freeze if it isn't protected.

CAUTION: *Never add large quantities of cold coolant to a hot engine. A cracked engine block may result. If it is absolutely necessary to add coolant to a hot engine do so only with the engine idling and add only small quantities at a time.*

Each year the cooling system should be serviced as follows:

1. Wash the radiator cap and filler neck with clean water.

2. Check the coolant for proper level and freeze protection.

3. Have the system pressure tested. If a replacement cap is installed, be sure that it conforms to the original specifications.

4. Tighten the hose clamps and inspect all hoses. Replace hoses that are swollen, cracked or otherwise deteriorated.

5. Clean the frontal area of the radiator

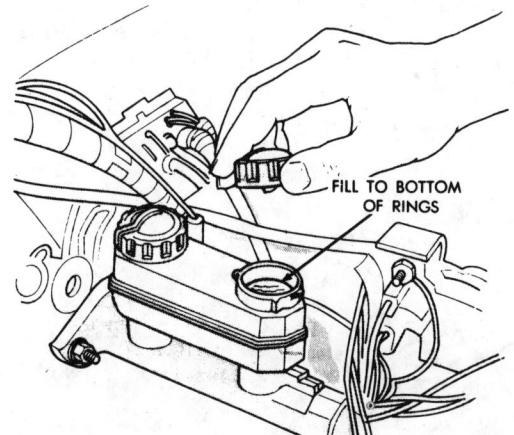

Checking the master cylinder fluid level

10 GENERAL INFORMATION AND MAINTENANCE

core and the air conditioning condenser, if so equipped.

After 3 years or 25,000 miles the system should be drained, flushed, and refilled. If the system is dirty, rusty, or contains sediment, clean and flush it with a reliable cooling system cleaner.

NOTE: *After this initial drain and refill, the service interval is reduced to 2 years or 15,000 miles.*

1. Run the engine with the cap removed and the heater on until operating temperature is reached (indicated by heat in the upper radiator hose).
2. With the engine stopped, open the radiator drain cock located at the bottom of the radiator, and (to speed the draining) the engine block drains, if any.
3. Completely drain the coolant, and close and drain cocks.
4. Add sufficient clean water to fill the system. Run the engine and drain and refill the system as often as necessary until the drain water is nearly colorless.
5. Add sufficient ethylene glycol coolant to provide the required freezing and corrosion protection (at least a 44% solution protecting to −20°F). Fill the radiator to the cold level. Run the engine with the cap removed until normal operating temperature is reached.
6. Check the hot level.
7. Install the cap.

DIFFERENTIAL FLUID CHECK

Under normal operating conditions, lubricant changes are not required for this unit. However, fluid level checks are required every 7500 miles or 12 months whichever comes first. The fluid level should be within ⅜ in. of the bottom of the fill plug.

NOTE: *A rod with a U bend at the end can be made to check the fluid level.*

If it becomes necessary to add or replace the fluid use only Dexron® II automatic transmission fluid.

STEERING GEAR

The manual steering gear is permanently lubricated at the factory and periodic lubrication is not needed.

POWER STEERING RESERVOIR

Maintain the proper fluid level as indicated on the cap of the reservoir. Check the level with the engine off and at normal ambient temperature. The dipstick should indicate "FULL COLD". If the reservoir needs fluid refill with power steering fluid, Part No. 2084329 or its equivalent.

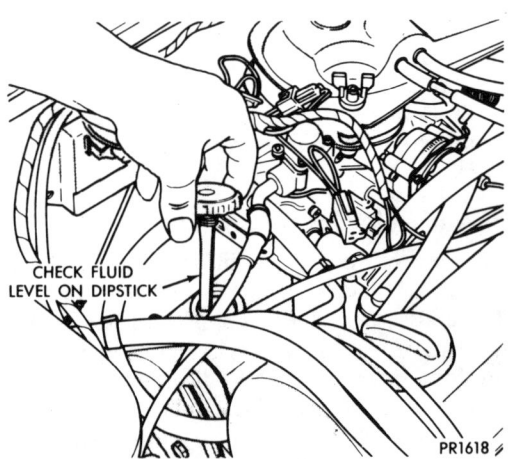

Checking the power steering fluid level

BATTERY

Two types of batteries are used, Standard and Maintenance Free.

Both batteries are equipped with a "Test Charge Indicator". This indicator is a built in hydrometer, which replaces one of the battery filler caps in the Standard battery and is permanently installed in the cover on the Maintenance Free battery.

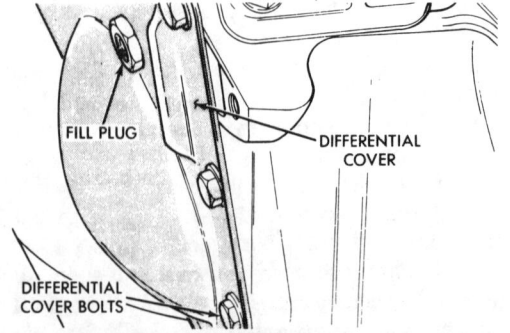

Differential (cover) fill plug location

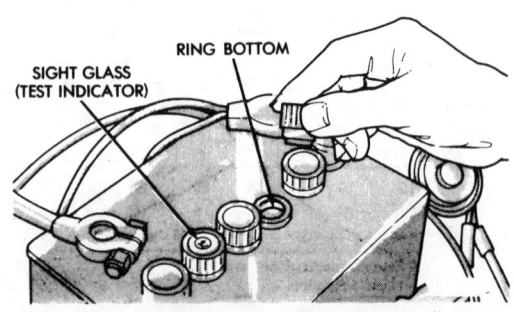

Check the fluid level—standard battery

GENERAL INFORMATION AND MAINTENANCE

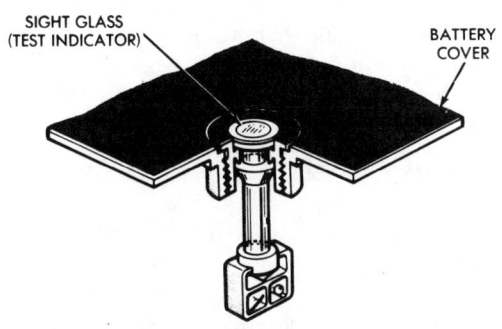

Test indicator—maintenance free battery

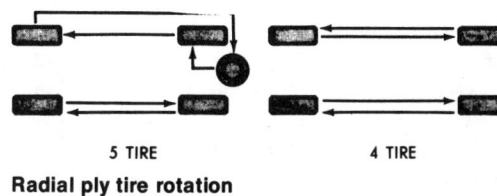

Radial ply tire rotation

Visual inspection of the indicator sight glass will aid in determining battery condition. The indicator shows green if the battery is above 75–80 percent of being fully charged, and "Dark" if it needs charging. A light yellow means the battery requires water or may need replacing.

For Standard batteries, check the fluid level in each cell every 2 months (more often in hot weather or on long trips). If the water is low, fill it to the bottom of the filler well with distilled water.

Tires

Check the air pressure in your car's tires every few weeks. Make sure that the tires cool, as you will get a false reading when the tires are heated because air pressure increases with temperature. A decal located on the glovebox door will tell you the proper tire pressure for the standard equipment tires. Naturally, when you replace tires you will want to get the correct tire pressures for the new ones from the dealer or manufacturer. It pays to buy a tire pressure gauge to keep in the car, since those at service stations are often inaccurate or broken.

While you are checking the tire pressure, take a look at the tread. The tread should be wearing evenly across the tire. Excessive wear in the center of the tread indicates overinflation. Excessive wear on the outer edges indicates underinflation. An irregular wear pattern is usually a sign of incorrect front wheel alignment or wheel balance. A front end that is out of alignment will usually pull the car to one side of a flat road when the steering wheel is released. Incorrect wheel balance is usually accompanied by high speed vibration. Front wheels which are out of balance will produce vibration in the steering wheel, while unbalanced rear wheels will result in floor or truck vibration.

Rotating the tires every 6000 miles or so will result in increased thread life. Use the correct pattern for your tire switching. Most automotive experts are in agreement that radial tires are better all around performers, giving prolonged wear and better handling. An added benefit which you should consider when purchasing tires is that radials have less rolling resistance and can give up to a 10% increase in fuel economy over a bias-ply tire.

Tires of different construction should never be mixed. Always replace tires in sets of four or five when switching tire types and never

Capacities

Year	Engine Displacement Cu In.	Engine Crankcase (qts) With Filter	Engine Crankcase (qts) Without Filter	Transaxle (pts) Manual	Transaxle (pts) Automatic	Differential (pts)	Gasoline Tank (gals)	Cooling System (qts) W/ AC	Cooling System (qts) W/O AC
1981	135	4	4	4	15	2①	13	7	7
1981	156	5	4½	4	17	2①	13	8½	8½
1982	135	4	4	4	15	2①	13	7	7
1982	156	5	4½	4	15	2①	13	8½	8½

GENERAL INFORMATION AND MAINTENANCE

substitute a belted tire for a bias-ply, a radial for a belted tire, etc. An occasional pressure check and periodic rotation could make your tires last much longer than a neglected set and maintain the safety margin which was designed into them.

Fuel Filter Replacement

There are two fuel filters in the present system. One is part of the gauge unit assembly located inside the fuel tank on the suction end of the tube. This filter normally does not need servicing, but may be replaced if necessary.

The second filter is an in-line paper element, disposable type, located in the fuel line just above the fuel pump.

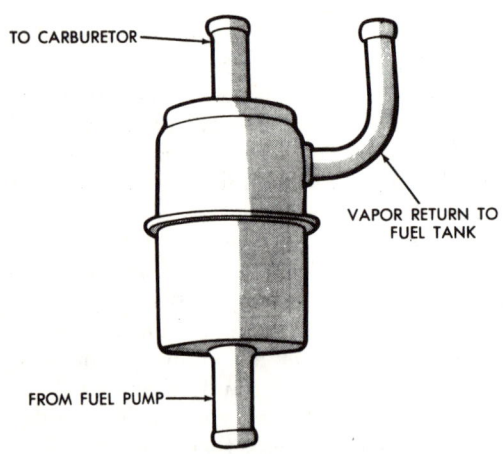

Fuel filter vapor separator 2.2L engine

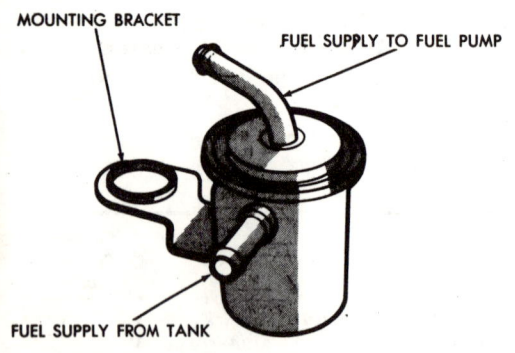

Fuel filter 2.6L engine

A plugged fuel filter can limit the speed at which a vehicle can be driven and cause hard starting.

Remove the filter as follows:
1. Remove the hose clamps from each end of the filter.
2. Remove the old filter and hoses.

3. Install the new filter, hoses, and tighten the hose clamps.
4. Start your vehicle and check for leaks.

LUBRICATION

Oil and Fuel Recommendations

Chrysler recommends the use of a high quality heavy-duty detergent oil having the proper viscosity for prevailing temperatures and an SE service rating. The SE rating will be printed on the top of the can. Under the classification system adopted by the American Petroleum Institute (API) in May, 1970, SE is the highest designation given for normal passenger car use. The S stands for passenger car and the second letter denotes a more specific application. SA oil, for instance, contains no additives and is suitable only for very light-duty. Oil designated MS may also be used, since this was the highest classification under the old API rating system. Pick your oil viscosity with regard to the anticipated temperatures during the period before your next oil change. Using the chart, choose the oil viscosity for the lowest expected temperature. You will be assured of easy cold starting and sufficient engine protection.

Oil Viscosity Selection Chart

	Anticipated Temperature Range	*SAE Viscosity*
Multi-grade	Above 32°F	10W—40 10W—50 20W—40 20W—50 10W—30
	May be used as low as −10°F	10W—30 10W—40
	Consistently below 10°F	5W—20 5W—30
Single-grade	Above 32°F	30
	Temperature between +32°F and −10°F	10W

Fuel should be selected for the brand and octane which performs without pinging. Find your exact engine model in the "General Engine Specifications" chart in Chapter 3.

GENERAL INFORMATION AND MAINTENANCE

Fuels of the same octane rating have varying anti-knock qualities. Thus, if your engine knocks or pings, try switching brands of gasoline before trying a more expensive higher octane fuel.

Your engine's fuel requirements can change with time, due to carbon buildup which changes the compression ratio. If switching brands or grades of gas doesn't work, check the ignition timing. If it is necessary to retard timing from specifications, don't change it more than about four degrees. Retarded timing will reduce power output and fuel mileage and increase engine temperature.

Fluid Changes

OIL CHANGES

The recommended mileage figures for Aries/Reliant oil and filter changes are 7,500 miles or 12 months whichever comes first, assuming normal driving conditions. If your vehicle is being used under dusty conditions, frequent trailer pulling, excessive idling, or stop and go driving, it is recommended to change the oil and filter at 3,000 miles.

Always drain the oil after the engine has been running long enough to bring it to operating temperature. Hot oil will flow easier and more contaminants will be removed along with the oil than if it were drained cold. You will need a large capacity drain pan, which you can purchase at any store which sells automotive parts. Another necessity is containers for the used oil. You will find that plastic bottles, such as those used for bleach or fabric softener, make excellent storage jugs. One ecologically desirable solution to the used oil disposal problem is to find a cooperative gas station owner who will allow you to dump your used oil into his tank. Another is to keep the oil for use around the house as a preservative on fences, railroad tie borders, etc.

Chrysler recommends changing both the oil and filter during the first oil change and the filter every other oil change thereafter. For the small price of an oil filter, it's cheap insurance to replace the filter at every oil change. One of the larger filter manufacturers points out in its advertisements that not changing the filter leaves one quart of dirty oil in the engine. This claim is true and should be kept in mind when changing your oil.

1. Run the engine until it reaches normal operating temperature.
2. Jack up the front of the car and support it on jack stands.
3. Slide a drain pan of at least 6 quarts capacity under the oil pan.
4. Loosen the drain plug. It is located in the lowest point of the oil pan. Turn the plug out by hand. By keeping an inward pressure on the plug as you unscrew it, oil won't escape past the threads and you can remove it without being burned by hot oil.
5. Allow the oil to drain completely and then install the drain plug. Don't overtighten the plug, or you'll be buying a new pan or a replacement plug for stripped threads.
6. Using a strap wrench, remove the oil filter. Keep in mind that it's holding about one quart of dirty, hot oil.
7. Empty the old filter into the drain pan and dispose of the filter.
8. Using a clean rag, wipe off the filter adapter on the engine block. Be sure that the rag doesn't leave any lint which could clog an oil passage.
9. Coat the rubber gasket on the filter with fresh oil. Spin it onto the engine *by hand;* when the gasket touches the adapter surface give it another ½–¾ turn. No more, or you'll squash the gasket and it will leak.
10. Refill the engine with the correct amount of fresh oil. See the "Capacities" chart.
11. Crank the engine over several times and then start it. Do not race the engine. If the oil pressure "idiot light" doesn't go out or the pressure gauge shows zero, shut the engine down and find out what's wrong.
12. If the oil pressure is OK and there are no leaks, shut the engine off and lower the car.
13. Wait a few minutes and check the oil level. Add oil, as necessary, to bring the level up to Fill.

TRANSMISSION

Manual

Under normal operating conditions the fluid installed at the factory will give satisfactory lubrication for the life of the vehicle. Oil changes therefore, are not necessary unless the lubricant has become contaminated with water.

Automatic

No service is required under normal operating conditions. If fluid is needed use only Dexron® II automatic transmission fluid.

14 GENERAL INFORMATION AND MAINTENANCE

DIFFERENTIAL

Under normal operating conditions, lubricant changes in the unit are not required. However, fluid level checks should be made at 7,500 miles or 12 months, whichever comes first.

Chassis Greasing

Chassis greasing can be performed with a pressurized grease gun or it can be performed at home using a hand-operated grease gun. Wipe the fittings clean before greasing, in order to prevent the possibility of forcing any dirt into the component.

Ball joint and steering linkage are semipermanently lubricated at the factory with a special grease. They should be regreased every 30,000 miles or 3 years whichever comes first.

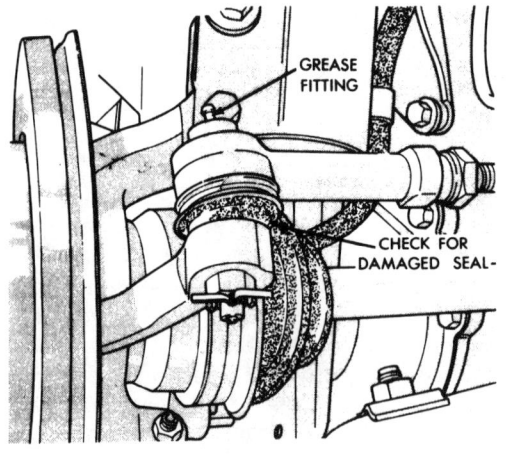

Tie rod seal and grease fitting

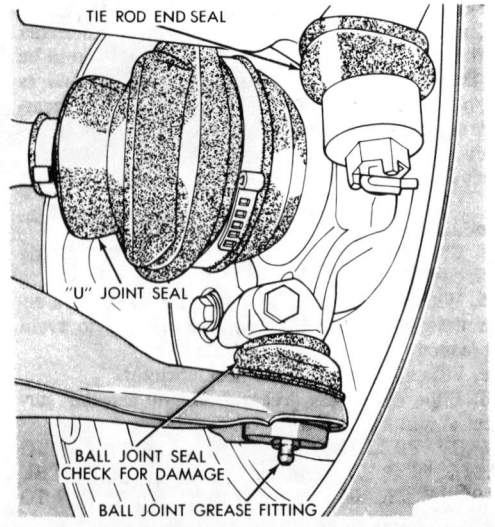

Front suspension ball joint seal and grease fitting

When regreasing is necessary, use only special long life chassis grease such as Multi-Mileage lubricant Part No. 2525035 or its equivalent.

Front Wheel Bearings

Your Aries or Reliant is equipped with permanently sealed front wheel bearings. There is no periodic adjustment for these units.

The rear wheel bearings should be inspected whenever the drums are removed to inspect or service the brakes, or at least every 30,000 miles. For lubrication procedures of these bearings refer to Chapter 8.

TOWING

The Aries or Reliant can be towed from either the front or rear. If the vehicle is towed from the front for an extended distance make sure the parking brake is completely released.

Manual transmission vehicles may be towed on the front wheels at speeds up to 35 mph, for a distances not to exceed 15 miles, provided the transmission is in neutral and the driveline has not been damaged. The steering wheel must be clamped in a straight ahead position.

CAUTION: *Do not use the steering column lock to secure front wheel position for towing.*

Automatic transmission vehicles may be towed on the front wheels at speeds not to exceed 25 mph for a period of 15 miles.

CAUTION: *If this requirement cannot be met the front wheels must be placed on a dolly.*

JACKING

The standard jack utilizes special receptacles located at the body sills to accept the scissors jack supplied with the vehicle for emergency road service. The jack supplied with the car should never be used for any service operation other than tire changing. Never get under the car while it is supported by only a jack. Always block the wheels when changing tires.

The service operations in this book often require that one end or the other, or both, of the car be raised and safely supported. The ideal method, of course, would be a hydraulic hoist. Since this is beyond both the

GENERAL INFORMATION AND MAINTENANCE

JUMP STARTING A DEAD BATTERY

The chemical reaction in a battery produces explosive hydrogen gas. This is the safe way to jump start a dead battery, reducing the chances of an accidental spark that could cause an explosion.

Jump Starting Precautions

1. Be sure both batteries are of the same voltage.
2. Be sure both batteries are of the same polarity (have the same grounded terminal).
3. Be sure the vehicles are not touching.
4. Be sure the vent cap holes are not obstructed.
5. Do not smoke or allow sparks around the battery.
6. In cold weather, check for frozen electrolyte in the battery.
7. Do not allow electrolyte on your skin or clothing.
8. Be sure the electrolyte is not frozen.

Jump Starting Procedure

1. Determine voltages of the two batteries; they must be the same.
2. Bring the starting vehicle close (they must not touch) so that the batteries can be reached easily.
3. Turn off all accessories and both engines. Put both cars in Neutral or Park and set the handbrake.
4. Cover the cell caps with a rag—do not cover terminals.
5. If the terminals on the run-down battery are heavily corroded, clean them.
6. Identify the positive and negative posts on both batteries and connect the cables in the order shown.
7. Start the engine of the starting vehicle and run it at fast idle. Try to start the car with the dead battery. Crank it for no more than 10 seconds at a time and let it cool off for 20 seconds in between tries.
8. If it doesn't start in 3 tries, there is something else wrong.
9. Disconnect the cables in the reverse order.
10. Replace the cell covers and dispose of the rags.

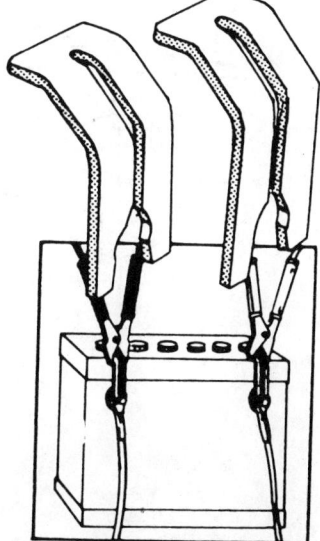

Side terminal batteries occasionally pose a problem when connecting jumper cables. There frequently isn't enough room to clamp the cables without touching sheet metal. Side terminal adaptors are available to alleviate this problem and should be removed after use.

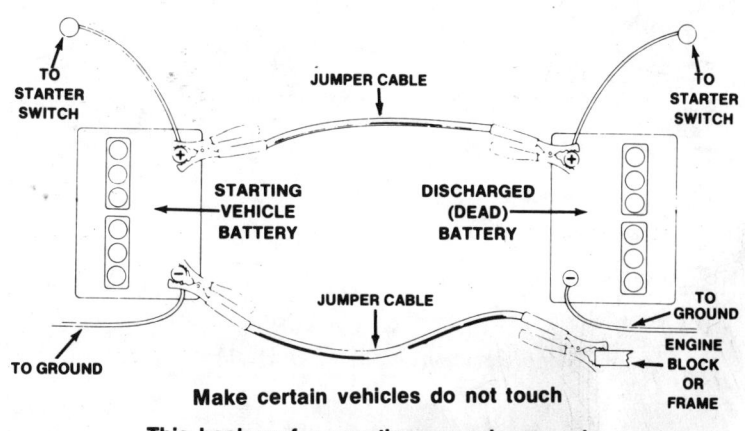

Make certain vehicles do not touch

This hook-up for negative ground cars only

16 GENERAL INFORMATION AND MAINTENANCE

resource and requirement of the do-it-yourselfer, a small hydraulic, screw or scissors jack will suffice for the procedures in this guide. Two sturdy jackstands should be acquired if you intend to work under the car at any time. An alternate method of raising the car would be drive-on ramps. These are available commercially or can be fabricated from heavy boards or steel. Be sure to block the wheels when using ramps.

CAUTION: *Concrete blocks are not recommended for supporting the car. They are likely to crumble if the load is not evenly distributed. Boxes and milk crates of any description must not be used to support the car!*

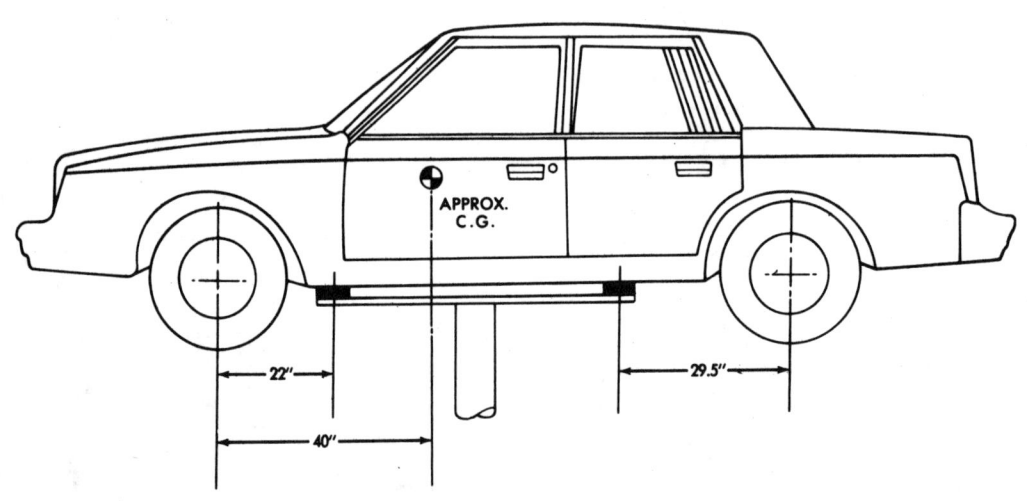

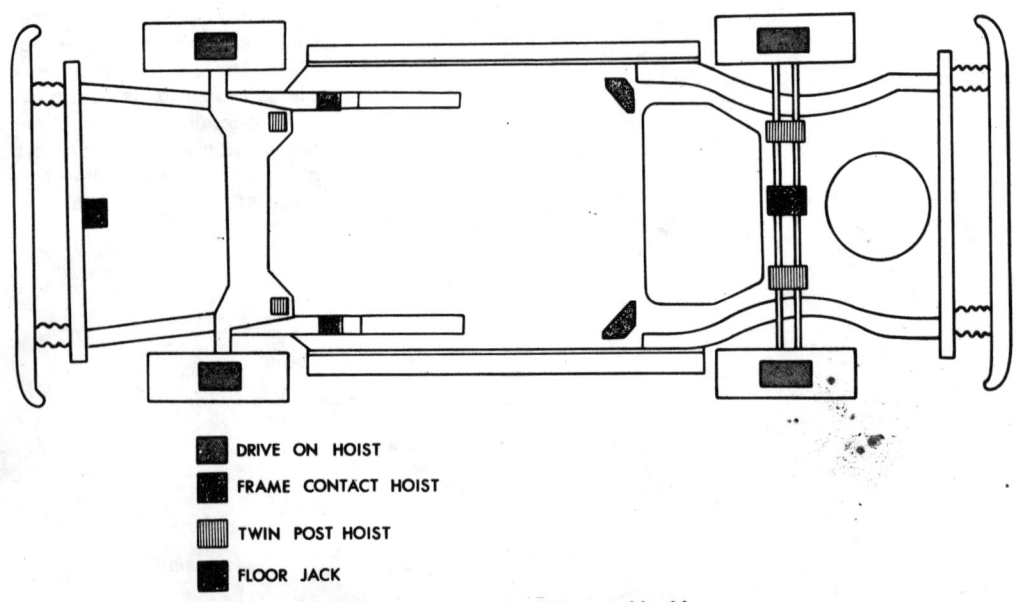

■ DRIVE ON HOIST
■ FRAME CONTACT HOIST
▥ TWIN POST HOIST
■ FLOOR JACK

Support locations for lifting and jacking

GENERAL INFORMATION AND MAINTENANCE

HOW TO BUY A USED CAR

Many people believe that a two or three year old used car is a better buy than a new car. This may be true; the new car suffers the heaviest depreciation in the first two years, but is not old enough to present a lot of costly repair problems. Whatever the age of the used car you might want to buy, this section and a little patience will help you select one that should be safe and dependable.

TIPS

1. First decide what model you want, and how much you want to spend.
2. Check the used car lots and your local newspaper ads. Privately owned cars are usually less expensive, however you will not get a warranty that, in most cases, comes with a used car purchased from a lot.
3. Never shop at night. The glare of the lights make it easy to miss faults on the body caused by accident or rust repair.
4. Try to get the name and phone number of the previous owner. Contact him/her and ask about the car. If the owner of the lot refuses this information, look for a car somewhere else.

A private seller can tell you about the car and maintenance. Remember, however, there's no law requiring honesty from private citizens selling used cars. There is a law that forbids the tampering with or turning back the odometer mileage. This includes both the private citizen and the lot owner. The law also requires that the seller or anyone transferring ownership of the car must provide the buyer with a signed statement indicating the mileage on the odometer at the time of transfer.

5. Write down the year, model and serial number before you buy any used car. Then dial 1-800-424-9393, the toll free number of the National Highway Traffic Safety Administration, and ask if the car has ever been included on any manufacturer's recall list. If so, make sure the needed repairs were made.
6. Use the "Used Car Checklist" in this section and check all the items on the used car you are considering. Some items are more important than others. You know how much money you can afford for repairs, and, depending on the price of the car, may consider doing any needed work yourself. Beware, however, of trouble in areas that will affect operation, safety or emission. Problems in the "Used Car Checklist" break down as follows:

1-8: Two or more problems in these areas indicate a lack of maintenance. You should beware.

9-13: Indicates a lack of proper care, however, these can usually be corrected with a tune-up or relatively simple parts replacement.

14-17: Problems in the engine or transmission can be very expensive. Walk away from any car with problems in both of these areas.

7. If you are satisfied with the apparent condition of the car, take it to an independent diagnostic center or mechanic for a complete check. If you have a state inspection program, have it inspected immediately before purchase, or specify on the bill of sale that the sale is conditional on passing state inspection.
8. Road test the car—refer to the "Road Test Checklist" in this section. If your original evaluation and the road test agree—the rest is up to you.

USED CAR CHECKLIST

NOTE: *The numbers on the illustrations refer to the numbers on this checklist.*

1. *Mileage:* Average mileage is about 12,000 miles per year. More than average mileage may indicate hard usage. 1975 and later catalytic converter equipped models may need converter service at 50,000 miles.
2. *Paint:* Check around the tailpipe, molding and windows for overspray indicating that the car has been repainted.
3. *Rust:* Check fenders, doors, rocker panels, window moldings, wheelwells, floorboards, under floormats, and in the trunk for signs of rust. Any rust at all will be a problem. There is no way to check the spread of rust, except to replace the part or panel.
4. *Body appearance:* Check the moldings, bumpers, grille, vinyl roof, glass, doors, trunk lid and body panels for general overall condition. Check for misalignment, loose holdown clips, ripples, scratches in glass, rips or patches in the top. Mismatched paint, welding in the trunk, severe misalignment of body panels or ripples may indicate crash work.
5. *Leaks:* Get down and look under the car. There are no normal "leaks", other than water from the air conditioning condenser.
6. *Tires;* Check the tire air pressure. A common trick is to pump the tire pressure up

18 GENERAL INFORMATION AND MAINTENANCE

to make the car roll easier. Check the tread wear, open the trunk and check the spare too. Uneven wear is a clue that the front end needs alignment. See the troubleshooting chapter for clues to the causes of tire wear.

7. *Shock absorbers:* Check the shock absorbers by forcing downward sharply on each corner of the car. Good shocks will not allow the car to bounce more than twice after you let go.

8. *Interior:* Check the entire interior. You're looking for an interior condition that agrees with the overall condition of the car. Reasonable wear is expected, but be suspicious of new seatcovers on sagging seats, new pedal pads, and worn armrests. These indicate an attempt to cover up hard use. Pull back the carpets and look for evidence of water leaks or flooding. Look for missing hardware, door handles, control knobs etc. Check lights and signal operations. Make sure all accessories (air conditioner, heater, radio etc.) work. Check windshield wiper operation.

9. *Belts and Hoses:* Open the hood and check all belts and hoses for wear, cracks or weak spots.

10. *Battery:* Low electrolyte level, corroded terminals and/or cracked case indicate a lack of maintenance.

11. *Radiator:* Look for corrosion or rust in the coolant indicating a lack of maintenance.

12. *Air filter:* A dirty air filter usually means a lack of maintenance.

13. *Ignition Wires:* Check the ignition wires for cracks, burned spots, or wear. Worn wires will have to be replaced.

14. *Oil level:* If the oil level is low, chances are the engine uses oil or leaks. Beware of water in the oil (cracked block), excessively thick oil (used to quiet a noisy engine), or thin, dirty oil with a distinct gasoline smell (internal engine problems).

15. *Automatic Transmission:* Pull the transmission dipstick out when the engine is running. The level should read "Full", and the fluid should be clear or bright red. Dark brown or black fluid that has distinct burnt odor, signals a transmission in need of repair or overhaul.

16. *Exhaust:* Check the color of the exhaust smoke. Blue smoke indicates, among other problems, worn rings; black smoke can indicate burnt valves or carburetor problems. Check the exhaust system for leaks; it can be expensive to replace.

17. *Spark Plugs:* Remove one of the spark plugs (the most accessible will do). An engine in good condition will show plugs with a light tan or gray deposit on the firing tip. See the color Tune-Up tips section for spark plug conditions.

ROAD TEST CHECK LIST

1. *Engine Performance:* The car should be peppy whether cold or warm, with adequate power and good pickup. It should respond smoothly through the gears.

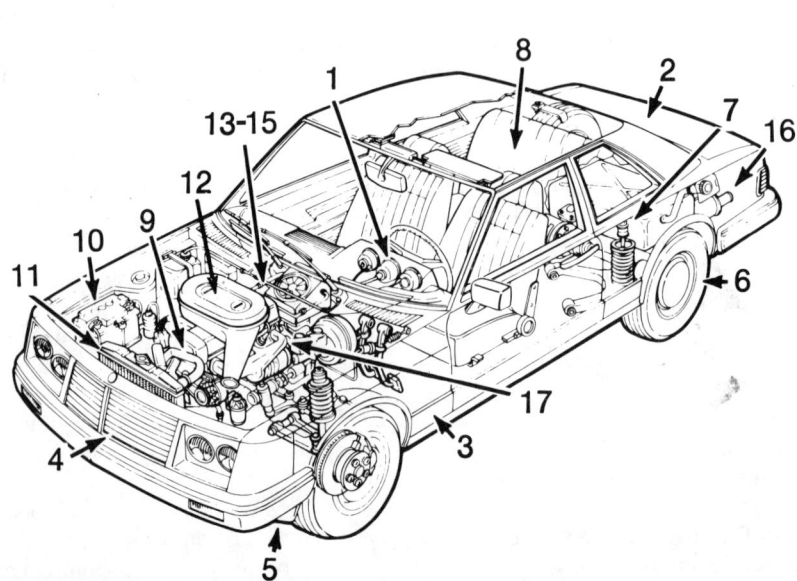

You should check these points when buying a used car. The "Used Car Checklist" gives an explanation of the numbered items

GENERAL INFORMATION AND MAINTENANCE

2. *Brakes:* They should provide quick, firm stops with no noise, pulling or brake fade.

3. *Steering:* Sure control with no binding, harshness, or looseness and no shimmy in the wheel should be expected. Noise or vibration from the steering wheel when turning the car means trouble.

4. *Clutch (Manual Transmission):* Clutch action should give quick, smooth response with easy shifting. The clutch pedal should have about 1–1½ inches of free-play before it disengages the clutch. Start the engine, set the parking brake, put the transmission in first gear and slowly release the clutch pedal. The engine should begin to stall when the pedal is one-half to three-quarters of the way up.

5. *Automatic Transmission:* The transmission should shift rapidly and smoothly, with no noise, hesitation, or slipping.

6. *Differential:* No noise or thumps should be present. Differentials have no "normal" leaks.

7. *Driveshaft, Universal Joints:* Vibration and noise could mean driveshaft problems. Clicking at low speed or coast conditions means worn U-joints.

8. *Suspension:* Try hitting bumps at different speeds. A car that bounces has weak shock absorbers. Clunks mean worn bushings or ball joints.

9. *Frame:* Wet the tires and drive in a straight line. Tracks should show two straight lines, not four. Four tire tracks indicate a frame bent by collision damage. If the tires can't be wet for this purpose, have a friend drive along behind you and see if the car appears to be traveling in a straight line.

Tune-Up

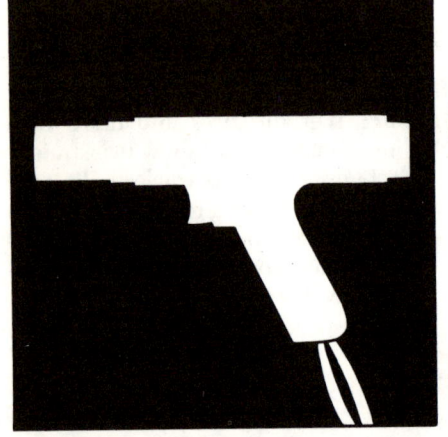

TUNE-UP PROCEDURES

Neither tune-up nor troubleshooting can be considered independently since each has a direct relationship with the other.

It is advisable to follow a definite and thorough tune-up procedure. Tune-up consists of three separate steps: Analysis, the process of determining whether normal wear is responsible for performance loss, and whether parts require replacement or service; parts replacement or service; and adjustment, where engine adjustments are performed.

The manufacturer's recommended interval for tune-ups is every 30,000 miles. This interval should be shortened if the car is subjected to severe operating conditions such as trailer pulling or stop and start driving, or if starting and running problems are noticed. It is assumed that the routine maintenance described in Chapter 1 has been kept up, as this will have an effect on the results of the tune-up. All the applicable tune-up steps should be followed, as each adjustment complements the effects of the others. If the tune-up (emission control) sticker in the engine compartment disagrees with the information presented in the "Tune-up Specifications" chart in this chapter, the sticker figures must be followed. The sticker information reflects running changes made by the manufacturer during production.

Troubleshooting is a logical sequence of procedures designed to locate a particular case of trouble. The "Troubleshooting" section in Chapter 10 is general in nature (applicable to most vehicles), yet specific enough to locate the problem.

It is advisable to read the entire chapter before beginning a tune-up, although those who are more familiar with tune-up procedures may wish to go directly to the instructions.

Spark Plugs

Rough idle, hard starting, frequent engine miss at high speeds and physical deterioration are all indications that the plugs should be replaced.

The electrode end of a spark plug is a good indicator of the internal condition of your car's engine. If a spark plug is fouled, causing the entine to misfire, the problem will have to be found and corrected. Often, "reading" the plugs will lead you to the cause of the problem. Spark plug conditions and probable causes are listed in the color section.

NOTE: *A small amount of light tan or rust*

TUNE-UP 21

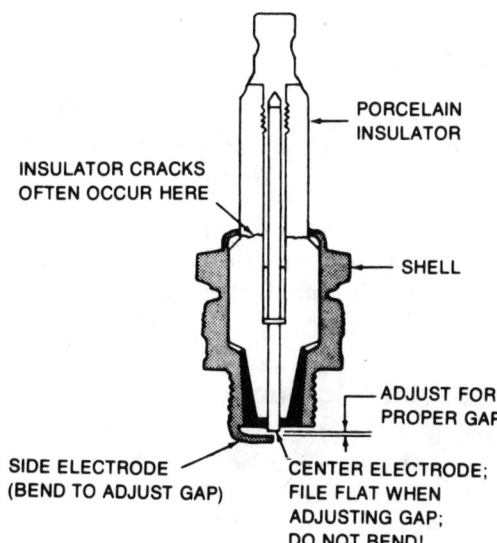

Cross section of a spark plug

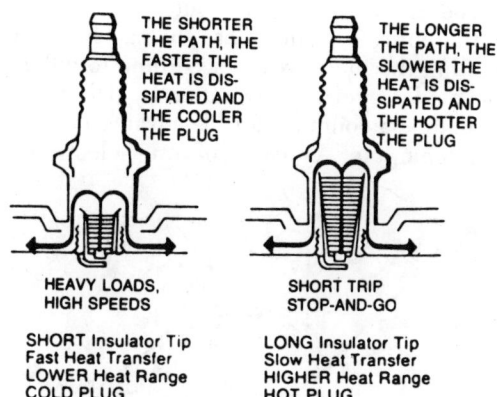

Spark plug heat range

are checked or newly installed. Never assume that new plugs are correctly gapped.

1. Before removing the spark plugs, number the plug wires so that the correct wire goes on the plug when replaced. This can be done with pieces of adhesive tape.
2. Next, clean the area around the plugs by brushing or blowing with compressed air. You can also loosen the plugs a few turns and crank the engine to blow the dirt away.
3. Disconnect the plug wires by twisting and pulling on the rubber cap, not on the wire.
4. Remove each plug with a rubber-insert spark plug socket. Make sure that the socket is all the way down on the plug to prevent it from slipping and cracking the porcelain insulator.
5. After removing each plug, evaluate its condition. A spark plug's useful life is approximately 30,000 miles with electronic ignition. Thus, it would make sense to replace a plug if it has been in service that long. If the plug is to be replaced, refer to the "Tune-up Specifications" chart for the proper spark plug type. The numbers indicate heat range; hotter running plugs have higher numbers.

Pull on the rubber boot to remove the spark plug wire, not the wire itself

red colored deposits at the electrode end of the plug is normal. These plugs need not be renewed unless they are severely worn.

Heat range is a term used to describe the cooling characteristcs of spark plugs. Plugs with longer nosed insulators take a longer time to dissipate heat than plugs with shorter nosed insulators. These are termed "hot" or "cold plugs, respectively. It is generally advisable to use the factory recommended plugs. However, in conditions of extremely hard use (cross-country driving in summer) going to the next cooler heat range may be advisable. If most driving is done in the city or over short distances, go to the next hotter heat range plug to eliminate fouling. If in doubt concerning the substitution of spark plugs, consult your Chrysler dealer.

Spark plugs should be gapped when they

Keep the socket straight on the plug

22 TUNE-UP

6. If the plugs are to be reused, file the center and side electrodes flat with a fine, flat point file. Heavy or baked on deposits can be carefully scraped off with a small knife blade or the scraper tool on a combination spark plug tool. It is often suggested that plugs be tested and cleaned on a service station sandblasting machine; however, this piece of equipment is becoming rare. Check the gap between the electrodes with a round wire spark plug gapping guage. Do not use a flat feeler gauge; it will give an inaccurate reading. If the gap is not as specified, use the bending tool on the spark plug gap gauge to bend the outside electrode. Be careful not to bend the electrode too far or too often, because excessive bending may cause the electrode to break off and fall into the combustion chamber. This would require removing the cylinder head to reach the broken piece, and could also result in cylinder wall, piston ring, or valve damage.

CAUTION: *Never bend the center electrode of the spark plug. This will break the insulator and render the plug useless.*

7. Clean the threads of old plugs with a wire brush. Lubricate the threads with a drop of oil.
8. Screw the plugs in finger tight, and then tighten them with the spark plug socket. Be very careful not to overtighten them. Just snug them in.
9. Reinstall the wires. If, by chance, you have forgotten to number the plug wires, refer to the "Firing Order" illustrations in Chapter 3.

Electronic Ignition

Models using the 2.2 Liter engine are equipped with the "Electronic Fuel Control System" This consists of a Spark Control Computer, various engine sensors, and a specially calibrated carburetor. The function of this system is to provide a way for the entine to burn a correct air-fuel mixture.

The Spark Control Computer is the heart of the entire system. It has the capability of igniting the fuel mixture according to different modes of engine operation by delivering an infinite amount of variable advance curves. The computer consists of one electronic

Use a wire gauge to check the electrode gap

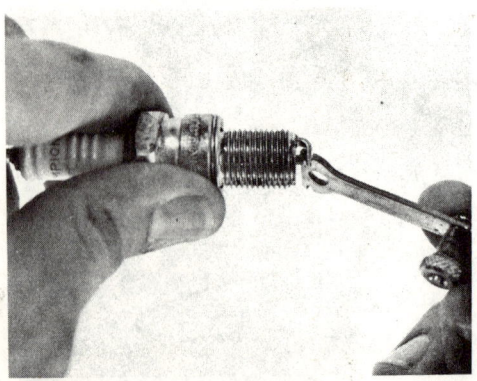
Adjust the electrode gap by bending the side electrode.

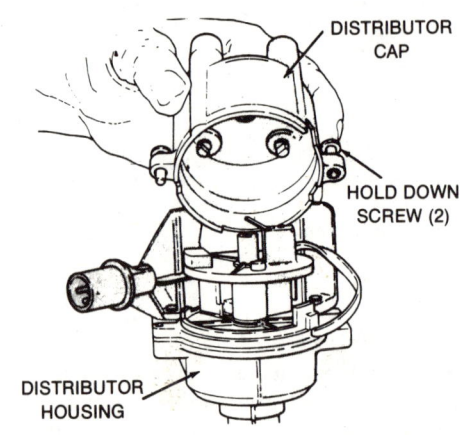
Distributor

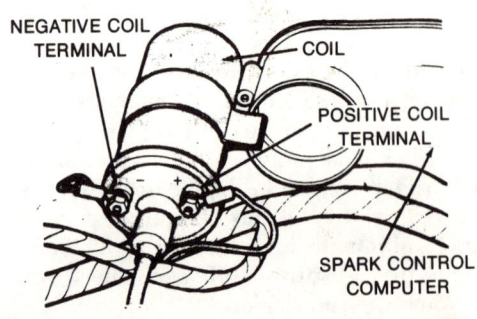
Ignition coil

Tune-Up Specifications

When analyzing compression test results, look for uniformity among cylinders rather than specific pressures.

Year	No. Cyl Displacement (cu. in.)	Spark plugs Type	Gap (in.)	Distributor Point Dwell (deg.)	Distributor Point Gap (in.)	Ignition timing (deg.) ▲ Man Trans	Ignition timing (deg.) ▲ Auto Trans ●	Valves Intake Opens ■ (deg.)	Fuel Pump Pressure (psi)	Idle speed (rpm) ▲ Man Trans	Idle speed (rpm) ▲ Auto Trans ●
1981	4-135	P65-PR4	.035	Electronic		10B	10B	12	4½-6	900	900
1981	4-156	P65-PR4	.035	Electronic		—	7B	25	4½-6	—	800
1982	4-135	P65-PR4	.035	Electronic		10B	10B	16	4½-6	900	900
1982	4-156	RN-12Y	.035	Electronic		—	7B	25	4½-6	—	800

▲ See text for procedure
● Figure in parentheses indicates California engine
■ All figures Before Top Dead Center

TUNE-UP 23

TUNE-UP

printed circuit board, which simultaneously receives signals from all the sensors and within milliseconds, analyzes them to determine how the engine is operating and then advances or retards the timing.

The 2.6 Liter engine uses a system that consists of the battery, ignition switch, coil, and IC igniter (electronic control unit), built into the distributor, spark plugs and inter-component wiring. Primary current is switched by the IC igniter in response to timing signals produced by a magnetic pickup.

The distributor is equipped with both centrifugal and vacuum advance mechanisms. The centrifugal advance is located below the rotor assembly, and has governor weights that move in and out with changes in engine speed. As speed increases the weights move outward and cause the reluctor to rotate ahead of the distributor shaft, this advances ignition timing.

The vacuum advance has a spring loaded diaphragm connected to the breaker assembly. The diaphragm is actuated against the spring pressure by carburetor vacuum pressure. When the vacuum increases, the diaphragm causes the movable breaker assembly to pivot in a direction opposite to distributor rotation, advancing the ignition timing.

Ignition Timing

Timing should be checked at each tune-up. Timing isn't likely to change very much with electronic ignition.

If your vehicle is equipped with the A-412 transaxle, the timing marks are located on the flywheel with the pointer on the access hole. All other manual and automatic transaxles have a notch on the torque converter or flywheel, with the numerical timing marks on the bell housing.

Models equipped with the 2.6 liter engine having the timing marks on the counter balance and the numerical pointer attached to the block.

A stroboscopic (dynamic) timing light must be used, because static lights are too inaccurate for emission controlled engines.

There are three basic types of timing light available. The first is a simple neon bulb with two wire connections. One wire connects to the spark plug terminal and the other plugs into the end of the spark plug wire for the No. 1 cylinder, thus connecting the light in series with the spark plug. This type of light

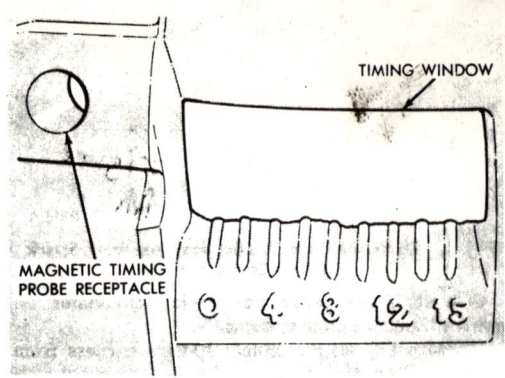

Timing mark location all manual and automatic transaxles except A-412

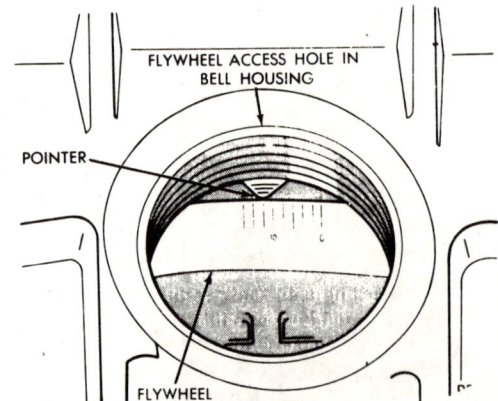

Timing mark location A-412 transaxle

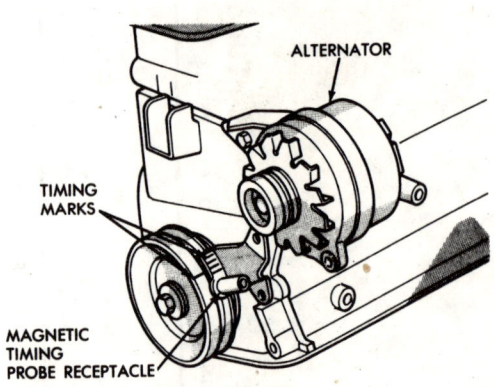

Timing marks 2.6L engine

is pretty dim and must be held close to the timing marks to be seen. It has the advantage of low price. The second type operates from the car's battery; two alligator clips connect to the battery terminals, while an adapter enables a third clip to be connected to the No. 1 spark plug and wire. This type provides a bright flash which can be seen even in bright sunlight. The third type replaces the battery current with 110 volt house current.

TUNE-UP 25

Some timing lights have other features built into them, such as dwell meters or tachometers. These are nice, in that they reduce the tangle of wires under the hood when you're working, but may duplicate the functions of tools you already have. One worthwhile feature, which is becoming more of a necessity with higher voltage ignition systems, is an inductive pickup. The inductive pickup clamps around the No. 1 spark plug wire, sensing the surges of high voltage electricity as they are sent to the plug. The advantage is that no mechanical connection is inserted between the wire and the plug, which eliminates false signals to the timing light. A timing light with an inductive pickup should be used on electronic ignition systems.

To check and adjust the timing:

1. Warm the engine to normal operating temperature. Shut off the engine and connect the timing light to the No. 1 spark plug. Do not under any circumstances pierce a wire to hook up a light.

2. Clean off the timing marks and mark the pulley or damper notch and the timing scale with white chalk or paint. The timing notch on the damper or pulley can be elusive. Bump the engine around with the starter or turn the crankshaft with a wrench on the front pulley bolt to get it to an accessible position.

NOTE: *The 2.2 Liter engine has its timing marks on the flywheel and bell housing.*

3. Disconnect and plug the vacuum advance hose at the distributor, to prevent any distributor advance. The vacuum line is the rubber hose connected to the metal cone-shaped canister on the side of the distributor. A short screw, pencil, or a golf tee can be used to plug the hose.

4. Start the engine and adjust the idle speed to that specified in the "Tune-Up Specifications" chart. Some cars require that the timing be set with the transmission in Neutral. You can disconnect the idle solenoid, if any, to get the speed down. Otherwise, adjust the idle speed screw. This is to prevent any centrifugal advance of timing in the distributor.

5. Aim the timing light at the timing marks. Be careful not to touch the fan, which may appear to be standing still. Keep your clothes and hair, and the light's wires clear of the fan, belts, and pulleys. If the pulley or damper notch isn't aligned with the proper timing mark (see the "Tune-Up Specifications" chart), the timing will have to be adjusted.

NOTE: *TDC or Top Dead Center corresponds to 0 degrees; B, or BTDC, or Before Top Dead Center, may be shown as BEFORE; A, or ATDC, or After Top Dead Center, may be shown as AFTER.*

6. Loosen the distributor base clamp locknut. You can buy special wrenches which will make this task easy. Turn the distributor slowly to adjust the timing, holding it by the body and not the cap. Turn the distributor in the direction of rotor rotation (found in the "Firing Order" illustration in Chapter 3) to retard, and against the direction to advance.

7. Tighten the locknut. Check the timing, in case the distributor moved as you tightened it.

8. Replace the distributor vacuum hose. Correct the idle speed.

9. Shut off the engine and disconnect the light.

Valve Lash

Valve adjustment determines how far the valves enter the cylinder and how long they stay open and closed.

If the valve clearance is too large, part of the lift of the camshaft will be used in removing the excessive clearance. Consequently, the valve will not be opening as far as it should. This condition has two effects: the valve train components will emit a tapping sound as they take up the excessive clearance and the engine will perform poorly because the valves don't open fully and allow the proper amount of gases to flow into and out of the engine.

If the valve clearance is too small, the intake valve and the exhaust valves will open too far and they will not fully seat on the cylinder head when they close. When a valve seats itself on the cylinder head, it does two things: it seals the combustion chamber so that none of the gases in the cylinder escape and it cools itself by transferring some of the heat it absorbs from the combustion in the cylinder to the clinder head and to the engine's cooling system. If the valve clearance is too small, the engine will run poorly because of the gases escaping from the combustion chamber. The valves will also become overheated and will warp, since they cannot transfer heat unless they are touching the valve seat in the cylinder head.

NOTE: *While all valve adjustments must be made as accurately as possible, it is better to have the valve adjustment slightly*

TUNE-UP

loose then slightly tight as a burned valve may result from overly tight adjustments.

2.2 Engine

The 2.2 liter engine uses hydraulic lash adjusters. No periodic adjustment or checking is necessary.

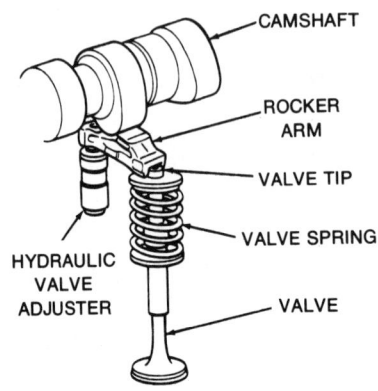

Hydraulic valve adjuster used on 2.2L engine

2.6 Engine

The 2.6 engine has a jet valve located beside the intake of each cylinder.
NOTE: *When adjusting valve clearances, the jet valve must be adjusted before the intake valve.*

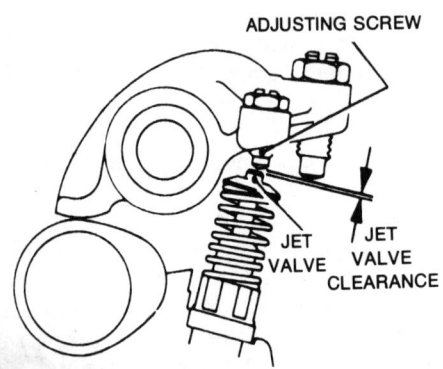

Adjusting the jet valve on 2.6L engines

1. Start the engine and allow it to reach normal operating temperature.
2. Stop the engine and remove the air cleaner and its hoses. Remove any other cables, hoses, wires, etc., which are attached to the valve cover, and remove the valve cover.
3. Disconnect the high tension coil-to-distributor wire at the coil.
4. Watch the rocker arms for No.1 cylin-

der and rotate the crankshaft until the exhaust valve is closing and the intake valve has just started to open. At this point, no. 4 cylinder will be at Top Dead Center (TDC) commencing its firing stroke.

5. Loosen the locknut on cylinder no. 4 intake valve adjusting screw 2 or more turns.
6. Loosen the locknut on the jet valve adjusting screw.
7. Turn the jet valve adjusting screw counter-clockwise and insert a 0.006 in. feeler gauge between the jet valve stem and the adjusting screw.
8. Tighten the adjusting screw until it touches the feeler gauge.

Take care not to press on the valve while adjusting because the jet valve spring is very weak.

NOTE: *If the adjusting screw is tight, special care must be taken to avoid pressing down on the jet valve when adjusting the clearance or a false reading will result.*

9. Tighten the locknut securely while holding the rocker arm adjusting screw with a screwdriver to prevent it from turning.

Adjusting the valve lash on 2.6L engines

10. Make sure that a 0.006 in. feeler gauge can be easily inserted between the jet valve and the rocker arm.
11. Adjust no. 4 cylinder's intake valve to 0.006 in. and its exhaust value to 0.010 in. Tighten the adjusting screw locknuts and recheck each clearance.
12. Perform step 4 in conjunction with the chart below to set up the remaining three cylinders for valve adjustments.
13. Replace the valve cover and all other components. Run the engine and check for oil leaks at the valve cover.

TUNE-UP

Exhaust Valve Closing	Adjust
No. 1 Cylinder	No. 4 Cylinder Valves
No. 2 Cylinder	No. 3 Cylinder Valves
No. 3 Cylinder	No. 2 Cylinder Valves
No. 4 Cylinder	No. 1 Cylinder Valves

Idle Speed and Mixture Adjustment

Chrysler recommends the use of propane enrichment procedure to adjust the mixture. The equipment needed for this procedure is not readily available to the general public. An alternate method recommended by Chrysler is with the use of an exhaust gas analyzer. If this equipment is not available, and a mixture adjustment must be performed, follow this procedure:

1. Run engine to normal operating temperature.
2. Place the transmission in neutral, turn off the lights and air conditioning and make certain that the electric cooling fan is operating.
3. Disconnect the EGR vacuum line, and ground the carburetor idle stop switch (if equipped) with a jumper wire.
4. Connect tachometer according to the manufacturer's instructions.
5. Adjust the idle screw to achieve the curb idle figure listed on the underhood sticker.
6. Back out the mixture screw to achieve the fastest possible idle.
7. Adjust the idle screw to the specified curb idle speed.

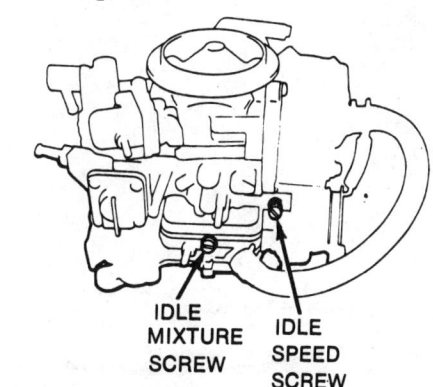

Location of idle speed and mixture adjusting screws on 2.6L engines

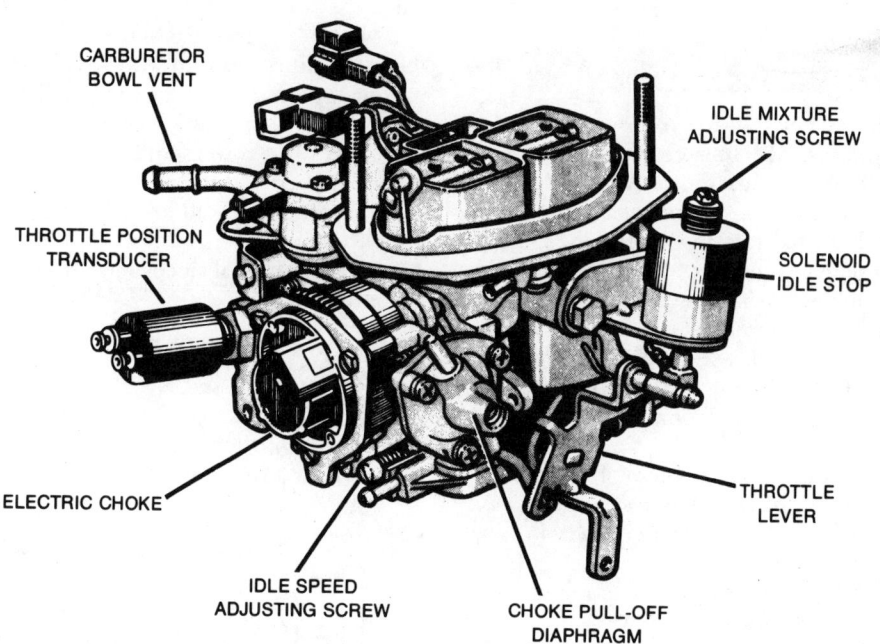

Details of the staged two-barrel carburetor

Engine and Engine Rebuilding

ENGINE ELECTRICAL

Distributor

REMOVAL AND INSTALLATION

1. Disconnect the distributor pickup lead wire at the harness connector.
2. Remove the distributor cap.
3. Rotate the engine crankshaft (in the direction of normal rotation) until No. 1 cylinder is at TDC on compression stroke. Make a mark on the block where the rotor points for installation reference.
4. Remove the distributor holddown bolt.
5. Carefully lift the distributor from the engine. The shaft will rotate slightly as the distributor is removed.
6. Installation is the reverse of removal.
NOTE: *The following procedure is to be used if the engine was cranked with the distributor removed.*

1. If the engine has been cranked over while the distributor was removed, rotate the crankshaft until the number one piston is at TDC on the compression stroke. This will be indicated by the O mark on the flywheel or crank pulley aligning with the pointer on the clutch housing or engine front cover. Position the rotor just ahead of the #1 terminal of the cap and lower the distributor into the engine. With the distributor fully seated, the rotor should be directly under the #1 terminal.
2. If the engine was not disturbed while the distributor was out, lower the distributor into the engine, engaging the gears and making sure that the gasket is properly seated in the block. The rotor should line up with the mark made before removal.
3. Tighten the holddown bolt and connect the wires.
4. Check and, if necessary, adjust the ignition timing.

Firing Order

To avoid confusion replace the spark plug wires one at a time.

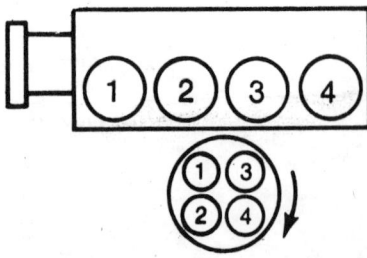

2.2L engine firing order: 1-3-4-2 distributor rotation: clockwise

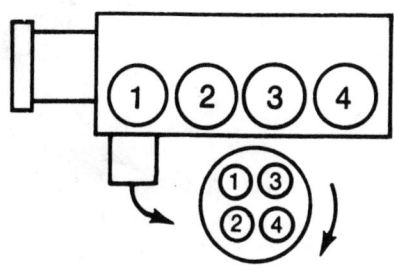

ENGINE AND ENGINE REBUILDING 29

2.6L engine firing order: 1-3-4-2 distribution rotation: clockwise

Alternator
REMOVAL AND INSTALLATION

1. Disconnect the negative battery terminal.
2. Disconnect the wiring and label it for easy reinstallation.
3. Loosen the alternator brace bolt.
4. Remove all necessary drive belts.
5. Remove the brace bolt and the mounting bolt.
6. Remove the alternator.
7. Installation is the reverse of removal. Adjust the belt tension to allow ½ in. of play on the longest run.

Regulator
REMOVAL AND INSTALLATION

NOTE: *The alternator on the 2.6 liter engine has an integral regulator. No adjustments are possible.*

1. Disconnect the negative battery terminal.
2. Remove the electrical connection.
3. Remove the bolts and remove the regulator.

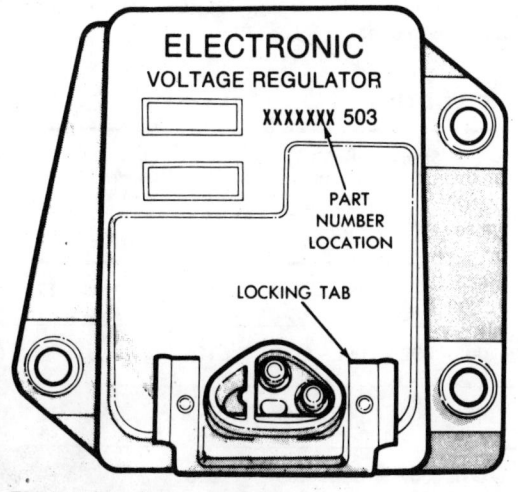

4. This regulator is not adjustable and must be replaced as a unit if found to be defective.
5. Installation is the reverse of removal.

Starter
REMOVAL AND INSTALLATION

1. Disconnect the negative battery terminal.
2. Remove the bolts attaching the starter to the flywheel housing and the rear bracket to the engine or transaxle.
3. On the 2.2 liter engine loosen the air pump tube at the exhaust manifold and move the tube bracket away from the starter.
4. Remove the heatshield and its clamp if so equipped.
5. Remove the electrical connections from the starter.
6. Remove the starter.
7. Installation is the reverse of removal.

SOLENOID REPLACEMENT

1. Remove the starter as previously outlined.
2. Disconnect the field coil wire from the solenoid.
3. Remove the solenoid mounting screws.
4. Remove the solenoid.
5. Installation is the reverse of removal.

Battery
REMOVAL AND INSTALLATION

1. Loosen the nuts which secure the cable ends to the battery terminals. Lift the battery cables from the terminals with a twisting motion.
2. If there is a battery cable puller available, make use of it.
3. Remove the hold-down nuts from the battery hold-down bracket and remove the bracket and the battery. Lift the battery straight up and out of the vehicle, being sure to keep the battery level to avoid spilling the battery acid.

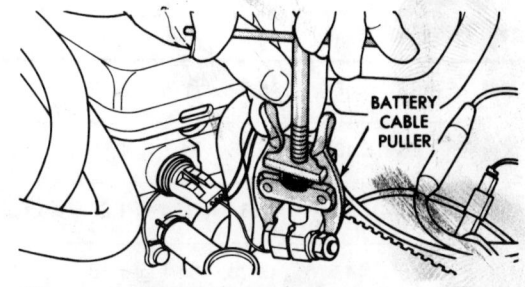

Electronic voltage regulator

Disconnecting the battery cables

ENGINE AND ENGINE REBUILDING

4. Before installing the battery in the vehicle, make sure that the battery terminals are clean and free from corrosion. Use a battery terminal cleaner on the terminals and on the inside of the battery cable ends. If a cleaner is not available, use coarse grade sandpaper to remove the corrosion. A mixture of baking soda and water poured over the terminals and cable ends will help remove and neutralize any acid buildup. Before installing the cables onto the terminals, cut a piece of felt cloth, or something similar into a circle about 3 in. across. Cut a hole in the middle about the size of the battery terminals at their base. Push the cloth pieces over the terminals so that they lay flat on the top of the battery. Soak the pieces of cloth with oil. This will keep the formation of oxidized acid to a minimum. Place the battery in the vehicle. Install the cables onto the terminals. Tighten the nuts on the cable ends. Smear a light coating of grease on the cable ends and tops of the terminals. This will further prevent the buildup of oxidized acid on the terminals and the cable ends. Install and tighten the nuts of the battery hold-down bracket.

Ring Gap
All measurements are given in inches

Year	Engine No. Cyl Displacement (cu. in.)	Top Compression	Bottom Compression	Oil Control
1981	135	.011–.021	.011–.021	.015–.055
	156	.011–.018	.011–.018	.0078–.035
1982	135	.011–.021	.011–.021	.015–.055
	156	.011–.018	.011–.018	.0078–.035

General Engine Specifications

Year	Engine Displacement Cu. In.	Carburetor Type	Advertised Horsepower @ rpm ■	Advertised Torque @ rpm (ft. lbs.) ■	Bore x Stroke (in.)	Compression Ratio	Oil Pressure
1981	135	2bbl	84 @ 4800	111 @ 2800	3.44 x 3.62	8.5:1	50
	156	2bbl	92 @ 4500	131 @ 2500	3.59 x 3.86	8.2:1	57
1982	135	2bbl	84 @ 4800	111 @ 2800	3.44 x 3.62	8.5:1	50
	156	2bbl	92 @ 4500	131 @ 2500	3.59 x 3.86	8.2:1	57

■ Horsepower and torque are SAE net, with all accessories installed and operating. Figure may vary from model-to-model and is intended to be representative rather than exact.

Valve Specifications

Year	Engine Displacement Cu. In.	Seat Angle (deg)	Face Angle (deg)	Spring Test Pressure (lbs @ in.)	Spring Installed Height (in.)	Stem to Guide Clearance (in.) Intake	Stem to Guide Clearance (in.) Exhaust	Stem Diameter (in.) Intake	Stem Diameter (in.) Exhaust
1981	135	45	45.5	175 @ 1.22	1.65	.001–.003	.002–.004	.312–.313	.311–.312
	156	43.75	45.25	34.1 @ 1.18	1.59	.001–.002	.002–.003	.315	.315
1982	135	45	45.5	175 @ 1.22	1.65	.001–.003	.002–.004	.312–.313	.311–.312
	156	43.75	45.22	34.1 @ 1.18	1.59	.001–.002	.002–.003	.315	.315

ENGINE AND ENGINE REBUILDING

Crankshaft and Connecting Rod Specifications
All measurements are given in inches

Year	Engine Displacement Cu. In.	Crankshaft Main Brg Journal Dia	Main Brg Oil Clearance	Shaft End-Play	Thrust on No.	Connecting Rod Journal Diameter	Oil Clearance	Side Clearance
1981	135	2.362–2.363	.0004–.0026	.002–.007	3	1.968–1.969	.0004–.0026	.005–.013
	156	2.3622	.0008–.0028	.002–.007	3	2.0866	.0008–.0028	.004–.010
1982	135	2.362–2.363	.0004–.0026	.002–.007	3	1.968–1.969	.0004–.0026	.005–.013
	156	2.3622	.0008–.0028	.002–.007	3	2.0866	.0004–.0026	.005–.013

Ring Side Clearance
All measurements are given in inches

Year	Engine	Top Compression	Bottom Compression	Oil Control
1981	135	.0015–.0031	.0015–.0037	NA
	156	.0024–.0039	.0008–.0024	NA
1982	135	.0015–.0031	.0015–.0037	NA
	156	.0024–.0039	.0008–.0024	NA

NA—Not available

Piston Clearance

Year	Engine No. Cyl. Displacement (cu. in.)	Piston to Bore Clearance (in.)
1981	135	.0005–.0240
	156	.0005–.0240
1982	135	.0005–.0240
	156	.0005–.0240

Torque Specifications
All readings in ft lbs

Year	Engine Displacement Cu In.	Cylinder Head Bolts	Rod Bearing Bolts	Main Bearing Bolts	Crankshaft Pulley Bolt	Flywheel-to-Crankshaft Bolts	Manifolds Intake	Manifolds Exhaust	Camshaft Cap Bolts
1981	135	120①	40②	30②	50	NA	17	17	14
	156	69③	34	58	87	97	13	13	13
1982	135	120①	40②	30②	50	NA	17	17	14
	156	69③	34	58	87	97	13	13	13

① Torque Sequence 30–45–120 plus ¼ turn
② Plus ¼ turn
③ Cold engine; Hot engine 76 ft. lbs.
NA—not available

ENGINE AND ENGINE REBUILDING

ENGINE MECHANICAL

Design

Two engines are used in Aries/Reliant models. A 135 cu. in. (2.2 Liter) engine is standard. The 156 cu. in. (2.6 Liter) engine is optional.

The 2.2 Liter engine is a four cylinder overhead camshaft power plant with a cast iron cylinder head. The crankshaft is supported by five main bearings. No vibration damper is used. A sintered iron timing belt sprocket is mounted on the crankshaft. The intake manifold and oil filter base are aluminum.

The 2.6 Liter optional engine is also a four cylinder overhead camshaft power plant with a cast iron block, aluminum head and a silent shaft system. The countershafts (silent shafts) are incorporated in the cylinder block to reduce noise and vibration. Its most distinguishing feature is a "jet valve" located beside the intake valve of each cylinder. This valve works off the intake valve rocker arm and injects a swirl of air into the combustion chamber to promote more complete combustion.

Engine Removal

NOTE: *The engine and transmission must be removed together, or the transmission should be completely removed from the car first. The following is for engine/transmission assembly removal.*

1. Disconnect and remove the battery.
2. Mark the hood hinge outline and remove the hood.
3. Drain the cooling system.
4. Remove the radiator hoses and remove the radiator and shroud assembly.
5. Remove the air cleaner and hoses.
6. Remove the power steering pump and set it aside, if so equipped.
7. Remove the oil filter.
8. Remove the alternator, and set it aside.
9. The air conditioning compressor does not have to be disconnected. Remove it from its bracket and position it out of the way. Securing it with wire is the best method.
10. Disconnect and label all wiring from the engine, alternator and carburetor.
11. Disconnect the fuel line, heater hoses and accelerator linkage.
12. Disconnect the air pump lines.
13. Remove the alternator.
14. Disconnect the clutch and speedometer cables.
15. Raise the vehicle and support it on jackstands.
16. Disconnect the driveshafts from the transmission and support them with wires.
17. Disconnect the exhaust pipe.
18. Remove the air pump.
19. Disconnect the transmission linkage.
20. Lower the vehicle.
21. Attach a lifting fixture and a shop crane to the engine. Raise the engine slightly to take up the weight and disconnect the engine mounts in this order: front, right, left. Lift the engine from the car.

Engine lifting device

Engine Installation

1. Lower the engine into place and loosely install all mounting bolts. When all mounts have been hand tightened, torque each to 40 ft. lbs.
2. Remove the lifting fixture and raise the vehicle, supporting it on jackstands.
3. Connect the driveshafts. Torque the bolts to 35 ft. lbs.
4. Connect the transmission linkage, install the air pump, connect the exhaust pipe and lower the vehicle.
5. Connect the clutch and speedometer cables.
6. Install the alternator.
7. Install the air pump lines.
8. Connect the fuel line, heater hoses and accelerator linkage.
9. Connect all wiring.
10. Mount the air conditioning compressor.
11. Install the air cleaner.
12. Install the radiator and hoses.
13. Fill the cooling system.
14. Install the hood.

ENGINE AND ENGINE REBUILDING

15. Connect the battery.
16. Start the engine and run it to normal operating temperature.
17. Check the timing and adjust if necessary. Adjust the carburetor idle speed and mixture, and the transmission linkage.

Cylinder Head
REMOVAL AND INSTALLATION
2.2 Engines

1. Disconnect the negative battery terminal.
2. Drain the cooling system.
3. Remove the air cleaner assembly.
4. Disconnect all lines, hoses and wires from the head, manifold and carburetor.
5. Disconnect the accelerator linkage.
6. Remove the distributor cap.
7. Disconnect the exhaust pipe.
8. Remove the carburetor.
9. Remove the intake and exhaust manifolds.
10. Remove the upper portion of the front cover.
11. Turn the engine by hand until all gear timing marks are aligned.
12. Loosen the drive belt tensioner and slip the belt off the camshaft gear.
13. If equipped with air conditioning, remove the compressor from the mounting brackets and support it out of the way with wires. Remove the mounting brackets from the head.
14. Remove the valve cover, gaskets and seals.
15. Remove head bolts in reverse order of the tightening sequence.
16. Lift off the head and discard the gasket.
17. Installation is the reverse of removal. Make certain all gasket surfaces are thoroughly cleaned and are free of deep nicks or scratches. Always use new gaskets and seals. Never reuse a gasket or seal, even if it looks good. When positioning the head on the block, insert bolts 8 and 10 (see illustration) to align the head. Tighten bolts in the order shown to specifications. Make sure all timing marks are aligned before installing the drive belt. The drive belt is correctly tensioned when it can be twisted 90° with the thumb and index finger midway between the camshaft and the intermediate shaft.

2.6 Engines

CAUTION: *Do not perform this operation on a warm engine. Remove the head bolts in the sequence shown in several steps. Loosen the head bolts evenly, not one at a time. Do not attempt to slide the cylinder head off the block, as it is located with dowel pins. Lift the head straight up and off the block.*

NOTE: *It is necessary to support the engine and remove the motor mount in order to remove the engine front cover.*

1. Disconnect the battery and drain the cooling system. Disconnect the upper radiator hose.
2. Remove the breather hoses and purge hose.
3. Remove the air cleaner and fuel line.
4. Remove the vacuum hose at the distributor and purge control valve.
5. Disconnect the spark plug wires after marking them for reinstallation.
6. Remove the distributor cap, and distributor by removing the retainer nut and pulling the unit out.
7. Disconnect the heater hose at the intake manifold.
8. Disconnect the water temperature gauge unit wire.
9. Place No. 1 piston in the Top Dead Center position to take pressure off the fuel pump rocker arm. Disconnect the fuel hoses and plug the line leading to the gas tank to prevent fuel leakage.
10. Remove the fuel pump mounting nuts or bolts and remove the pump assembly. Remove the insulator and gaskets.
11. Disconnect the exhaust pipe at the exhaust manifold flange.
12. Remove the rocker cover.
13. Remove its breather and semi-circular seal.
14. After slightly loosening the camshaft sprocket bolt, turn the crankshaft until No. 1 piston is at TDC on compression stroke (both valves closed).

NOTE: *Never turn the engine over using the camshaft bolt; it puts undue strain on the chain and other components.*

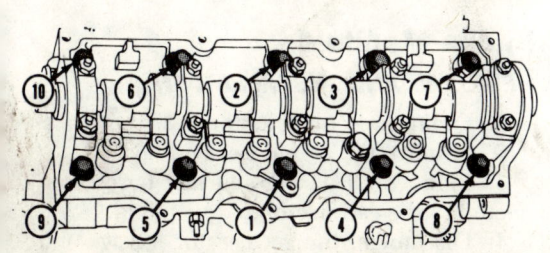

2.2L cylinder head bolt tightening sequence

ENGINE AND ENGINE REBUILDING

15. Remove the camshaft sprocket bolt and distributor drive gear. Remove the camshaft sprocket and allow it to rest in the chain on the holder below.

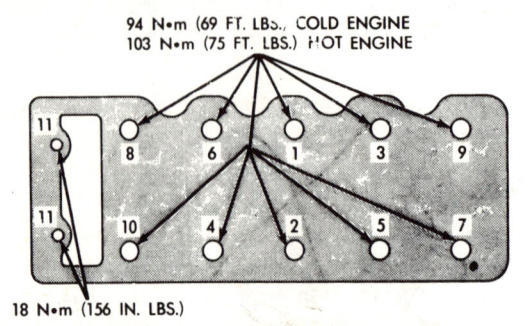

94 N•m (69 FT. LBS.) COLD ENGINE
103 N•m (75 FT. LBS.) HOT ENGINE

18 N•m (156 IN. LBS.)

2.6L cylinder head bolt tightening sequence

16. Remove the cylinder head bolts in reverse of the sequence shown. Head bolts should be loosened in two or three stages to prevent head warpage.
17. Remove the cylinder head and cylinder head gasket.

Installation is performed in the following manner.

18. Clean all gasket surfaces of cylinder block and cylinder head.
19. Install a new cylinder head gasket. Install the cylinder head assembly.

NOTE: *Do not apply sealant to the head gasket and do not reuse an old head gasket.*
NOTE: *The head gasket has the number "54" stamped at the front of the upper surface.*

20. Install the ten cylinder head bolts. Starting at top center, tighten all cylinder head bolts to specifications.
21. Tighten the two front bolts to 11–15 ft. lb.
22. Verify that No. 1 cylinder is at TDC. Align the dowel pin in the end of the camshaft sprocket with the groove in the top of the front camshaft bearing cap and install the camshaft sprocket and chain while pulling up on the sprocket.
23. Install the distributor drive gear and the sprocket bolt.
24. Turn the crankshaft about 90° back, and tighten the camshaft sprocket bolt back to 37–43 ft. lb.

Very slowly turn the engine over two times to make sure the valve timing is correct. If the engine locks at a certain point in these two revolutions, the valve timing is not correct. Repeat steps 22–24.

CAUTION: *At this point, do not turn the engine over using the starter. If the valve timing is off, several of the valves could be bent.*

25. Install the breather and semicircular seal to the cylinder head after applying sealant to surface contact points. Install the rocker cover with a new gasket.
26. Connect the exhaust pipe to the exhaust manifold flange. Tighten the bolts to 11–18 ft. lb.
27. Put No. 1 cylinder at TDC and install the fuel pump with a new gasket and insulator. Connect all hoses.
28. Connect the water temperature gauge unit wire. Connect the heater hose to the intake manifold.
29. Install the distributor and spark plug cables.
30. Connect the vacuum hose to the distributor and purge control valve. Connect the upper radiator hose and fill the cooling system.

Valve Guides

Because of the special tools needed to remove the valve guides, this work should be done by a qualified repair shop.

VALVE SPRING REMOVAL AND INSTALLATION

1. Remove the cylinder head as previously outlined.
2. Compress the valve spring using special tool C-3422A or its equivalent.
3. Remove the valve retaining locks, spring retainers, valve stem seal, and the valve spring.
4. If a valve should drop out of the head, make sure it is replaced in the same position from which it came.
5. Installation is the reverse of removal.

Rocker Shafts

REMOVAL AND INSTALLATION

Refer to the camshaft removal and installation procedure.

Intake Manifold

REMOVAL AND INSTALLATION

1. Drain the cooling system.
2. Remove the air cleaner and hoses.
3. Remove all wiring and any hoses connected to the carburetor and manifold.
4. Disconnect the accelerator linkage and shift linkage (if equipped).

ENGINE AND ENGINE REBUILDING

5. Remove the intake-to-exhaust manifold bolts.
6. Remove the manifold-to-head bolts and lift out the intake manifold.
7. Clean all gasket surfaces and install the intake manifold using new gaskets.
8. Connect all hoses and wires, and install the air cleaner.
9. Connect the accelerator linkage and shift linkage (if equipped).

Exhaust Manifold

REMOVAL AND INSTALLATION

2.2 Engine

1. Follow the intake manifold removal procedure above.
2. Disconnect the exhaust pipe.
3. Unbolt and remove the exhaust manifold.
4. Clean the gasket surfaces, and use a new gasket.
5. Installation is the reverse of removal.

2.6 Engines

1. Remove air cleaner.
2. Remove the heat shield from the exhaust manifold. Remove the EGR lines and reed valve, if equipped.
3. Unbolt the exhaust flange connection.
4. Remove the nuts holding manifold to the cylinder head.
5. Remove the manifold.
6. Installation is the reverse of removal. Tighten flange connection bolts to 11–18 ft. lb. Tighten manifold bolts to 11–14 ft. lb.

Timing Gear Cover

REMOVAL AND INSTALLATION

2.2 Engines

1. Loosen the alternator mounting bolts, pivot the alternator and remove the drive belt.
2. Do the same thing with the air conditioning compressor.
3. Remove the cover retaining nuts, washers and spacers.
4. Remove the cover.
5. Installation is the reverse of removal.

Timing Belt

REMOVAL AND INSTALLATION

1. Remove the timing belt cover.
2. While holding the large hex on the tension pulley, loosen the pulley nut.
3. Remove the belt from the tensioner.
4. Slide the belt off the three toothed pulleys.
5. Using the larger bolt on the crankshaft pulley, turn the engine until the #1 cylinder is at TDC of the compression stroke. At this point the valves for the #1 cylinder will be closed and the timing mark will be aligned with the pointer on the flywheel housing. Make sure that the dots on the cam sprocket and cylinder head are aligned.
6. Check that the V-notch in the crankshaft pulley aligns with the dot mark on the intermediate shaft.

CAUTION: *If the timing marks are not perfectly aligned, poor engine performance and probable engine damage will result!*

7. Install the belt on the pulleys.
8. Adjust the tensioner by turning the large tensioner hex to the right. Tension is correct when the belt can be twisted 90° with the thumb and forefinger, midway between the camshaft and intermediate pulleys.
9. Tighten the tensioner locknut to 32 ft. lb.
10. Install the timing belt cover and check the ignition timing.

Adjusting drive belt tension on 2.2L engines

Timing Chain, Cover, "Silent Shafts" and Tensioner

REMOVAL AND INSTALLATION

2.6 Engines

NOTE: *All 2.6 engines are equipped with two "Silent Shafts" which concel the vertical vibrating force of the engine and the secondary vibrating forces, which include the sideways rocking of the engine due to the turning direction of the crankshaft and other rolling parts. The shafts are driven*

ENGINE AND ENGINE REBUILDING

by a duplex chain and are turned by the crankshaft. The silent shaft chain assembly is mounted in front of the timing chain assembly and must be removed to service the timing chain.

1. Disconnect the negative battery terminal.
2. Drain the radiator and remove it from the vehicle.
3. Remove the cylinder head.
4. Remove the cooling fan, spacer, water pump pulley and belt.
5. Remove the alternator and water pump.
6. Raise the front of the vehicle and support it on jack stands.
7. Remove the oil pan and screen. Remove the crankshaft pulley.
8. Remove the timing case cover.
9. Remove the chain guides, side (A), top (B), bottom (C), from the "B" chain (outer).
10. Remove the locking bolts from the "B" chain sprockets.
11. Remove the crankshaft sprocket, silent shaft sprocket and the outer chain.
12. Remove the crankshaft and camshaft sprockets and the timing chain.
13. Remove the camshaft sprocket holder and the chain guides, both left and right.
14. Remove the tensioner.
15. Remove the sleeve from the oil pump. Remove the oil pump by first removing the bolt locking the oil pump driven gear and the right silent shaft, then remove the oil pump mounting bolts. Remove the silent shaft from the engine block.

NOTE: *If the bolt locking the oil pump and the silent shaft is hard to loosen, remove the oil pump and the shaft as a unit.*

16. Remove the left silent shaft thrust washer and take the shaft from the engine block.

Installation is performed in the following manner:

1. Install the right silent shaft into the engine block.
2. Install the oil pump assembly. Do not lose the woodruff key from the end of the silent shaft. Torque the oil pump mounting bolts from 6 to 7 ft. lbs.
3. Tighten the silent shaft and the oil pump driven gear mounting bolt.

NOTE: *The silent shaft and the oil pump can be installed as a unit, if necessary.*

4. Install the left silent shaft into the engine block.
5. Install a new "O" ring on the thrust plate and install the unit into the engine block, using a pair of bolts without heads, as alignment guides.

CAUTION: *If the thrust plate is turned to align the bolt holes, the "O" ring may be damaged.*

6. Remove the guide bolts and install the regular bolts into the thrust plate and tighten securely.
7. Rotate the crankshaft to bring No. 1 piston to TDC.

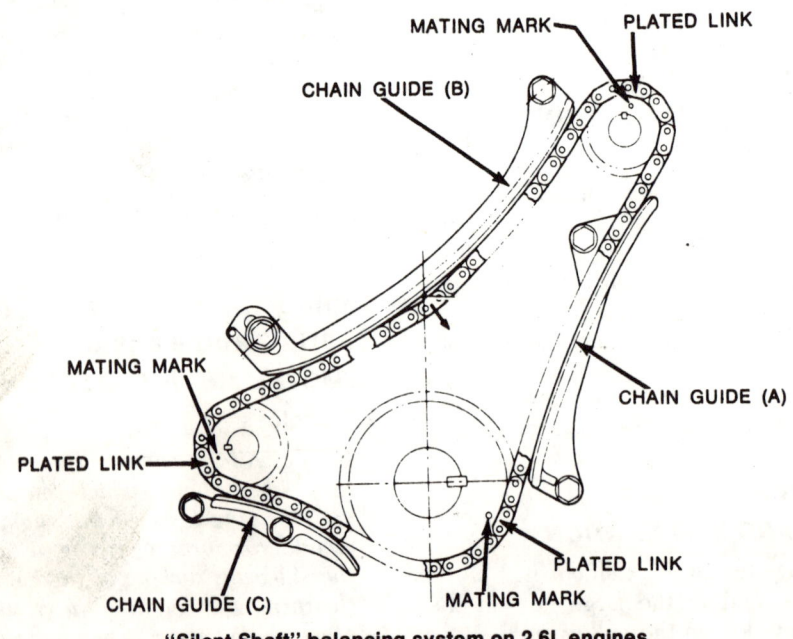

"Silent Shaft" balancing system on 2.6L engines

ENGINE AND ENGINE REBUILDING

8. Install the cylinder head.
9. Install the sprocket holder and the right and left chain guides.
10. Install the tensioner spring and sleeve on the oil pump body.
11. Install the camshaft and crankshaft sprockets on the timing chain, aligning the sprocket punch marks to the plated chain links.
12. While holding the sprocket and chain as a unit, install the crankshaft sprocket over the crankshaft and align it with the keyway.
13. Keeping the dowel pin hole on the camshaft in a vertical position, install the camshaft sprocket and chain on the camshaft.

NOTE: *The sprocket timing mark and the plated chain link should be at the 2 to 3 o'clock position when correctly installed.*

CAUTION: *The chain must be aligned in the right and left chain guides with the tensioner pushing against the chain. The tension for the inner chain is determined by spring tension.*

14. Install the crankshaft sprocket for the outer or "B" chain.
15. Install the two silent shaft sprockets and align the punched mating marks with the plated links of the chain.
16. Holding the two shaft sprockets and chain, install the outer chain in alignment with the mark on the crankshaft sprocket. Install the shaft sprockets on the silent shaft and the oil pump driver gear. Install the lock bolts and recheck the alignment of the punch marks and the plated links.
17. Temporarily install the chain guides, *Side* (A), *Top* (B), and *Bottom* (C).
18. Tighten *Side* (A) chain guide securely.
19. Tighten *Bottom* (B) chain guide securely.
20. Adjust the position of the *Top* (B) chain guide, after shaking the right and left sprockets to collect any chain slack, so that when the chain is moved toward the center, the clearance between the chain guide and the chain links will be approximately 9/64 inch. Tighten the *Top* (B) chain guide bolts.
21. Install the timing chain cover using a new gasket, being careful not to damage the front seal.
22. Install the oil screen and the oil pan, using a new gasket. Torque the bolts to 4.5 to 5.5 ft. lbs.
23. Install the crankshaft pulley, alternator and accessory belts, and the distributor.
24. Install the oil pressure switch, if removed, and install the battery ground cable.

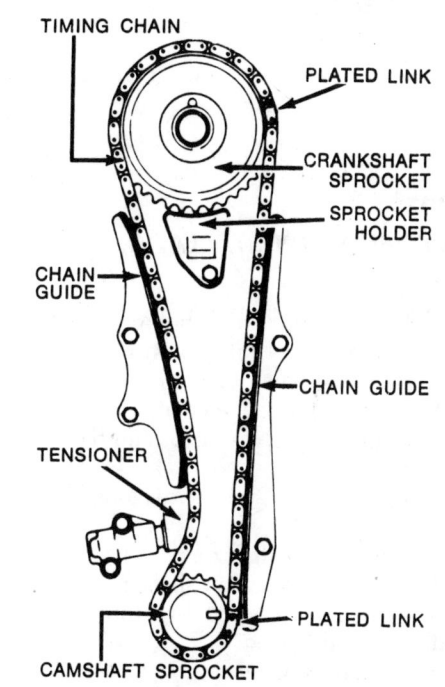

Timing chain installation on 2.2L engines. Align the plated links with the punch marks on the cam and crankshaft sprockets.

25. Install the fan blades, radiator, fill the system with coolant and start the engine.

Timing Gears

REMOVAL AND INSTALLATION

2.2 Engines

The camshaft, intermediate shaft, and crankshaft pulleys are located by keys on their respective shafts and each is retained by a bolt. To remove any or all of the pulleys, first remove the timing belt cover and belt and then use the following procedure.

NOTE: *When removing the crankshaft pulley, don't remove the four socket head bolts which retain the outer belt pulley to the timing belt pulley.*

1. Remove the center bolt.
2. Gently pry the pulley off the shaft.
3. If the pulley is stubborn in coming off, use a gear puller. Don't hammer on the pulley.
4. Remove the pulley and key.
5. Install the pulley in the reverse order of removal.
6. Tighten the center bolt to 58 ft. lbs.
7. Install the timing belt, check valve timing, tension belt, and install the cover.

38 ENGINE AND ENGINE REBUILDING

2.6 Engines
See the procedures under Timing Chain, Cover and Silent Shafts.

Camshaft
REMOVAL AND INSTALLATION
2.2 Engines

1. Remove the timing belt cover.
2. Remove the timing belt.
3. Remove the air cleaner assembly.
4. Remove the valve cover.
5. Remove the Nos. 1, 3, and 5 camshaft bearing caps.
6. Loosen caps 2 and 4 diagonally and in increments.
7. Lift the camshaft out.
8. Lubricate the camshaft journals and lobes with engine assembly lubricant and position it in the head.
9. Install a new oil seal.
10. Install the Nos. 1, 3, 5 bearing caps and torque the nuts to 14 ft. lbs.
11. Install the Nos. 2 and 4 caps and diagonally torque the nuts to 14 ft. lbs.

CAUTION: *All bearing caps are slightly offset. They should be installed so the numbers on the cap read right side up from the drivers seat.*

12. Position a dial indicator so that the feeler touches the front end of the camshaft. Check for end play. Play should not exceed .006 in.
13. Place a new seal on the #1 bearing cap. If necessary, replace the end plug in the head.
14. Follow the procedures under Timing Belt Removal and Installation for belt installation and timing.
15. Check the valve clearance and ignition timing.

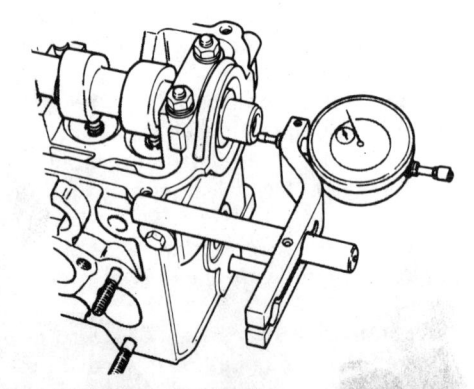

Checking camshaft end play

2.6 Engines

1. Remove the breather hoses and purge hose.
2. Remove the air cleaner and fuel line.
3. Remove the fuel pump. Remove the distributor.
4. Disconnect the spark plug cables.
5. Remove the rocker cover.
6. Remove the breather and semi-circular seal.
7. After slightly loosening the camshaft sprocket bolt, turn the crankshaft until No. 1 piston is at Top Dead Center on compression stroke (both valves closed).
8. Remove the camshaft sprocket bolt and distributor drive gear.
9. Remove the camshaft sprocket with chain and allow it to rest on the camshaft sprocket holder.
10. Remove the camshaft bearing cap tightening bolts. Do not remove the front and rear bearing cap bolts altogether, but keep them inserted in the bearing caps so that the rocker assembly can be removed as a unit.
11. Remove the rocker arms, rocker shafts and bearing caps as an assembly.
12. Remove the camshaft.
13. Installation is the reverse of removal. Lubricate the camshaft lobes and bearings and fit camshaft into head. Install the assembled rocker arm shaft assembly. The camshaft should be positioned so that the dowel pin on the front end of the cam is in the 12 o'clock position and in line with the notch in the top of the front bearing cap.

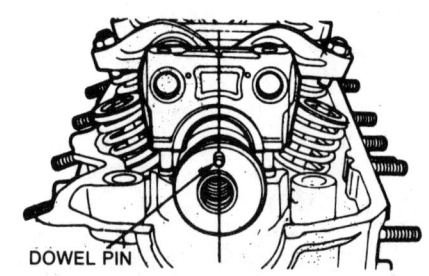

Install the camshaft on 2.6L engines by aligning the dowel pin with the notch in the top of the front bearing cap

Pistons and Connecting Rods
IDENTIFICATION

The pistons used in the 2.2 Liter engine have notches in them to indicate the proper installed position. The notch faces the front of

ENGINE AND ENGINE REBUILDING

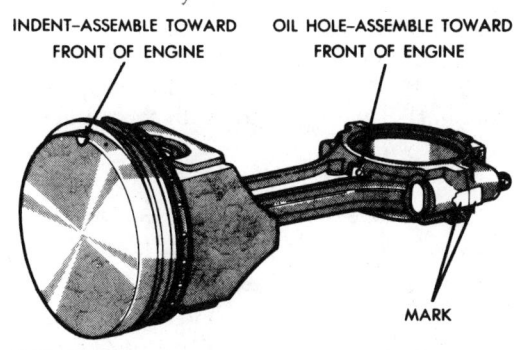

INDENT–ASSEMBLE TOWARD FRONT OF ENGINE

OIL HOLE–ASSEMBLE TOWARD FRONT OF ENGINE

MARK

2.2L pistons

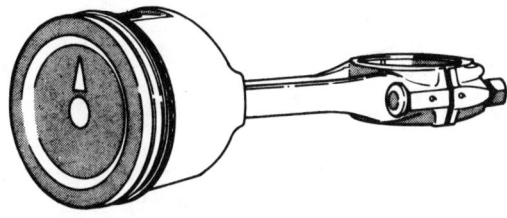

2.6L pistons with connecting rod markings

the engine, when installed. Connecting rods have no markings.

2.6 Liter engines have arrows on the pistons. These arrows must face front when installed in the engine. The connecting rods are numbered for easy identification.

REMOVAL AND INSTALLATION

Piston and connecting rod removal/installation and piston ring removal/installation are detailed in the Engine Rebuilding section at the end of this chapter. Removal and installation is outlined with the engine out of the car, but the same procedures may be used with block in the chassis. Remove the cylinder heads and oil pan for piston and connecting rod removal.

Engine Lubrication

All engines have pressurized lubrication systems with full-flow oil filters.

Oil Pump

REMOVAL AND INSTALLATION

2.2 Engines

1. Remove the oil pan.
2. Remove the two pump mounting bolts.
3. Pull the pump down and out of the engine.
4. Installation is the reverse of removal. Torque the pump mounting bolts to 17 ft. lbs.

2.6 Engines

See Timing Chain, Cover, "Silent Shaft" and Tensioner removal and installation procedure.

Oil Pan

REMOVAL AND INSTALLATION

1. Drain the engine oil.
2. Support the pan and remove the attaching bolts.
3. Lower the pan and remove the gasket.
4. Clean all gasket surfaces thoroughly. Install the pan using gasket sealer and a new gasket.

NOTE: *The 2.2 Liter engine uses a form-in-place type gasket. Chrysler Part Number 4205918 or its equivalent RTV gasket material must be used.*

5. Torque the pan bolts to 17 ft. lbs. (2.2 Liter) and 5 ft. lbs. (2.6 Liter).
6. Refill the engine with oil, start the engine, and check for leaks.

Rear Main Seal

REMOVAL AND INSTALLATION

2.2 Engines

The rear main seal is located in a housing on the rear of the block. To replace the seal it is necessary to remove the engine.

1. Remove the transmission and flywheel.

CAUTION: *Before removing the transmission, align the dimple on the flywheel with the pointer on the flywheel housing. The transmission will not mate with the engine during installation unless this alignment is observed.*

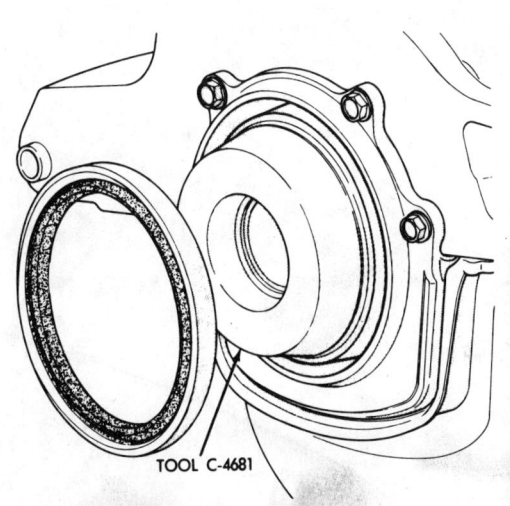

TOOL C-4681

Installing rear oil seal

40　ENGINE AND ENGINE REBUILDING

2. Very carefully, pry the oil seal out of the support ring. Be careful not to nick or damage the crankshaft flange seal surface or retainer bore.

3. Place special tool #C-4681 or its equivalent on the crankshaft.

4. Lightly coat the outside diameter of the seal with Loctite Stud N' Bearing Mount® or its equivalent. Also coat the inside of the seal with engine oil.

5. Place the seal over tool #C-4681 and gently tap it into place with a plastic hammer.

6. Reinstall the remaining parts in the reverse order of removal.

2.6 Engines

The rear main oil seal is located in a housing on the rear of the block. To replace the seal, remove the transmission and do the work from underneath the vehicle or remove the engine and do the work on the bench.

1. Remove the housing from the block.
2. Remove the separator from the housing.
3. Pry out the old seal.
4. Lightly oil the replacement seal. The oil seal should be installed so that the seal plate fits into the inner contact surface of the seal case. Install the separator with the oil holes facing down.

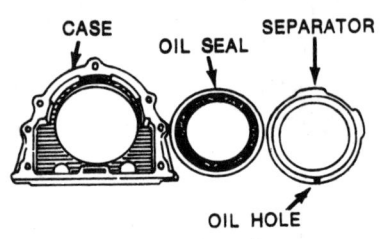

Rear main oil seal on 2.6L engines

COOLING SYSTEM

The cooling system consists of a radiator, fan shroud, if equipped with air conditioning, overflow tank, water pump, thermostat, coolant temperature switch, electric fan and radiator fan switch. The use of an electric fan is necessitated by the transversely mounted engine. A radiator bypass system is used for faster warmup.

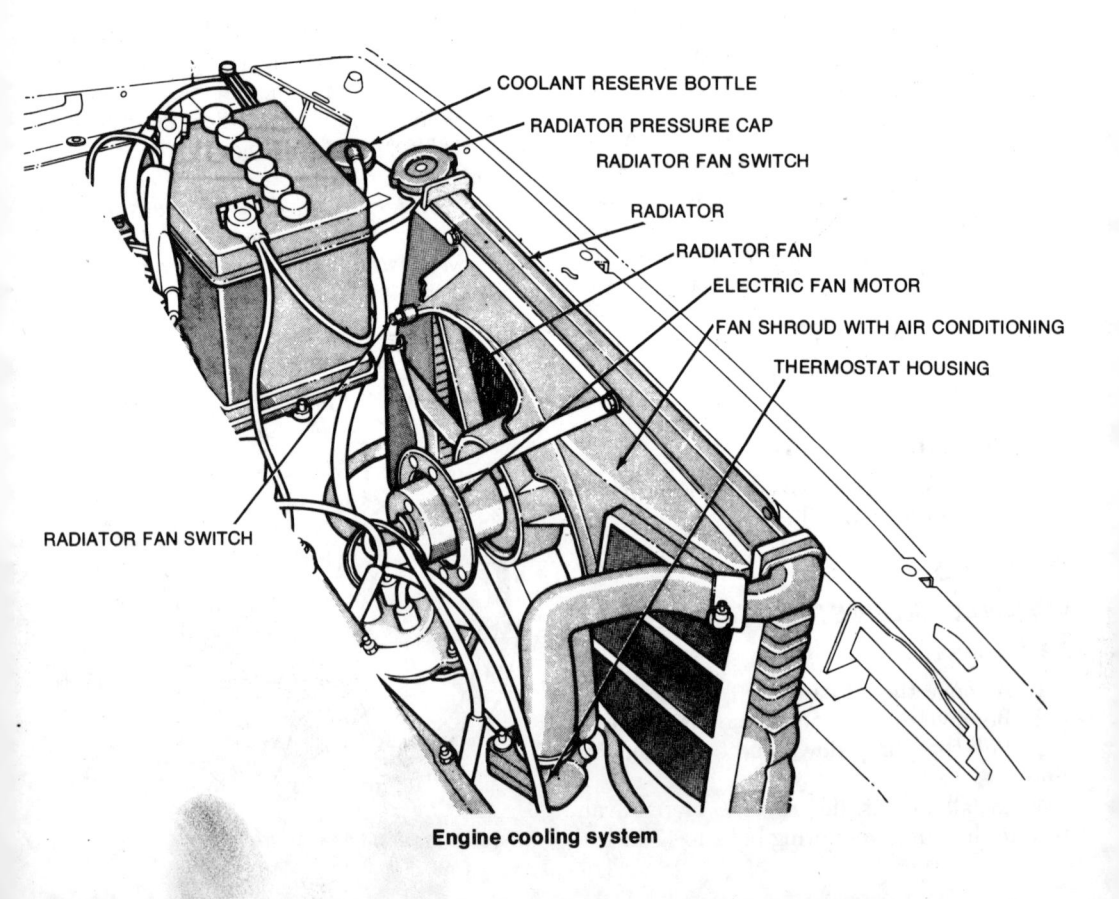

Engine cooling system

ENGINE AND ENGINE REBUILDING

Radiator

REMOVAL AND INSTALLATION

1. Move the temperature selector to full on.
2. Open the radiator drain cock.
3. When the coolant reserve tank is empty, remove the radiator cap.
4. Remove the hoses.
5. If equipped with automatic transmission, disconnect and plug the fluid cooler lines.
6. Remove the upper and lower mounting brackets.
7. Remove the shroud.
8. Remove the fan motor attaching bolts.
9. Remove the top radiator attaching bolts.
10. Remove the bottom radiator attaching bolts.
11. Lift the radiator from the engine compartment.
12. Installation is the reverse of removal.

Water Pump

REMOVAL AND INSTALLATION

1. Drain the cooling system.
2. Remove the drive belts.
3. Remove the water pump pulley.
4. Unbolt the compressor and/or air pump brackets from the water pump and secure them out of the way.
5. Position the bypass hose lower clamp in the center of the hose and disconnect the heater hose.
6. Unbolt and remove the water pump. Discard the gasket and clean the gasket surfaces.
7. Installation is the reverse of removal. Torque the water pump bolts to 25–40 ft. lbs., the alternator adjusting bolt to 30–50 ft. lbs.; the pulley bolts to 85–125 in. lbs.

Thermostat

REMOVAL AND INSTALLATION

The thermostat on the 2.2 Liter engine is located in the thermostat housing on the cylinder head. 2.6 Liter engines have the thermostat housing near the intake manifold.

1. Drain the cooling system to a level below the thermostat.
2. Remove the hose from the thermostat housing.
3. Remove the thermostat housing.
4. Remove the thermostat and discard the gasket. Clean both gasket surfaces thoroughly.
5. Position the thermostat in the housing. Install a new gasket and the upper half of the housing. Make sure that the thermostat is properly seated.
6. Refill the cooling system, start the engine, and check for leaks.

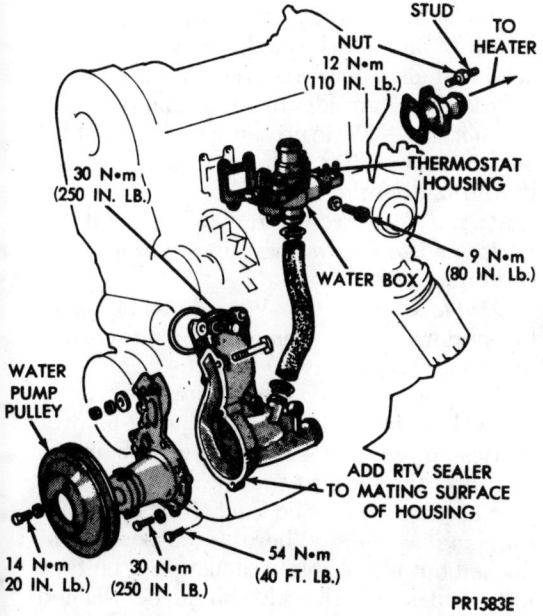

Thermostat Housing and Water Pump—1.7L Engine

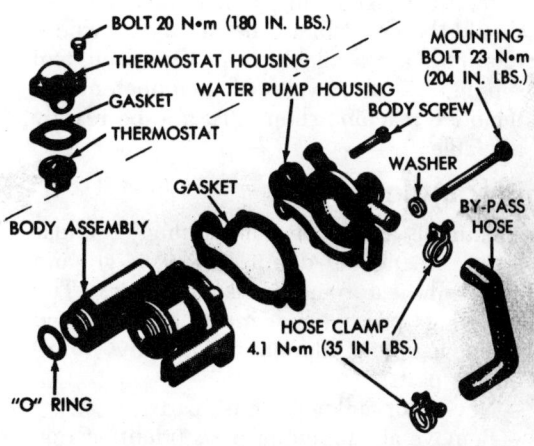

Thermostat Housing and Water Pump—2.6L Engine

ENGINE REBUILDING

Most procedures involved in rebuilding an engine are fairly standard, regardless of the type of engine involved. This section is a guide to accepted rebuilding procedures. Examples of standard rebuilding practices are illustrated and should be used along with specific details concerning your particular engine, found earlier in this chapter.

The procedures given here are those used by any competent rebuilder. Obviously some of the procedures cannot be performed by the do-it-yourself mechanic, but are provided so that you will be familiar with the services that should be offered by rebuilding or machine shops. As an example, in most instances, it is more profitable for the home mechanic to remove the cylinder heads, buy the necessary parts (new valves, seals, keepers, keys, etc.) and deliver these to a machine shop for the necessary work. In this way you will save the money to remove and install the cylinder head and the mark-up on parts.

On the other hand, most of the work involved in rebuilding the lower end is well within the scope of the do-it-yourself mechanic. Only work such as hot-tanking, actually boring the block or Magnafluxing (invisible crack detection) need be sent to a machine shop.

Tools

The tools required for basic engine rebuilding should, with a few exceptions, be those included in a mechanic's tool kit. An accurate torque wrench, and a dial indicator (reading in thousandths) mounted on a universal base should be available. Special tools, where required, are available from the major tool suppliers. The services of a competent automotive machine shop must also be readily available.

Precautions

Aluminum has become increasingly popular for use in engines, due to its low weight and excellent heat transfer characteristics. The following precautions must be observed when handling aluminum (or any other) engine parts:
—Never hot-tank aluminum parts.
—Remove all aluminum parts (identification tags, etc.) from engine parts before hot-tanking (otherwise they will be removed during the process).
—Always coat threads lightly with engine oil or anti-seize compounds before installation, to prevent seizure.
—Never over-torque bolts or spark plugs in aluminum threads. Should stripping occur, threads can be restored using any of a number of thread repair kits available (see next section).

Inspection Techniques

Magnaflux and Zyglo are inspection techniques used to locate material flaws, such as stress cracks. Magnaflux is a magnetic process, applicable only to ferrous materials. The Zyglo process coats the material with a fluorescent dye penetrant, and any material may be tested using Zyglo. Specific checks of suspected surface cracks may be made at lower cost and more readily using spot check dye. The dye is sprayed onto the suspected area, wiped off, and the area is then sprayed with a developer. Cracks then will show up brightly.

Overhaul

The section is divided into two parts. The first, Cylinder Head Reconditioning, assumes that the cylinder head is removed from the engine, all manifolds are removed, and the cylinder head is on a workbench. The camshaft should be removed from overhead cam cylinder heads. The second section, Cylinder Block Reconditioning, covers the block, pistons, connecting rods and crankshaft. It is assumed that the engine is mounted on a work stand, and the cylinder head and all accessories are removed.

Procedures are identified as follows:
Unmarked—Basic procedures that must be performed in order to successfully complete the rebuilding process.
Starred (*)—Procedures that should be performed to ensure maximum performance and engine life.
Double starred (**)—Procedures that may be performed to increase engine performance and reliability.

When assembling the engine, any parts that will be in frictional contact must be pre-lubricated, to provide protection on initial start-up. Any product specifically formulated for this purpose may be used. NOTE: *Do not use engine oil.* Where semi-permanent (locked but removable) installation of bolts or nuts is desired, threads should be cleaned and located with Loctite® or a similar product (non-hardening).

ENGINE AND ENGINE REBUILDING 43

Repairing Damaged Threads

Several methods of repairing damaged threads are available. Heli-Coil® (shown here), Keenserts® and Microdot® are among the most widely used. All involve basically the same principle—drilling out stripped threads, tapping the hole and installing a pre-wound insert—making welding, plugging and oversize fasteners unnecessary.

Two types of thread repair inserts are usually supplied—a standard type for most Inch Coarse, Inch Fine, Metric Coarse and Metric Fine thread sizes and a spark plug type to fit most spark plug port sizes. Consult the individual manufacturer's catalog to determine exact applications. Typical thread repair kits will contain a selection of pre-wound threaded inserts, a tap (corresponding to the outside diameter threads of the insert) and an installation tool. Spark plug inserts usually differ because they require a tap equipped with pilot threads and a combined reamer/tap section. Most manufacturers also supply blister-packed thread repair inserts separately in addition to a master kit containing a variety of taps and inserts plus installation tools.

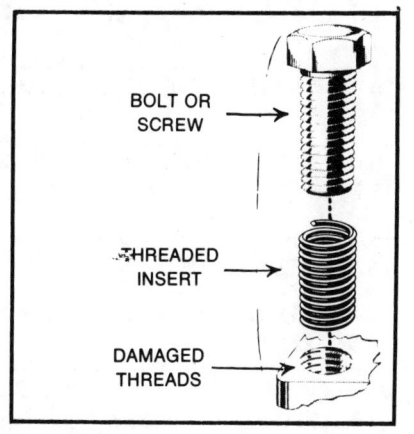

Before effecting a repair to a threaded hole, remove any snapped, broken or damaged bolts or studs. Penetrating oil can be used to free frozen threads; the offending item can be removed with locking pliers or with a screw or stud extractor. After the hole is clear, the thread can be repaired, as follows:

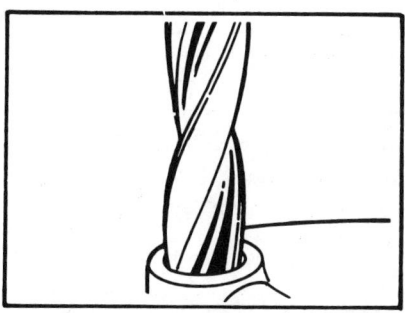

Drill out the damaged threads with specified drill. Drill completely through the hole or to the bottom of a blind hole

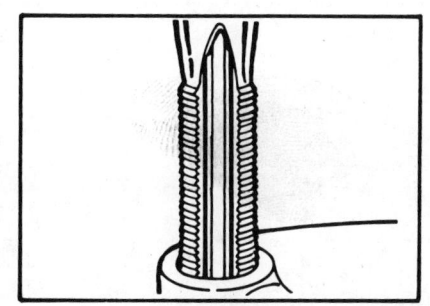

With the tap supplied, tap the hole to receive the thread insert. Keep the tap well oiled and back it out frequently to avoid clogging the threads

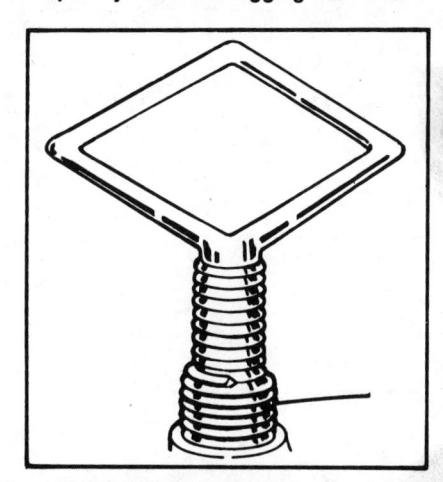

Damaged bolt holes can be repaired with thread repair inserts

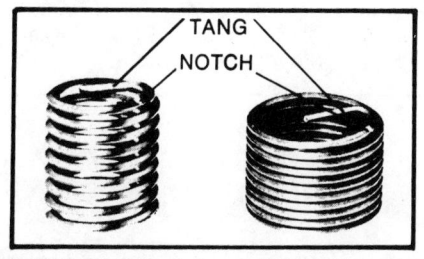

Standard thread repair insert (left) and spark plug thread insert (right)

Screw the threaded insert onto the installation tool until the tang engages the slot. Screw the insert into the tapped hole until it is ¼–½ turn below the top surface. After installation break off the tang with a hammer and punch

44 ENGINE AND ENGINE REBUILDING

Standard Torque Specifications and Fastener Markings

The Newton-metre has been designated the world standard for measuring torque and will gradually replace the foot-pound and kilogram-meter. In the absence of specific torques, the following chart can be used as a guide to the maximum safe torque of a particular size/grade of fastener.

- There is no torque difference for fine or coarse threads.
- Torque values are based on clean, dry threads. Reduce the value by 10% if threads are oiled prior to assembly.
- The torque required for aluminum components or fasteners is considerably less.

U. S. BOLTS

SAE Grade Number	1 or 2			5			6 or 7		
Bolt Markings Manufacturer's marks may vary—number of lines always 2 less than the grade number.									
Usage	Frequent			Frequent			Infrequent		
Bolt Size (inches)—(Thread)	Maximum Torque			Maximum Torque			Maximum Torque		
	Ft-Lb	kgm	Nm	Ft-Lb	kgm	Nm	Ft-Lb	kgm	Nm
1/4—20	5	0.7	6.8	8	1.1	10.8	10	1.4	13.5
—28	6	0.8	8.1	10	1.4	13.6			
5/16—18	11	1.5	14.9	17	2.3	23.0	19	2.6	25.8
—24	13	1.8	17.6	19	2.6	25.7			
3/8—16	18	2.5	24.4	31	4.3	42.0	34	4.7	46.0
—24	20	2.75	27.1	35	4.8	47.5			
7/16—14	28	3.8	37.0	49	6.8	66.4	55	7.6	74.5
—20	30	4.2	40.7	55	7.6	74.5			
1/2—13	39	5.4	52.8	75	10.4	101.7	85	11.75	115.2
—20	41	5.7	55.6	85	11.7	115.2			
9/16—12	51	7.0	69.2	110	15.2	149.1	120	16.6	162.7
—18	55	7.6	74.5	120	16.6	162.7			
5/8—11	83	11.5	112.5	150	20.7	203.3	167	23.0	226.5
—18	95	13.1	128.8	170	23.5	230.5			
3/4—10	105	14.5	142.3	270	37.3	366.0	280	38.7	379.6
—16	115	15.9	155.9	295	40.8	400.0			
7/8— 9	160	22.1	216.9	395	54.6	535.5	440	60.9	596.5
—14	175	24.2	237.2	435	60.1	589.7			
1— 8	236	32.5	318.6	590	81.6	799.9	660	91.3	894.8
—14	250	34.6	338.9	660	91.3	849.8			

ENGINE AND ENGINE REBUILDING

METRIC BOLTS

NOTE: *Metric bolts are marked with a number indicating the relative strength of the bolt. These numbers have nothing to do with size.*

Description Thread size x pitch (mm)	Torque ft-lbs (Nm) Head mark—4		Head mark—7	
6 x 1.0	2.2–2.9	(3.0–3.9)	3.6–5.8	(4.9–7.8)
8 x 1.25	5.8–8.7	(7.9–12)	9.4–14	(13–19)
10 x 1.25	12–17	(16–23)	20–29	(27–39)
12 x 1.25	21–32	(29–43)	35–53	(47–72)
14 x 1.5	35–52	(48–70)	57–85	(77–110)
16 x 1.5	51–77	(67–100)	90–120	(130–160)
18 x 1.5	74–110	(100–150)	130–170	(180–230)
20 x 1.5	110–140	(150–190)	190–240	(160–320)
22 x 1.5	150–190	(200–260)	250–320	(340–430)
24 x 1.5	190–240	(260–320)	310–410	(420–550)

NOTE: *This engine rebuilding section is a guide to accepted rebuilding procedures. Typical examples of standard rebuilding procedures are illustrated. Use these procedures along with the detailed instructions earlier in this chapter, concerning your particular engine.*

Cylinder Head Reconditioning

Procedure	Method
Remove the cylinder head:	See the engine service procedures earlier in this chapter for details concerning specific engines.
Identify the valves:	Invert the cylinder head, and number the valve faces front to rear, using a permanent felt-tip marker.
Remove the camshaft:	See the engine service procedures earlier in this chapter for details concerning specific engines.
Remove the valves and springs:	Using an appropriate valve spring compressor (depending on the configuration of the cylinder head), compress the valve springs. Lift out the keepers with needlenose pliers, release the compressor, and remove the valve, spring, and spring retainer. See the engine service procedures earlier in this chapter for details concerning specific engines.
Check the valve stem-to-guide clearance: Check the valve stem-to-guide clearance	Clean the valve stem with lacquer thinner or a similar solvent to remove all gum and varnish. Clean the valve guides using solvent and an expanding wire-type valve guide cleaner. Mount a dial indicator so that the stem is at 90° to the valve stem, as close to the valve guide as possible. Move the valve off its seat, and measure the valve guide-to-stem clearance by rocking the stem back and forth to actuate the dial indicator. Measure the valve stems using a micrometer, and compare to specifications, to determine whether stem or guide wear is responsible for excessive clearance. NOTE: *Consult the Specifications tables earlier in this chapter.*

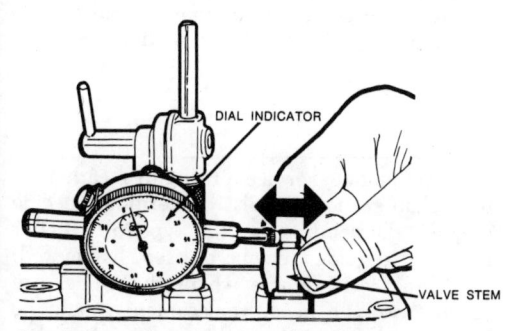

46 ENGINE AND ENGINE REBUILDING

Cylinder Head Reconditioning

Procedure	Method
De-carbon the cylinder head and valves:	Chip carbon away from the valve heads, combustion chambers, and ports, using a chisel made of hardwood. Remove the remaining deposits with a stiff wire brush. NOTE: *Be sure that the deposits are actually removed, rather than burnished.*

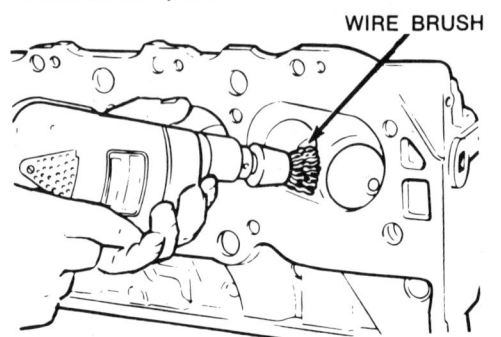

Remove the carbon from the cylinder head with a wire brush and electric drill

Hot-tank the cylinder head (cast iron heads only): CAUTION: *Do not hot-tank aluminum parts.*	Have the cylinder head hot-tanked to remove grease, corrosion, and scale from the water passages. NOTE: *In the case of overhead cam cylinder heads, consult the operator to determine whether the camshaft bearings will be damaged by the caustic solution.*
Degrease the remaining cylinder head parts:	Clean the remaining cylinder head parts in an engine cleaning solvent. Do not remove the protective coating from the springs.
Check the cylinder head for warpage:	Place a straight-edge across the gasket surface of the cylinder head. Using feeler gauges, determine the clearance at the center of the straight-edge. If warpage exceeds .003" in a 6" span, or .006" over the total length, the cylinder head must be resurfaced. NOTE: *If warpage exceeds the manufacturer's maximum tolerance for material removal, the cylinder head must be replaced.* When milling the cylinder heads of V-type engines, the intake manifold mounting position is altered, and must be corrected by milling the manifold flange a proportionate amount.

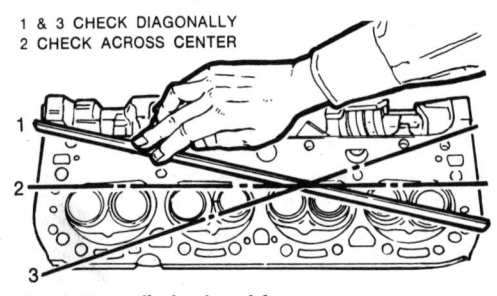

1 & 3 CHECK DIAGONALLY
2 CHECK ACROSS CENTER

Check the cylinder head for warpage

| *Knurl the valve guides: | *Valve guides which are not excessively worn or distorted may, in some cases, be knurled rather than replaced. Knurling is a process in which metal is displaced and raised, thereby reducing clearance. Knurling also provides excellent oil control. The possibility of knurling rather than replacing valve guides should be discussed with a machinist. |

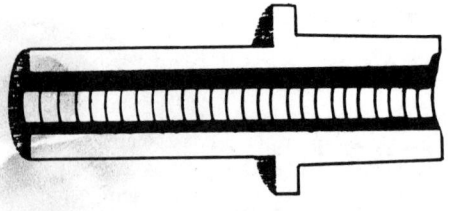

Cut-away view of a knurled valve guide

| Replace the valve guides:
NOTE: *Valve guides should only be replaced if damaged or if an oversize valve stem is not available.* | See the engine service procedures earlier in this chapter for details concerning specific engines. Depending on the type of cylinder head, valve guides may be pressed, hammered, or shrunk in. In cases where the guides are shrunk into the head, replacement should be left to an equipped machine shop. In other |

ENGINE AND ENGINE REBUILDING 47

Cylinder Head Reconditioning

Procedure	Method
	cases, the guides are replaced using a stepped drift (see illustration). Determine the height above the boss that the guide must extend, and obtain a stack of washers, their I.D. similar to the guide's O.D., of that height. Place the stack of washers on the guide, and insert the guide into the boss. NOTE: *Valve guides are often tapered or beveled for installation.* Using the stepped installation tool (see illustration), press or tap the guides into position. Ream the guides according to the size of the valve stem.

A—VALVE GUIDE I.D.   B—LARGER THAN THE VALVE GUIDE O.D.

WASHERS

A—VALVE GUIDE I.D.   B—LARGER THAN THE VALVE GUIDE O.D.

Valve guide installation tool using washers for installation

Replace valve seat inserts:	Replacement of valve seat inserts which are worn beyond resurfacing or broken, if feasible, must be done by a machine shop.
Resurface (grind) the valve face:	Using a valve grinder, resurface the valves according to specifications given earlier in this chapter. CAUTION: *Valve face angle is not always identical to valve seat angle.* A minimum margin of 1/32" should remain after grinding the valve. The valve stem top should also be squared and resurfaced, by placing the stem in the V-block of the grinder, and turning it while pressing lightly against the grinding wheel. NOTE: *Do not grind sodium filled exhaust valves on a machine. These should be hand lapped.*

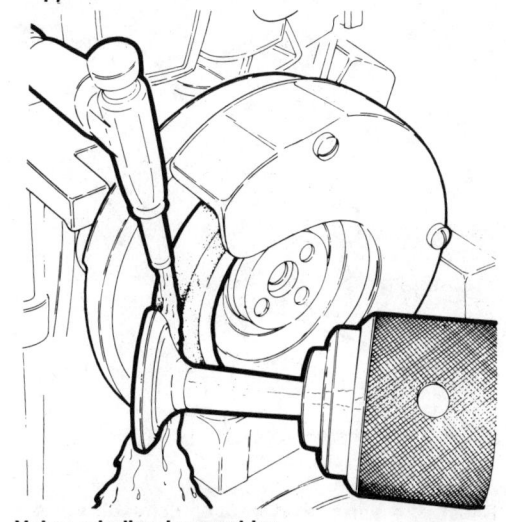

FOR DIMENSIONS, REFER TO SPECIFICATIONS

CHECK FOR BENT STEM

DIAMETER

VALVE FACE ANGLE

1/32" MINIMUM

THIS LINE PARALLEL WITH VALVE HEAD

Critical valve dimensions

Valve grinding by machine

ENGINE AND ENGINE REBUILDING

Cylinder Head Reconditioning

Procedure	Method
Resurface the valve seats using reamers or grinder: *Valve seat width and centering* *Reaming the valve seat with a hand reamer*	Select a reamer of the correct seat angle, slightly larger than the diameter of the valve seat, and assemble it with a pilot of the correct size. Install the pilot into the valve guide, and using steady pressure, turn the reamer clockwise. **CAUTION:** *Do not turn the reamer counterclockwise.* Remove only as much material as necessary to clean the seat. Check the concentricity of the seat (following). If the dye method is not used, coat the valve face with Prussian blue dye, install and rotate it on the valve seat. Using the dye marked area as a centering guide, center and narrow the valve seat to specifications with correction cutters. **NOTE:** *When no specifications are available, minimum seat width for exhaust valves should be 5/64", intake valves 1/16".* After making correction cuts, check the position of the valve seat on the valve face using Prussian blue dye. To resurface the seat with a power grinder, select a pilot of the correct size and coarse stone of the proper angle. Lubricate the pilot and move the stone on and off the valve seat at 2 cycles per second, until all flaws are gone. Finish the seat with a fine stone. If necessary the seat can be corrected or narrowed using correction stones.
Check the valve seat concentricity: *Check the valve seat concentricity with a dial gauge*	Coat the valve face with Prussian blue dye, install the valve, and rotate it on the valve seat. If the entire seat becomes coated, and the valve is known to be concentric, the seat is concentric. * Install the dial gauge pilot into the guide, and rest of the arm on the valve seat. Zero the gauge, and rotate the arm around the seat. Run-out should not exceed .002".

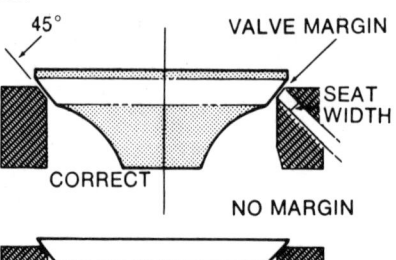

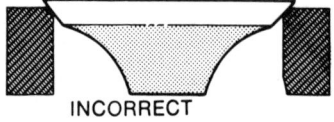

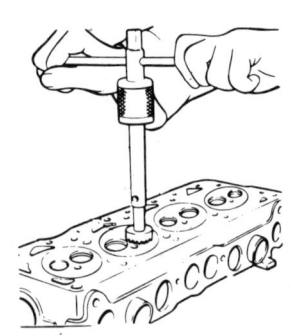

ENGINE AND ENGINE REBUILDING   49

Cylinder Head Reconditioning

Procedure	Method
*Lap the valves: NOTE: *Valve lapping is done to ensure efficient sealing of resurfaced valves and seats.*	Invert the cyclinder head, lightly lubricate the valve stems, and install the valves in the head as numbered. Coat valve seats with fine grinding compound, and attach the lapping tool suction cup to a valve head. NOTE: *Moisten the suction cup.* Rotate the tool between the palms, changing position and lifting the tool often to prevent grooving. Lap the valve until a smooth, polished seat is evident. Remove the valve and tool, and rinse away all traces of grinding compound.
	**Fasten a suction cup to a piece of drill rod, and mount the rod in a hand drill. Proceed as above, using the hand drill as a lapping tool. CAUTION: *Due to the higher speeds involved when using the hand drill, care must be exercised to avoid grooving the seat.* Lift the tool and change direction of rotation often.

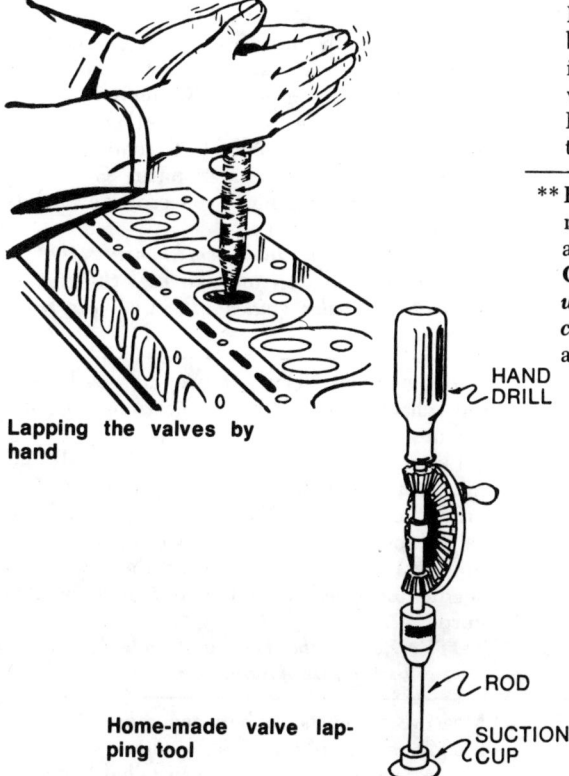

Lapping the valves by hand

Home-made valve lapping tool

Check the valve springs:	Place the spring on a flat surface next to a square. Measure the height of the spring, and rotate it against the edge of the square to measure distortion. If spring height varies (by comparison) by more than $1/16''$ or if distortion exceeds $1/16''$, replace the spring.
	**In addition to evaluating the spring as above, test the spring pressure at the installed and compressed (installed height minus valve lift) height using a valve spring tester. Springs used on small displacement engines (up to 3 liters) should be ∓ 1 lb of all other springs in either position. A tolerance of ∓ 5 lbs is permissible on larger engines.

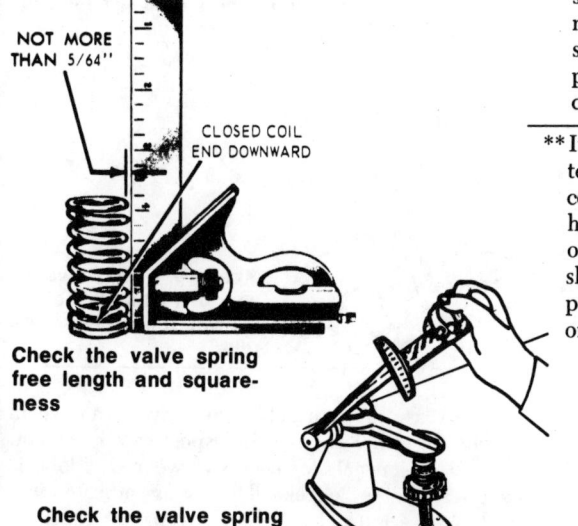

NOT MORE THAN 5/64″

CLOSED COIL END DOWNWARD

Check the valve spring free length and squareness

Check the valve spring test pressure

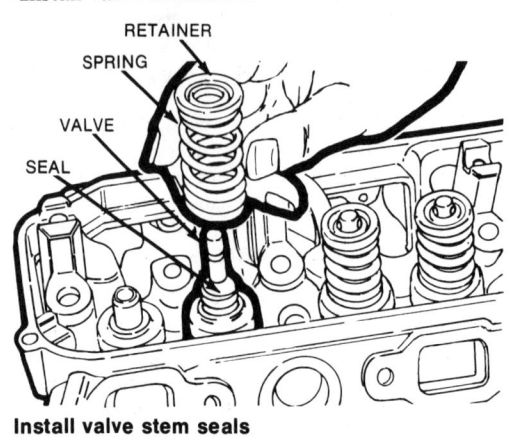

ENGINE AND ENGINE REBUILDING

Cylinder Head Reconditioning

Procedure	Method
*Install valve stem seals: **Install valve stem seals**	*Due to the pressure differential that exists at the ends of the intake valve guides (atmospheric pressure above, manifold vacuum below), oil is drawn through the valve guides into the intake port. This has been alleviated somewhat since the addition of positive crankcase ventilation, which lowers the pressure above the guides. Several types of valve stem seals are available to reduce blow-by. Certain seals simply slip over the stem and guide boss, while others require that the boss be machined. Recently, Teflon guide seals have become popular. Consult a parts supplier or machinist concerning availability and suggested usages. NOTE: *When installing seals, ensure that a small amount of oil is able to pass the seal to lubricate the valve guides; otherwise, excessive wear may result.*
Install the valves:	See the engine service procedures earlier in this chapter for details concerning specific engines. Lubricate the valve stems, and install the valves in the cylinder head as numbered. Lubricate and position the seals (if used) and the valve springs. Install the spring retainers, compress the springs, and insert the keys using needlenose pliers or a tool designed for this purpose. NOTE: *Retain the keys with wheel bearing grease during installation.*
Check valve spring installed height: **Valve spring installed height (A)**	Measure the distance between the spring pad the lower edge of the spring retainer, and compare to specifications. If the installed height is incorrect, add shim washers between the spring pad and the spring. CAUTION: *Use only washers designed for this purpose.* **Measure the valve spring installed height (A) with a modified steel rule**
Clean and inspect the camshaft:	Degrease the camshaft, using solvent, and clean out all oil holes. Visually inspect cam lobes and bearing journals for excessive wear. If a lobe is questionable, check all lobes as indicated below. If a journal or lobe is worn, the camshaft must be reground or replaced.

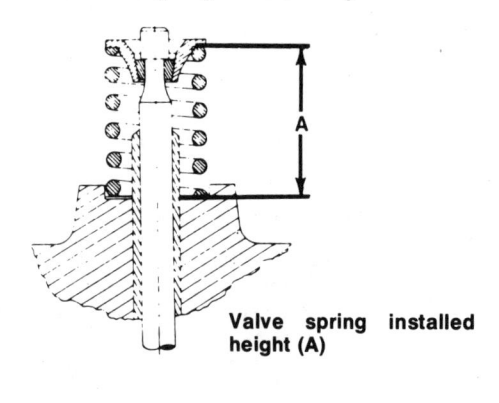

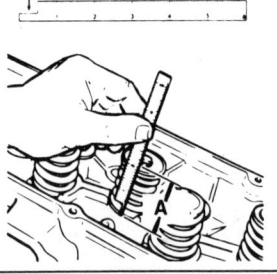

ENGINE AND ENGINE REBUILDING 51

Cylinder Head Reconditioning

Procedure	Method
	NOTE: *If a journal is worn, there is a good chance that the bushings are worn.* If lobes and journals appear intact, place the front and rear journals in V-blocks, and rest a dial indicator on the center journal. Rotate the camshaft to check straightness. If deviation exceeds .001", replace the camshaft. *Check the camshaft lobes with a micrometer, by measuring the lobes from the nose to base and again at 90° (see illustration). The lift is determined by subtracting the second measurement from the first. If all exhaust lobes and all intake lobes are not identical, the camshaft must be reground or replaced.
Check the camshaft for straightness	**Camshaft lobe measurement**
Install the camshaft:	See the engine service procedures earlier in this chapter for details concerning specific engines.
Install the rocker arms:	See the engine service procedures earlier in this chapter for details concerning specific engines.

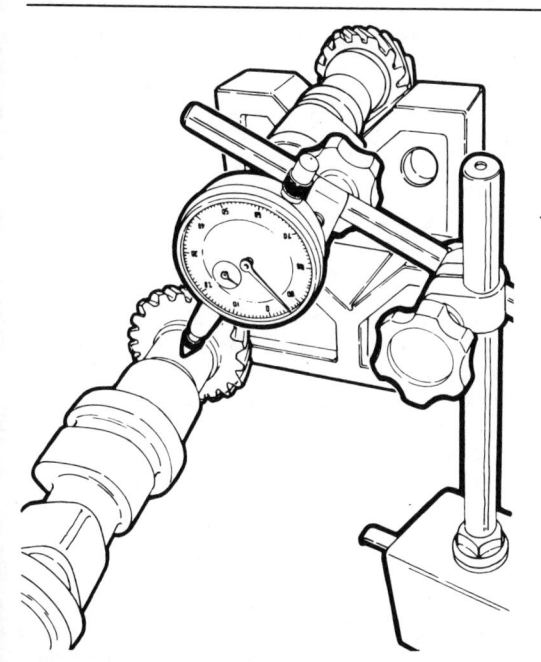

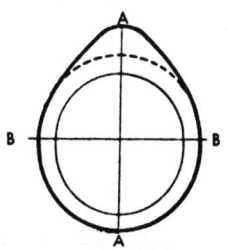

Cylinder Block Reconditioning

Procedure	Method
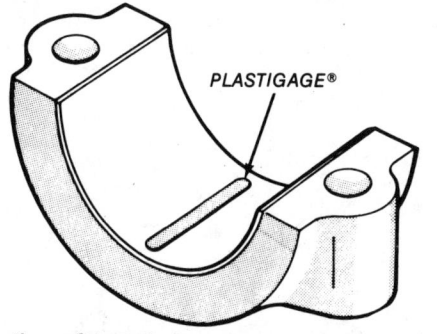 Checking the main bearing clearance:	Invert engine, and remove cap from the bearing to be checked. Using a clean, dry rag, thoroughly clean all oil from crankshaft journal and bearing insert. NOTE: *Plastigage® is soluble in oil; therefore, oil on the journal or bearing could result in erroneous readings.* Place a piece of Plastigage along the full length of journal, reinstall cap, and torque to specifications. NOTE: *Specifications are given in the engine specifications earlier in this chapter.* Remove bearing cap, and determine bearing clearance by comparing width of Plastigage to the scale on Plastigage envelope. Journal taper is determined by comparing width of the Plastigage strip near its ends. Rotate crankshaft 90° and retest, to determine journal eccentricity. NOTE: *Do not rotate crankshaft with Plastigage installed.* If bearing insert and journal appear in-
Plastigage® installed on the lower bearing shell	

52 ENGINE AND ENGINE REBUILDING

Cylinder Block Reconditioning

Procedure	Method
Measure Plastigage® to determine main bearing clearance	tact, and are within tolerances, no further main bearing service is required. If bearing or journal appear defective, cause of failure should be determined before replacement. *Remove crankshaft from block (see below). Measure the main bearing journals at each end twice (90° apart) using a micrometer, to determine diameter, journal taper and eccentricity. If journals are within tolerances, reinstall bearing caps at their specified torque. Using a telescope gauge and micrometer, measure bearing I.D. parallel to piston axis and at 30° on each side of piston axis. Subtract journal O.D. from bearing I.D. to determine oil clearance. If crankshaft journals appear defective, or do not meet tolerances, there is no need to measure bearings; for the crankshaft will require grinding and/or undersize bearings will be required. If bearing appears defective, cause for failure should be determined prior to replacement.
Check the connecting rod bearing clearance:	Connecting rod bearing clearance is checked in the same manner as main bearing clearance, using Plastigage. Before removing the crankshaft, connecting rod side clearance also should be measured and recorded. *Checking connecting rod bearing clearance, using a micrometer, is identical to checking main bearing clearance. If no other service is required, the piston and rod assemblies need not be removed.
Remove the crankshaft: 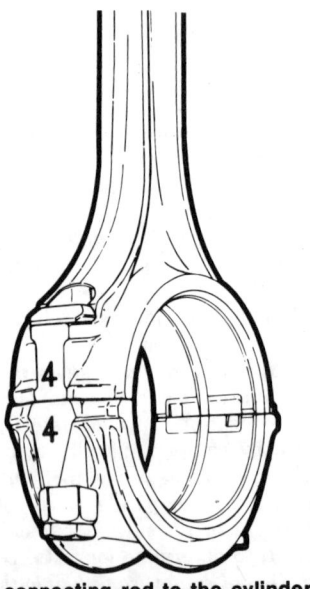 **Match the connecting rod to the cylinder with a number stamp**	Using a punch, mark the corresponding main bearing caps and saddles according to position (i.e., one punch on the front main cap and saddle, two on the second, three on the third, etc.). Using number stamps, identify the corresponding connecting rods and caps, according to cylinder (if no numbers are present). Remove the main and connecting rod caps, and replace sleeves of plastic tubing or vacuum hose over the connecting rod bolts, to protect the journals as the crankshaft is removed. Lift the crankshaft out of the block. 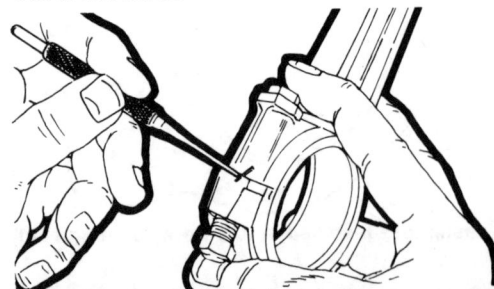 **Match the connecting rod and cap with scribe marks**

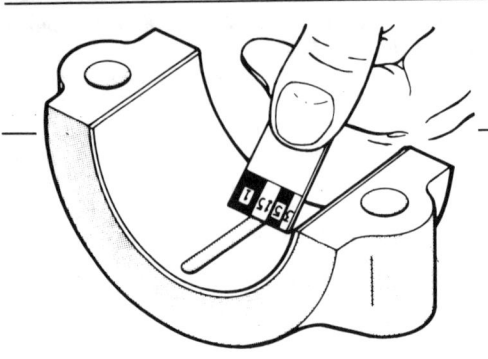

ENGINE AND ENGINE REBUILDING

Cylinder Block Reconditioning

Procedure	Method
Remove the ridge from the top of the cylinder: 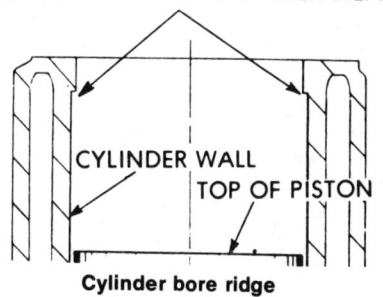 RIDGE CAUSED BY CYLINDER WEAR CYLINDER WALL TOP OF PISTON **Cylinder bore ridge**	In order to facilitate removal of the piston and connecting rod, the ridge at the top of the cylinder (unworn area; see illustration) must be removed. Place the piston at the bottom of the bore, and cover it with a rag. Cut the ridge away using a ridge reamer, exercising extreme care to avoid cutting too deeply. Remove the rag, and remove cuttings that remain on the piston. CAUTION: *If the ridge is not removed, and new rings are installed, damage to rings will result.*
Remove the piston and connecting rod: 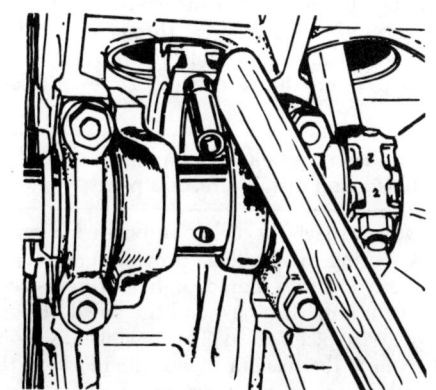 **Push the piston out with a hammer handle**	Invert the engine, and push the pistons and connecting rods out of the cylinders. If necessary, tap the connecting rod boss with a wooden hammer handle, to force the piston out. CAUTION: *Do not attempt to force the piston past the cylinder ridge* (see above).
Service the crankshaft:	Ensure that all oil holes and passages in the crankshaft are open and free of sludge. If necessary, have the crankshaft ground to the largest possible undersize.
	**Have the crankshaft Magnafluxed, to locate stress cracks. Consult a machinist concerning additional service procedures, such as surface hardening (e.g., nitriding, Tuftriding) to improve wear characteristics, cross drilling and chamfering the oil holes to improve lubrication, and balancing.
Removing freeze plugs:	Drill a small hole in the middle of the freeze plugs. Thread a large sheet metal screw into the hole and remove the plug with a slide hammer.
Remove the oil gallery plugs:	Threaded plugs should be removed using an appropriate (usually square) wrench. To remove soft, pressed in plugs, drill a hole in the plug, and thread in a sheet metal screw. Pull the plug out by the screw using pliers.
Hot-tank the block: NOTE: *Do not hot-tank aluminum parts.*	Have the block hot-tanked to remove grease, corrosion, and scale from the water jackets. NOTE: *Consult the operator to determine whether the camshaft bearings will be damaged during the hot-tank process.*

54 ENGINE AND ENGINE REBUILDING

Cylinder Block Reconditioning

Procedure	Method

Check the block for cracks:	Visually inspect the block for cracks or chips. The most common locations are as follows:
	    Adjacent to freeze plugs.
	    Between the cylinders and water jackets.
	    Adjacent to the main bearing saddles.
	    At the extreme bottom of the cylinders.
	Check only suspected cracks using spot check dye (see introduction). If a crack is located, consult a machinist concerning possible repairs.

	** Magnaflux the block to locate hidden cracks. If cracks are located, consult a machinist about feasibility of repair.
Install the oil gallery plugs and freeze plugs:	Coat freeze plugs with sealer and tap into position using a piece of pipe, slightly smaller than the plug, as a driver. To ensure retention, stake the edges of the plugs. Coat threaded oil gallery plugs with sealer and install. Drive replacement soft plugs into block using a large drift as a driver.
	* Rather than reinstalling lead plugs, drill and tap the holes, and install threaded plugs.
Check the bore diameter and surface:	Visually inspect the cylinder bores for roughness, scoring, or scuffing. If evident, the cylinder bore must be bored or honed oversize to eliminate imperfections, and the smallest possible oversize piston used. The new pistons should be given to the machinist with the block, so that the cylinders can be bored or honed exactly to the piston size (plus clearance). If no flaws are evident, measure the bore diameter using a telescope gauge and micrometer, or dial gauge, parallel and perpendicular to the engine centerline, at the top (below the ridge) and bottom of the bore. Subtract the bottom measurements from the top to determine taper, and the parallel to the centerline measurements from the perpendicular measurements to determine eccentricity. If the measurements are not within specifications, the cylinder must be bored or honed, and an oversize piston installed. If the measurements are within specifications the cylinder may

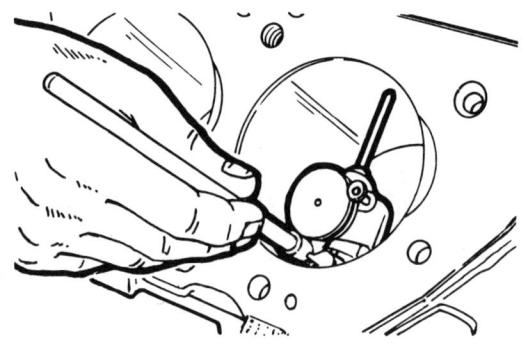

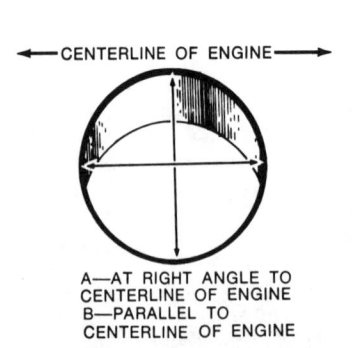

Measure the cylinder bore with a dial gauge

Cylinder bore measuring points
A—AT RIGHT ANGLE TO CENTERLINE OF ENGINE
B—PARALLEL TO CENTERLINE OF ENGINE

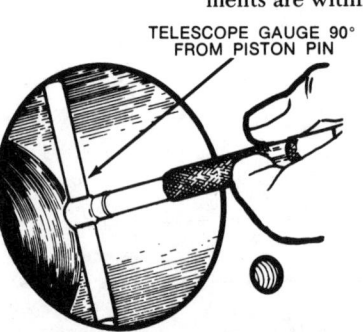

Measure the cylinder bore with a telescope gauge

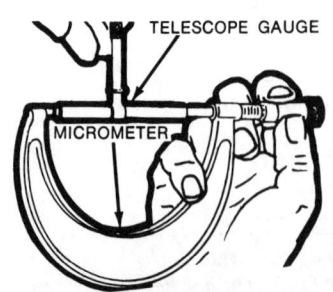

Measure the telescope gauge with a micrometer to determine the cylinder bore

ENGINE AND ENGINE REBUILDING

Cylinder Block Reconditioning

Procedure	Method
	be used as is, with only finish honing (see below). **NOTE:** *Prior to submitting the block for boring, perform the following operation(s).*
Check the cylinder block bearing alignment: Check the main bearing saddle alignment	Remove the upper bearing inserts. Place a straightedge in the bearing saddles along the centerline of the crankshaft. If clearance exists between the straightedge and the center saddle, the block must be alignbored.
*Check the deck height:	The deck height is the distance from the crankshaft centerline to the block deck. To measure, invert the engine, and install the crankshaft, retaining it with the center maincap. Measure the distance from the crankshaft journal to the block deck, parallel to the cylinder centerline. Measure the diameter of the end (front and rear) main journals, parallel to the centerline of the cylinders, divide the diameter in half, and subtract it from the previous measurement. The results of the front and rear measurements should be identical. If the difference exceeds .005", the deck height should be corrected. **NOTE:** *Block deck height and warpage should be corrected at the same time.*
Check the block deck for warpage:	Using a straightedge and feeler gauges, check the block deck for warpage in the same manner that the cylinder head is checked (see Cylinder Head Reconditioning). If warpage exceeds specifications, have the deck resurfaced. **NOTE:** *In certain cases a specification for total material removal (cylinder head and block deck) is provided. This specification must not be exceeded.*
Clean and inspect the pistons and connecting rods: RING EXPANDER Remove the piston rings	Using a ring expander, remove the rings from the piston. Remove the retaining rings (if so equipped) and remove piston pin. **NOTE:** *If the piston pin must be pressed out, determine the proper method and use the proper tools; otherwise the piston will distort.* Clean the ring grooves using an appropriate tool, exercising care to avoid cutting too deeply. Thoroughly clean all carbon and varnish from the piston with solvent. **CAUTION:** *Do not use a wire brush or caustic solvent on pistons.* Inspect the pistons for scuffing, scoring, cracks, pitting, or excessive ringsgroove wear. If wear is evident, the piston must be replaced. Check the connecting rod length by measuring

56 ENGINE AND ENGINE REBUILDING

Cylinder Block Reconditioning

Procedure	Method
RING GROOVE CLEANER **Clean the piston ring grooves**	the rod from the inside of the large end to the inside of the small end using calipers (see illustration). All connecting rods should be equal length. Replace any rod that differs from the others in the engine.
	* Have the connecting rod alignment checked in an alignment fixture by a machinist. Replace any twisted or bent rods.
Check the connecting rod length (arrow)	* Magnaflux the connecting rods to locate stress cracks. If cracks are found, replace the connecting rod.
Fit the pistons to the cylinders: 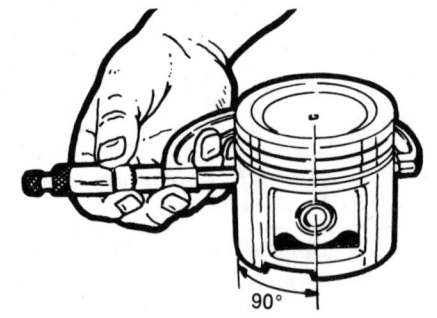 90° **Measure the piston prior to fitting**	Using a telescope gauge and micrometer, or a dial gauge, measure the cylinder bore diameter perpendicular to the piston pin, 2½" below the deck. Measure the piston perpendicular to its pin on the skirt. The difference between the two measurements is the piston clearance. If the clearance is within specifications or slightly below (after boring or honing), finish honing is all that is required. If the clearance is excessive, try to obtain a slightly larger piston to bring clearance within specifications. Where this is not possible, obtain the first oversize piston, and hone (of if necessary, bore) the cylinder to size.
Assemble the pistons and connecting rods: 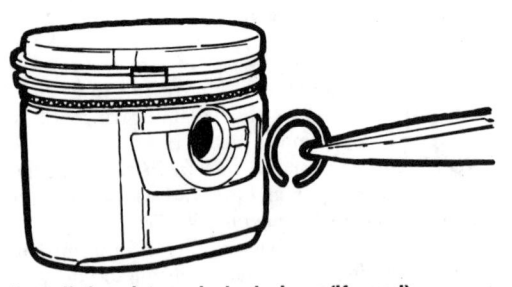 **Install the piston pin lock-rings (if used)**	Inspect piston pin, connecting rod small end bushing, and piston bore for galling, scoring, or excessive wear. If evident, replace defective part(s). Measure the I.D. of the piston boss and connecting rod small end, and the O.D. of the piston pin. If within specifications, assemble piston pin and rod. **CAUTION:** *If piston pin must be pressed in, determine the proper method and use the proper tools; otherwise the piston will distort.* Install the lock rings; ensure that they seat properly. If the parts are not within specifications, determine the service method for the type of engine. In some cases, piston and pin are serviced as an assembly when either is defective. Others specify reaming the piston and connecting rods for an oversize pin. If the connecting rod bushing is worn, it may in many cases be replaced. Reaming the piston and replacing the rod bushing are machine shop operations.

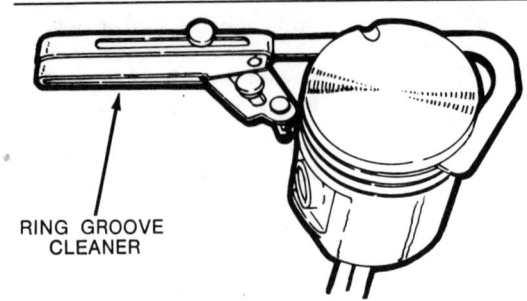

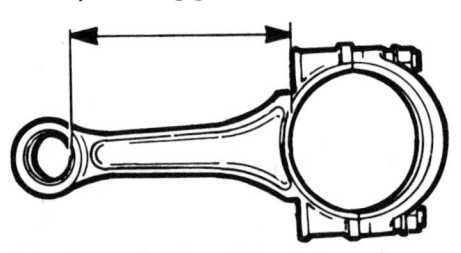

ENGINE AND ENGINE REBUILDING

Cylinder Block Reconditioning

Procedure	Method
Finish hone the cylinders:	Chuck a flexible drive hone into a power drill, and insert it into the cylinder. Start the hone, and move it up and down in the cylinder at a rate which will produce approximately a 60° cross-hatch pattern. **NOTE:** *Do not extend the hone below the cylinder bore.* After developing the pattern, remove the hone and recheck piston fit. Wash the cylinders with a detergent and water solution to remove abrasive dust, dry, and wipe several times with a rag soaked in engine oil.
Check piston ring end-gap: Check the piston ring end gap	Compress the piston rings to be used in a cylinder, one at a time, into that cylinder, and press them approximately 1" below the deck with an inverted piston. Using feeler gauges, measure the ring end-gap, and compare to specifications. Pull the ring out of the cylinder and file the ends with a fine file to obtain proper clearance. **CAUTION:** *If inadequate ring end-gap is utilized, ring breakage will result.*
Install the piston rings: Check the piston ring side clearance	Inspect the ring grooves in the piston for excessive wear or taper. If necessary, recut the groove(s) for use with an overwidth ring or a standard ring and spacer. If the groove is worn uniformly, overwidth rings, or standard rings and spaces may be installed without recutting. Roll the outside of the ring around the groove to check for burrs or deposits. If any are found, remove with a fine file. Hold the ring in the groove, and measure side clearance. If necessary, correct as indicated above. **NOTE:** *Always install any additional spacers above the piston ring.* The ring groove must be deep enough to allow the ring to seat below the lands (see illustration). In many cases, a "go-no-go" depth gauge will be provided with the piston rings. Shallow grooves may be corrected by recutting, while deep

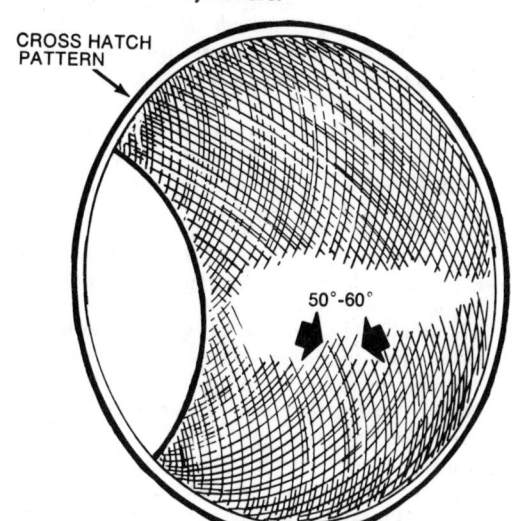

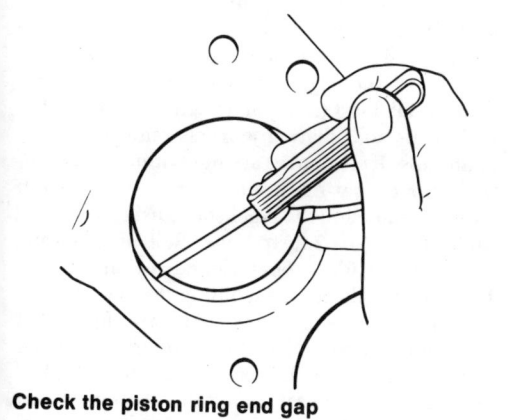

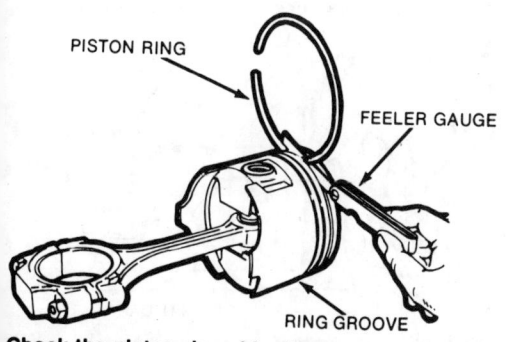

ENGINE AND ENGINE REBUILDING

Cylinder Block Reconditioning

Procedure	Method
	grooves require some type of filler or expander behind the piston. Consult the piston ring supplier concerning the suggested method. Install the rings on the piston, lowest ring first, using a ring expander. **NOTE:** *Position the rings as specified by the manufacturer.* Consult the engine service procedures earlier in this chapter for details concerning specific engines.
Install the rear main seal:	See the engine service procedures earlier in this chapter for details concerning specific engines.
Install the crankshaft: Remove or install the upper bearing insert using a roll-out pin Home-made bearing roll-out pin	Thoroughly clean the main bearing saddles and caps. Place the upper halves of the bearing inserts on the saddles and press into position. **NOTE:** *Ensure that the oil holes align.* Press the corresponding bearing inserts into the main bearing caps. Lubricate the upper main bearings, and lay the crankshaft in position. Place a strip of Plastigage on each of the crankshaft journals, install the main caps, and torque to specifications. Remove the main caps, and compare the Plastigage to the scale on the Plastigage envelope. If clearances are within tolerances, remove the Plastigage, turn the crankshaft 90°, wipe off all oil and retest. If all clearances are correct, remove all Plastigage, thoroughly lubricate the main caps and bearing journals, and install the main caps. If clearances are not within tolerance, the upper bearing inserts may be removed, without removing the crankshaft, using a bearing roll out pin (see illustration). Roll in a bearing that will provide proper clearance, and retest. Torque all main caps, excluding the thrust bearing cap, to specifications. Tighten the thrust bearing cap finger tight. To properly align the thrust bearing, pry the crankshaft the extent of its axial travel several times, the last movement held toward the front of the engine, and torque the thrust bearing cap to specifications. Determine the crankshaft end-play (see below), and bring within tolerance with thrust washers.
Aligning the thrust bearing	
Measure crankshaft end-play:	Mount a dial indicator stand on the front of the block, with the dial indicator stem resting on the

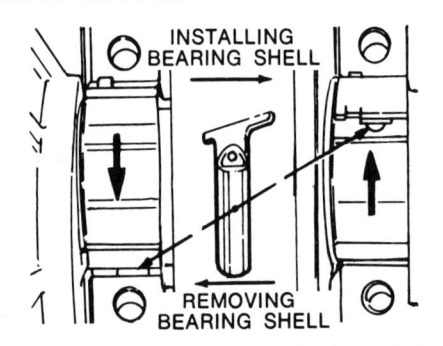

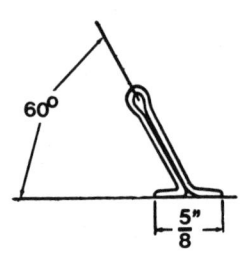

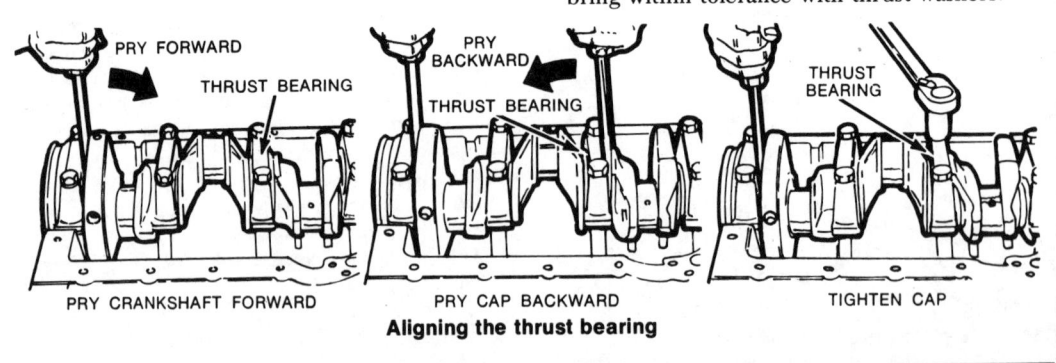

ENGINE AND ENGINE REBUILDING

Cylinder Block Reconditioning

Procedure	Method

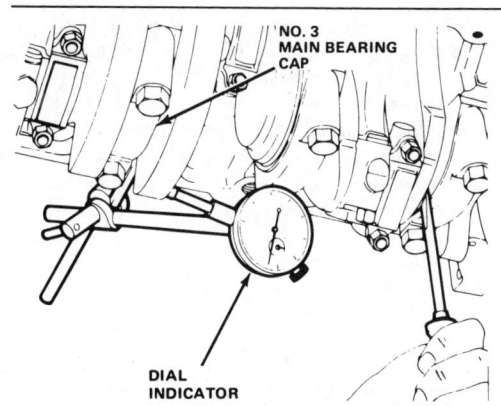

Check the crankshaft end-play with a dial indicator

Check the crankshaft end-play with a feeler gauge

nose of the crankshaft, parallel to the crankshaft axis. Pry the crankshaft the extent of its travel rearward, and zero the indicator. Pry the crankshaft forward and record crankshaft end-play.
NOTE: *Crankshaft end-play also may be measured at the thrust bearing, using feeler gauges* (see illustration).

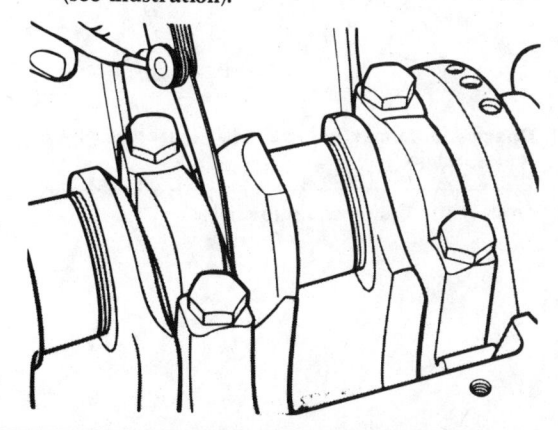

Install the pistons:

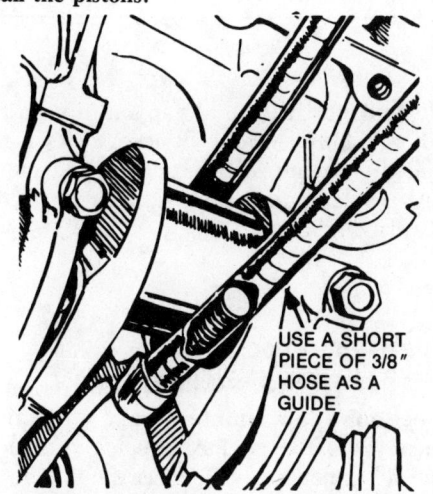

Use lengths of vacuum hose or rubber tubing to protect the crankshaft journals and cylinder walls during piston installation

Press the upper connecting rod bearing halves into the connecting rods, and the lower halves into the connecting rod caps. Position the piston ring gaps according to specifications (see car section), and lubricate the pistons. Install a ring compressor on a piston, and press two long (8″) pieces of plastic tubing over the rod bolts. Using the tubes as a guide, press the pistons into the bores and onto the crankshaft with a wooden hammer handle. After seating the rod on the crankshaft journal, remove the tubes and install the cap finger tight. Install the remaining pistons in the same manner. Invert the engine and check the bearing clearance at two points (90° apart) on each journal with Plastigage.
NOTE: *Do not turn the crankshaft with Plastigage installed.*

If clearance is within tolerances, remove *all* Plastigage, thoroughly lubricate the journals, and torque the rod caps to specifications. If clearance is not within specifications, install different thickness bearing inserts and recheck.
CAUTION: *Never shim or file the connecting rods or caps.*

Always install plastic tube sleeves over the rod bolts when the caps are not installed, to protect the crankshaft journals.

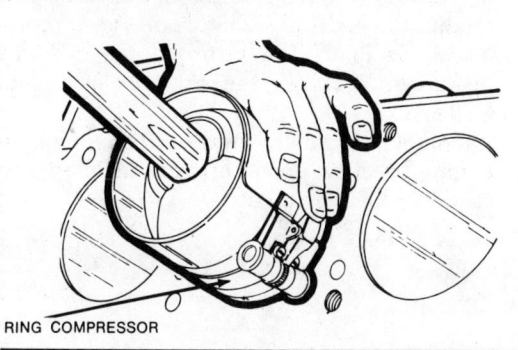

Install the piston using a ring compressor

ENGINE AND ENGINE REBUILDING

Cylinder Block Reconditioning

Procedure	Method
Check connecting rod side clearance: Check the connecting rod side clearance with a feeler gauge	Determine the clearance between the sides of the connecting rods and the crankshaft using feeler gauges. If clearance is below the minimum tolerance, the rod may be machined to provide adequate clearance. If clearance is excessive, substitute an unworn rod, and recheck. If clearance is still outside specifications, the crankshaft must be welded and reground, or replaced.
Inspect the timing chain (or belt):	Visually inspect the timing chain for broken or loose links, and replace the chain if any are found. If the chain will flex sideways, it must be replaced. Install the timing chain as specified. Be sure the timing belt is not stretched, frayed or broken. NOTE: *If the original timing chain is to be reused, install it in its original position.* See the engine service procedures earlier in this chapter for details concerning specific engines.

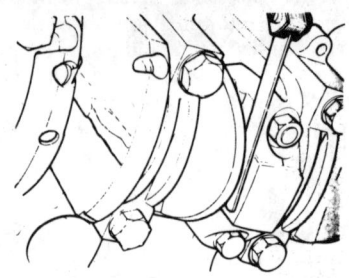

Completing the Rebuilding Process

Following the above procedures, complete the rebuilding process as follows:

Fill the oil pump with oil, to prevent cavitating (sucking air) on initial engine start up. Install the oil pump and the pickup tube on the engine. Coat the oil pan gasket as necessary, and install the gasket and the oil pan. Mount the flywheel and the crankshaft vibration damper or pulley on the crankshaft.
NOTE: *Always use new bolts when installing the flywheel.* Inspect the clutch shaft pilot bushing in the crankshaft. If the bushing is excessively worn, remove it with an expanding puller and a slide hammer, and tap a new bushing into place.

Position the engine, cylinder head side up. Install the cylinder head, and torque it as specified. Install the rocker arms and adjust the valves.

Install the intake and exhaust manifolds, the carburetor(s), the distributor and spark plugs. Adjust the point gap and the static ignition timing. Mount all accessories and install the engine in the car. Fill the radiator with coolant, and the crankcase with high quality engine oil.

Break-in Procedure

Start the engine, and allow it to run at low speed for a few minutes, while checking for leaks. Stop the engine, check the oil level, and fill as necessary. Restart the engine, and fill the cooling system to capacity. Check the point dwell angle and adjust the ignition timing and the valves. Run the engine at low to medium speed (800–2500 rpm) for approximately ½ hour, and retorque the cylinder head bolts. Road test the car, and check again for leaks.

Follow the manufacturer's recommended engine break-in procedure and maintenance schedule for new engines.

Emission Controls and Fuel System

EMISSION CONTROL SYSTEMS

Several different systems are used on each car. Most require no service and those which may require service also require sophisticated equipment for testing purposes.

Catalytic Converter

Two catalysts are used on each car: A small one located just after the exhaust manifold and a larger one located under the car body. Catalysts promote complete oxidation of exhaust gases through the effect of a platinum coated mass in the catalyst shell. Two things act to destroy the catalyst, functionally: excessive heat and leaded gas. Excessive heat during misfiring and prolonged testing with the ignition system in any way altered is the most common occurence. Test procedures should be accomplished as quickly as possible, and the car, should not be driven when misfiring is noted.

Heated Air Inlet System

All engines are equipped with a vacuum device located in the carburetor air cleaner air intake. A small door is operated by a vacuum diaphragm and a thermostatic spring. When the air temperature outside is 40°F or lower, the door will block off air entering from outside and allow air channelled from the exhaust manifold area to enter the intake. This air is heated by the hot manifold. At 65°F or above, the door fully blocks off the heated air. At temperatures in between, the door is operated in intermediate positions. During acceleration the door is controlled by engine vacuum to allow the maximum amount of air to enter the carburetor.

Exhaust Gas Recirculation System

This system reduces the amount of oxides of nitrogen in the exhaust by allowing a prede-

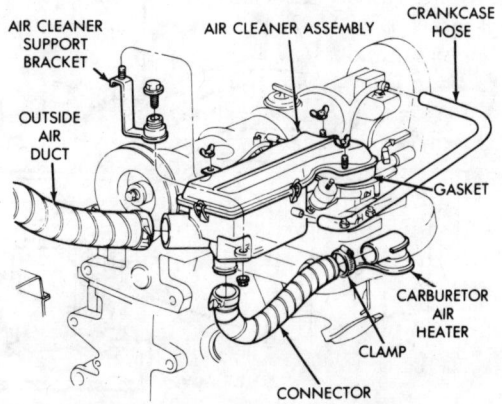

Heated inlet air system—2.2L engine

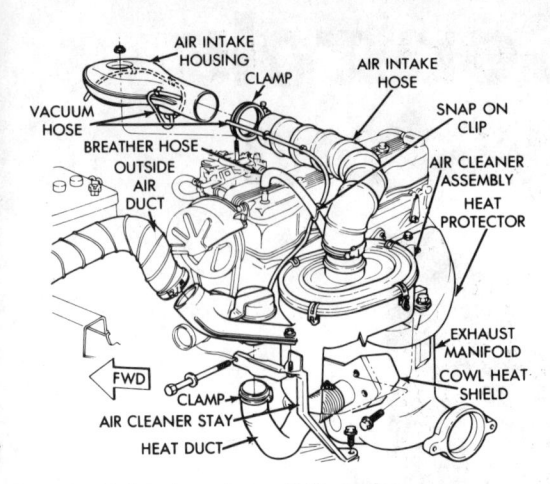

62 EMISSION CONTROLS AND FUEL SYSTEM

Heated inlet air system—2.6L engine

termined amount of hot exhaust gases to recirculate and dilute the incoming fuel/air mixture. The principal components of the system are the EGR valve and the Coolan Control Exhaust Gas Recirculation Valve (CCEGR). The former is located in the intake manifold and directly regulates the flow of exhaust gases into the intake. The latter is located in the thermostat housing and overrides the EGR valve when coolant temperature is below 125°F.

Ported Vacuum Control System

The ported vacuum control system utilizes a type port in the carburetor throttle body which is exposed to an increasing percentage of manifold vacuum as the throttle opens. This throttle bore is connected through an external nipple directly to the EGR valve. Flow rate is dependent on manifold vacuum, throttle position, and exhaust gas back pressure. Recycle at wide open throttle is eliminated by calibrating the valve opening point above manifold vacuums available at wide open throttle, since port vacuum cannot exceed manifold vacuum. The elimination of wide open throttle recycle provides maximum performance.

Air Injection System

This system is used on all 1981 and later 2.2 Liter engines. Its job is to reduce carbon monoxide and hydrocarbons to required levels. It adds a controlled amount of air to exhaust gases, causing oxidation of the gases and a reduction of carbon monoxide and hydrocarbons.

The air injection system on the 2.2 Liter engine also includes an air switching system. It has been designed so that air injection will not interfere with the EGR system to control NOx emissions, and on vehicles equipped with an oxygen sensor, to insure proper air-fuel distribution for maximum fuel economy.

The vehicles produced for sale in the 50 states pump air into the base of the exhaust manifold. The Canadian system pumps air through the head at the exhaust port.

The air injection system consists of a belt-driven air pump, a diverter valve (Canadian

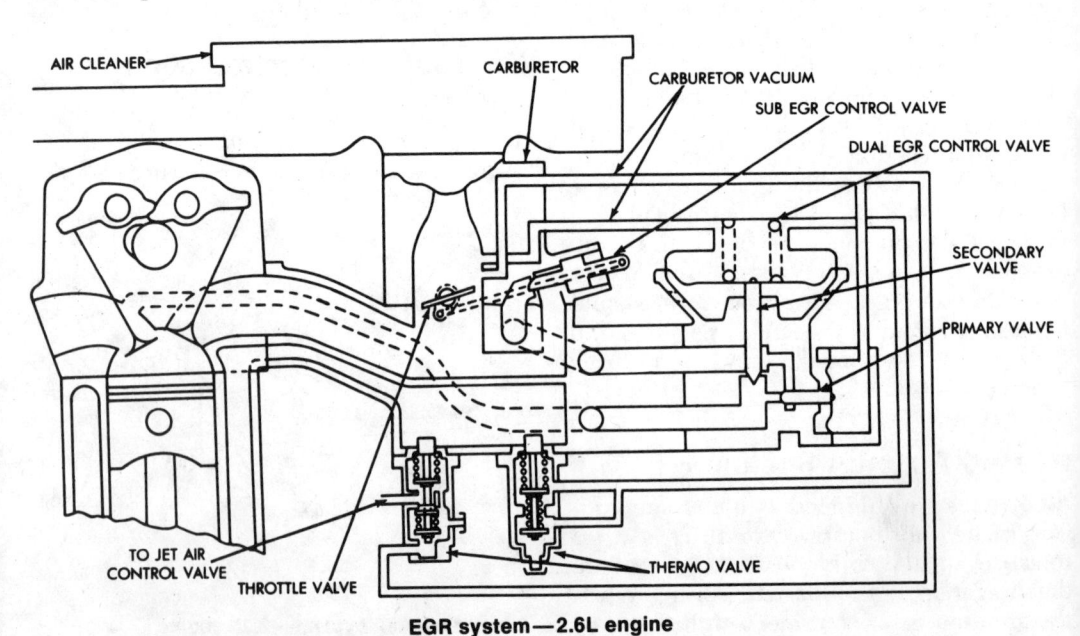

EGR system—2.6L engine

EMISSION CONTROLS AND FUEL SYSTEM

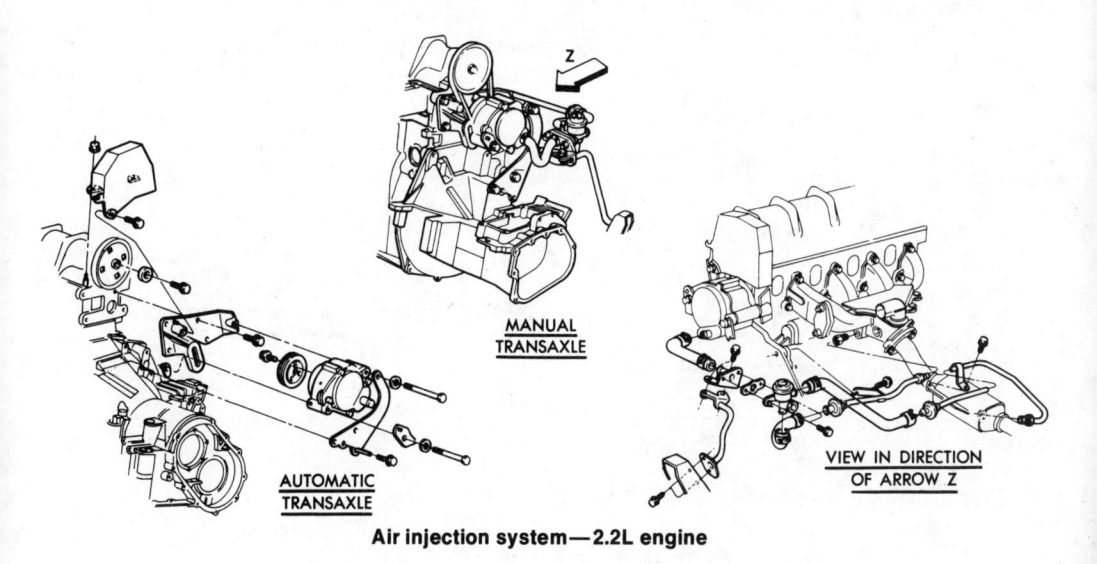

Air injection system—2.2L engine

Air injection system—2.2L engine Canada

engines only) a switch-relief valve, rubber hoses, and check valve tube assemblies to protect the hoses and other components from high temperature exhaust gases.

Pulse Air Feeder System

2.6 Liter Engines

Pulse Air Feeder (PAF) is used for supplying secondary air into the exhaust system between the front and rear catalytic converters, for the purpose of promoting oxidation of exhaust emissions in the rear converter.

The PAF consists of a main reed valve and a sub reed valve.

The main reed valve is actuated in response to movement of a diaphragm, which is activated by pressure generated when the piston is in the compression stroke. The sub reed valve is opened on the exhaust stroke.

To inspect the system, remove the hose connected to the air cleaner and check for vacuum, with the engine running. If vacuum is not present, check the lines for leaks and evidence of oil leaks. Periodic maintenance of this system is not required.

64 EMISSION CONTROLS AND FUEL SYSTEM

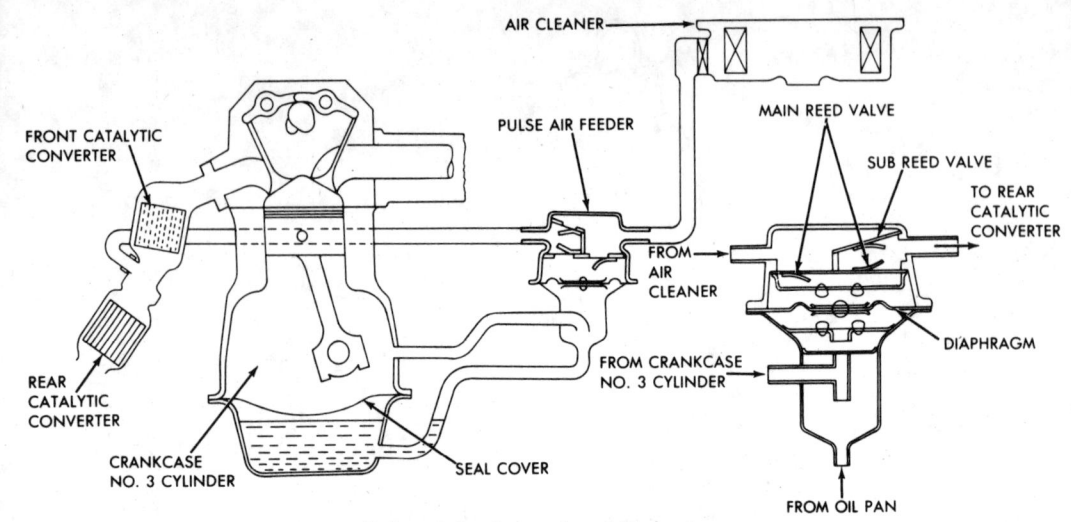

Pulse air feeder system 2.6L engine

Evaporation Control System

This system prevents the release of gasoline vapors from the fuel tank and the carburetor into the atmosphere. The system is vacuum operated and draws the fumes into a charcoal canister where they are temporarily held until they are drawn into the intake manifold for burning. For proper operation of the system and to prevent gas tank failure, the lines

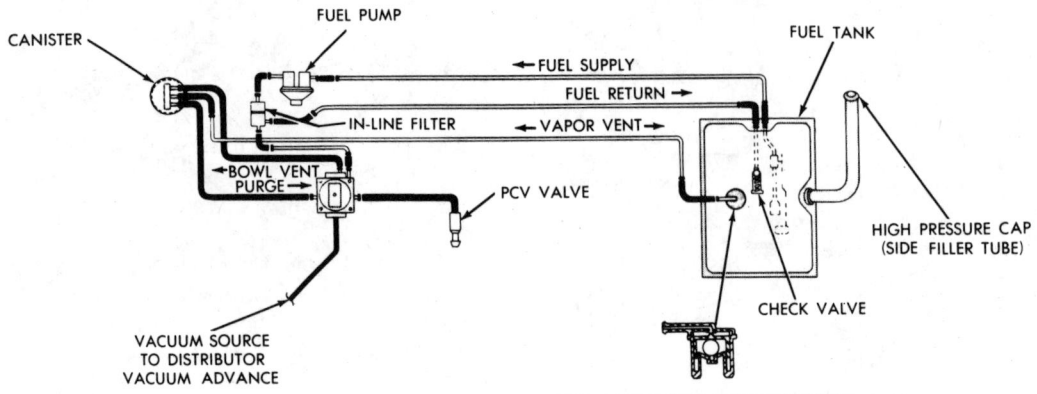

Evaporation control system—2.2L engine

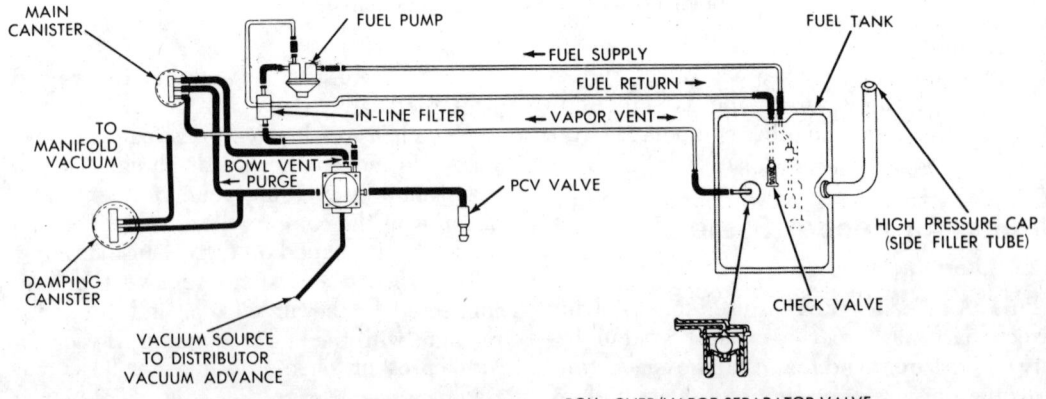

Evaporation control system—2.6L engine

EMISSION CONTROLS AND FUEL SYSTEM

should never be plugged, and no cap other than the one specified should be used on the fuel tank filler neck.

Diverter Valve

The purpose of the diverter valve is to prevent backfire in the exhaust system during sudden deceleration.

Sudden throttle closure at the beginning of deceleration temporarily creates an air-fuel mixture too rich to burn. This mixture becomes burnable when it reaches the exhaust area and combines with injector air. The next firing of the cylinder will ignite this air-fuel mixture. The valve senses the sudden increase in manifold vacuum causing the valve to open, allowing air from the pump to pass through the valve into the atmosphere.

A pressure relief valve incorporated in the same housing as the diverter valve, controls pressure within the system by diverting excessive pump output at high engine speed to the atmosphere.

Switch-Relief Valve

The purpose of this valve is two-fold. First of all, the valve directs the air injection flow to either the exhaust port location or to the downstream injection point. Second, the valve regulates system pressure by controlling the output of the air pump at high speeds. When the pressure reaches a certain level, some of the output is vented to the atmosphere through the silencer.

Check Valve

A check valve is located in the injection tube assemblies that lead to the exhaust manifold and the catalyst injection points on the 50 state engines and to the exhaust port area, through four hollow bolts on the Canadian engines.

This valve has a one-way diaphragm which prevents hot exhaust gases from backing up into the hose and pump. It also protects the system in the event of pump belt failure, excessively high exhaust system pressure, or air hose ruptures.

Deceleration Spark Advance System

The deceleration spark advance system consists of a solenoid valve and an engine speed sensor.

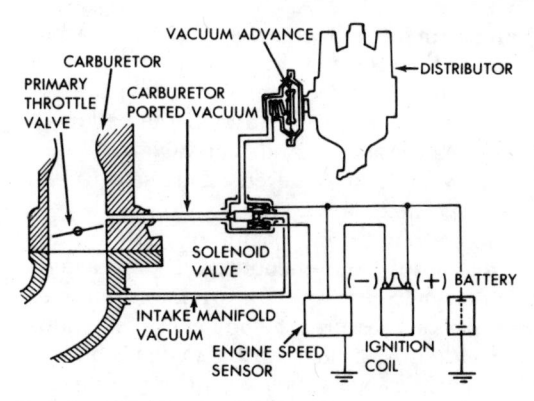

Deceleration spark advance system

During vehicle deceleration, ignition timing is advanced by intake manifold vacuum acting on the distributor advance through the solenoid valve. However, when the engine speed sensor detects engine speed at or below 1300 rpm the vacuum acting on the vacuum advance, is changed from the intake manifold to the carburetor ported vacuum by the solenoid valve movement, in order to maintain smooth vechicle operation.

High Altitude Compensation System

A high altitude compensation system is installed on California vehicles. This modification affects the primary metering system as follows:

A small cylindrical bellows chamber mounted on the body panel in the engine

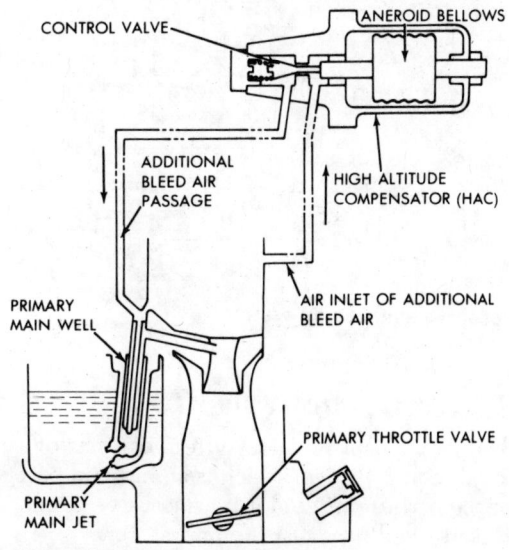

High altitude compensation system

EMISSION CONTROLS AND FUEL SYSTEM

compartment and connected to the carburetor with hoses, is vented to the atmosphere at the top of the carburetor. Atmostpheric pressure expands and contracts the bellows.

A small brass tapered-seat valve regulates air flow when it is raised off its seat by expanding the bellows.

Some time during engine operation, rarefied atmosphere is encountered, producing a rich airfuel mixture. At a predetermined atmospheric pressure, the bellows open, allowing additional air to enter the main air bleeds. The auxiliary air, along with the present air source, provides the system with the proper amount of air necessary to maintain the correct air-fuel mixture.

Throttle Opener (Idle-UP System)

This system consists of a throttle opener assembly, a solenoid valve, an engine speed sensor, and a compressor switch for the air conditioner unit.

When the compressor switch is turned on and the speed sensor detects engine speed at or below its present level, the solenoid valve is opened slightly by the throttle opener. Consequently, the engine idle speed increases to compensate for the compressor load. When the compressor switch is turned off the throttle stops working and returns to normal idle.

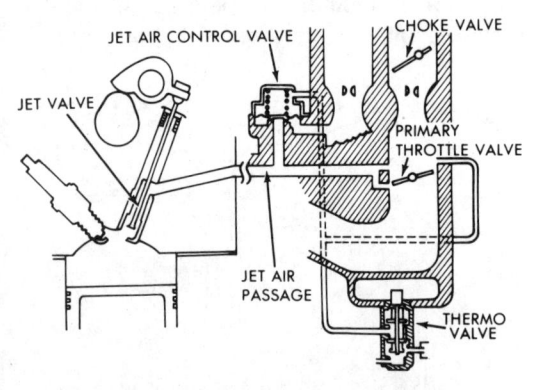

Jet air volume control system

Jet Air Control Valve (JACV)

The jet air control valve system consists of a jet air control valve, which is an integral part of the carburetor, and a thermo-valve which is controlled by coolant temperature.

Its purpose is to help decrease hydrocarbons and carbon monoxide during engine warm-up while the choke is operating.

Carburetor vacuum opens the valve thereby allowing air to flow into the jet air passage preventing an overly rich air-fuel mixture.

The function of the thermo-valve is to stop the jet valve operation when the coolant temperature is above or below a pre-set value.

Sub EGR Control Valve

This valve is an integral part of the carburetor, and is directly opened and closed by linkage connected to the throttle valve. In conjunction with the standard EGR system the sub EGR more closely modulates EGR flow in response to the throttle valve opening.

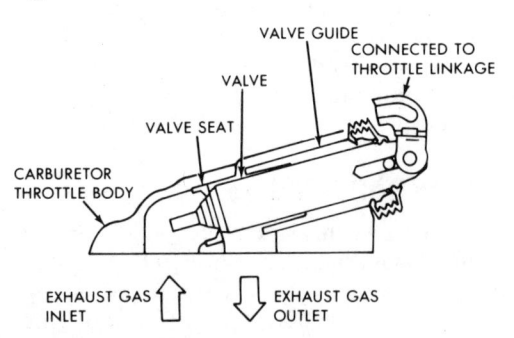

Sub EGR control valve

FUEL SYSTEM

Mechanical Fuel Pump

The fuel pump located on the left side of the engine is a mechanical type with an integral

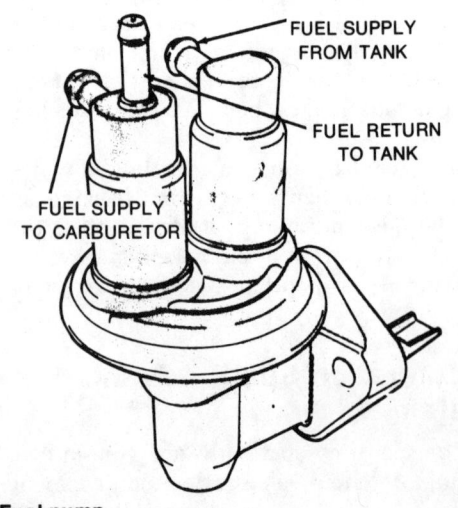

Fuel pump

EMISSION CONTROLS AND FUEL SYSTEM 67

vapor separator for satisfactory hot weather performance. The fuel pump is driven by an eccentric cam that is cast on the accessory driveshaft.

REMOVAL AND INSTALLATION

1. Disconnect the fuel and vapor lines.
2. Plug the lines to prevent fuel leaks.
3. Remove the attaching bolts and remove the fuel pump.
4. Installation is the reverse of removal.

NOTE: *The pump is not repairable. It must be replaced as a complete unit.*

Always use a new gasket when installing the pump and make certain that the gasket surfaces are clean.

Carburetors

REMOVAL AND INSTALLATION

NOTE: *When removing the carburetor on the 2.2 Liter engine, it should not be necessary to disturb the isolator, unless it has been determined that there is a leak in it.*

1. Disconnect the negative battery terminal.

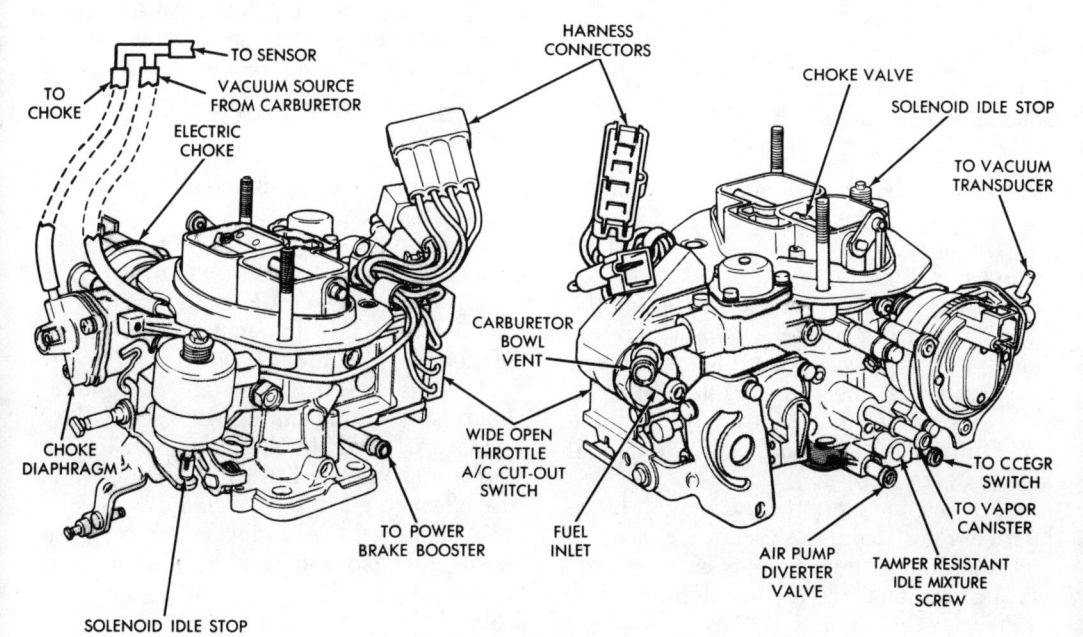

Details of the 2.2L carburetor

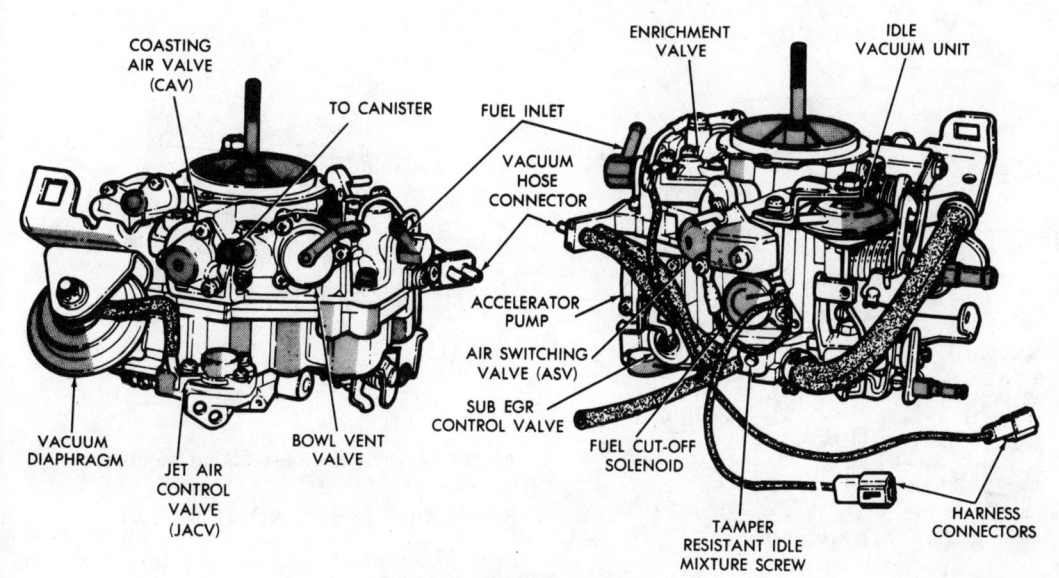

Details of the 2.6L carburetor

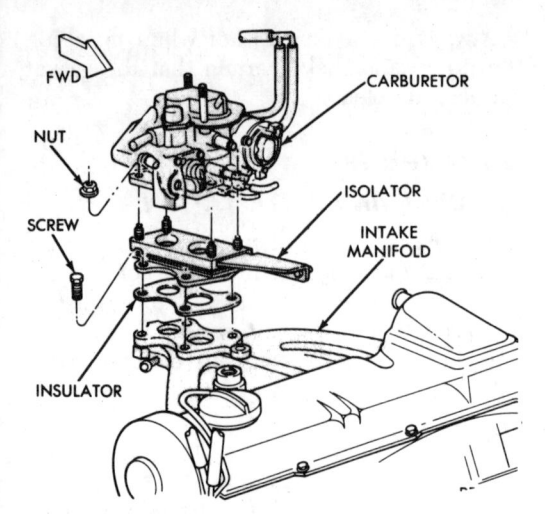

68 EMISSION CONTROLS AND FUEL SYSTEM

Carburetor—2.2L engine

2. Remove the air cleaner.
3. Remove the gas cap.
4. Disconnect the fuel inlet line and all necessary wiring.

NOTE: *It may be necessary to drain the coolant on the 2.6 Liter engine before removing the coolant lines at the carburetor.*

5. Disconnect the coolant lines from the carburetor, (2.6 Liter engines only).
6. Disconnect the throttle linkage and all vacuum hoses.
7. Remove the mounting nuts and remove the carburetor. Hold the carburetor level to avoid spilling fuel from the bowl.
8. Installation is the reverse of removal.

Before checking and adjusting any idle speed, check the ignition timing and adjust if necessary. Disconnect and plug the EGR vacuum hose. Unplug the connector at the radiator fan and install a jumper wire so the fan will run continously. Remove the PCV valve. Allow the PCV valve to draw under hood air and plug the 3/16 in. diameter hose at the canister. Connect a tachometer and start the engine.

NOTE: *Do not remove the air cleaner.*

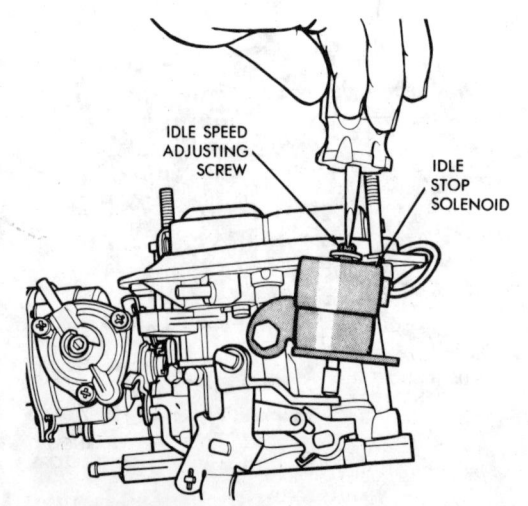

IDLE ADJUSTMENT

1. On air conditioned vehicles, allow the engine to stabilize after performing the idle speed adjustments.
2. If your tachometer indicates the rpm is not set to specifications, turn the idle speed screw until the correct rpm is achieved. See the under hood sticker for correct idle speed.

AIR CONDITIONING IDLE SPEED ADJUSTMENT

1. Turn the air conditioner on and set the blower on low.
2. Remove the adjusting screw and spring from the top of the air conditioning solenoid.
3. Insert a 1/8 in. Allen wrench into the solenoid and adjust to obtain the correct idle speed as per the under hood sticker.
4. Make sure that the air conditioning clutch is operating during the speed adjustments. Air conditioning compressor head pressure should be 250 psi since head pressure affects the loading on the engine.
5. Replace the adjusting screw and spring on the solenoid and turn off the air conditioner.

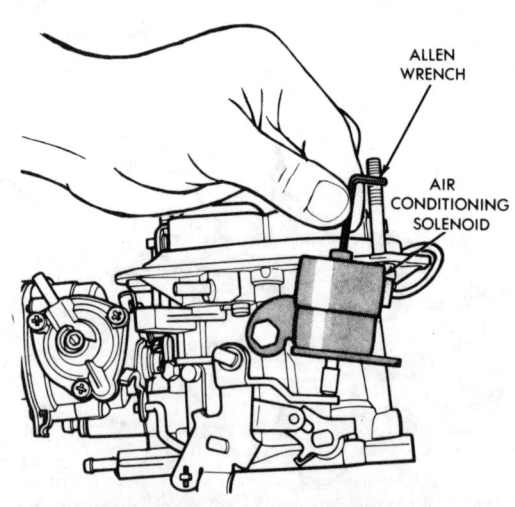

Idle set rpm adjustment

Air conditioning idle speed adjustment

FAST IDLE SPEED ADJUSTMENT

1. Disconnect the two-way electrical connector at the carburetor (red and tan wires).

EMISSION CONTROLS AND FUEL SYSTEM

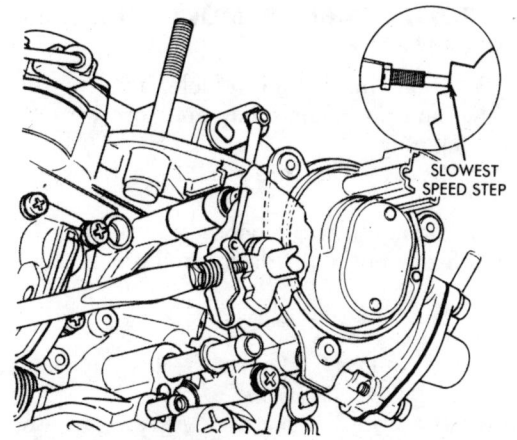

Fast idle speed adjustment

2. Open the throttle slightly and place the adjustment screw on the slowest speed step of the fast idle cam. With the choke fully open adjust the fast idle speed to comply with the under-hood sticker. Return the vehicle to idle, then replace the adjusting screw on the slowest speed step of the fast idle cam to verify fast idle speed. Re-adjust as necessary.

4. Turn the engine off, remove the jumper wire and reconnect the fan. Reinstall the PCV valve and remove the tachometer.

MIXTURE ADJUSTMENT

Chrysler recommends the use of a propane enrichment procedure to adjust the mixture. The equipment needed for this procedure is not readily available to the general public.

NOTE: *Mixture screws are sealed under tamperproof plugs. The only time mixture adjustments are necessary is during a major carburetor overhaul. Refer to the instructions supplied with the overhaul kit.*

OVERHAUL

Efficient carburetion depends greatly on careful cleaning and inspection during overhaul, since dirt, gum, water, or varnish in or on the carburetor parts are often responsible for poor performance.

Overhaul your carburetor in a clean, dust-free area. Carefully disassemble the carburetor, referring often to the exploded views and directions packaged with the rebuilding kit. Keep all similar and look-alike parts segregated during disassembly and cleaning to avoid accidental interchange during assembly. Make a note of all jet sizes.

When the carburetor is disassembled, wash all parts (except diaphragms, electric choke units, pump plunger, and any other plastic, leather, fiber, or rubber parts) in clean carburetor solvent. Do not leave parts in the solvent any longer than is necessary to sufficiently loosen the deposits. Excessive cleaning may remove the special finish from the float bowl and choke valve bodies, leaving these parts unfit for service. Rinse all parts in clean solvent and blow them dry with compressed air or allow them to air dry. Whipe clean all cork, plastic, leather, and fiber parts with a clean, lint-free cloth.

Blow out all passages and jets with compressed air and be sure that there are no restrictions or blockages. Never use wire or similar tools to clean jets, fuel passages, or air bleeds. Clean all jets and valves separately to avoid accidental interchange.

Check all parts for wear or damage. If wear or damage is found, replace the defective parts. Especially check the following.

1. Check the float needle and seat for wear. If wear is found, replace the complete assembly.

2. Check the float hinge pin for wear and the float(s) for dents or distortion. Replace the float if fuel has leaked into it.

3. Check the throttle and choke shaft bores for wear or an out-of-round condition. Damage or wear to the throttle arm, shaft, or shaft bore will often require replacement of the throttle body. These parts require a close tolerance of fit; wear may allow air leakage, which could affect starting and idling.

NOTE: *Throttle shafts and bushings are not included in overhaul kits. They can be purchased separately.*

4. Inspect the idle mixture adjusting needles for burrs or grooves. Any such condition requires replacement of the needle, since you will not be able to obtain a satisfactory idle.

5. Test the accelerator pump check valves. They should pass air one way but not the other. Test for proper seating by blowing and sucking on the valve. Replace the valve as necessary. If the valve is satisfactory, wash the valve again to remove breath moisture.

6. Check the bowl cover for warped surfaces with a straightedge.

7. Closely inspect the valves and seats for wear and damage, replacing as necessary.

8. After the carburetor is assembled, check the choke valve for freedom of operation.

Carburetor overhaul kits are recommended for each overhaul. These kits contain all gaskets and new parts to replace those which deteriorate most rapidly. Failure to

70 EMISSION CONTROLS AND FUEL SYSTEM

replace all parts supplied with the kit (especially gaskets) can result in poor performance later.

Some carburetor manufacturers supply overhaul kits of three basic types: minor repair; major repair; and gasket kits. Basically, they contain the following:

Minor Repair Kits:
- All gaskets
- Float needle valve
- All diaphragms
- Spring for the pump diaphragm

Major Repair Kits:
- All jets and gaskets
- All diaphragms
- Float needle valve
- Pump ball valve
- Float
- Complete intermediate rod
- Intermediate pump lever
- Some cover hold-down screws and washers

Gasket Kits:
- All gaskets

After cleaning and checking all components, reassemble the carburetor, using new parts and referring to the exploded view. When reassembling, make sure that all screws and jets are tight in their seats, but do not overtighten as the tips will be distorted. Tighten all screws gradually, in rotation. Do not tighten needle valves into their seats; uneven jetting will result. Always use new gaskets. Be sure to adjust the float level when reassembling.

THROTTLE CABLE REMOVAL AND INSTALLATION

1. From inside the vehicle, remove the cable housing retainer clip and core wire retaining plug.
2. Remove the core wire from the pedal shaft.
3. From under the hood, pull the housing end-fitting out of the dash panel grommet.

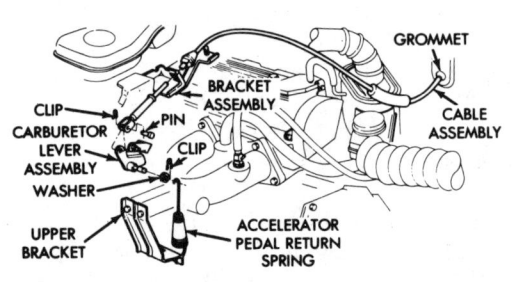

Throttle cable attachment to carburetor 2.6L engine

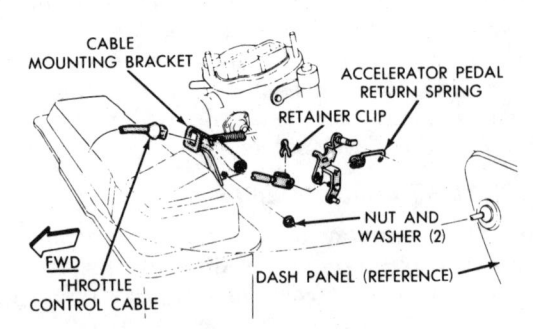

Throttle cable attachment 2.2L engine

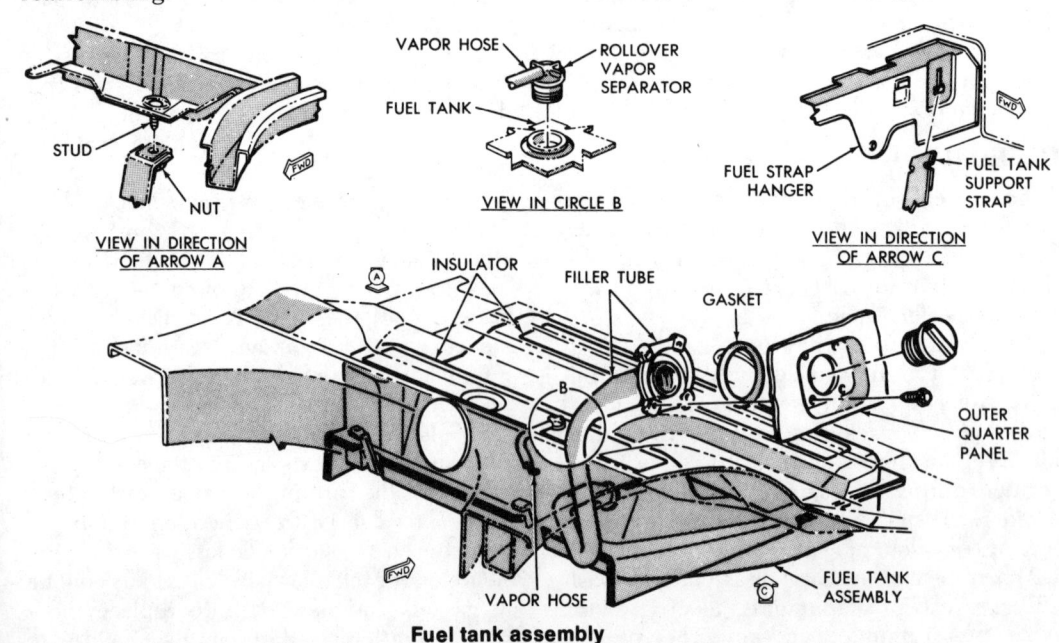

Fuel tank assembly

4. Remove the cable clevis from the carburetor lever stud. Now the cable mounting bracket will separate by using wide-jaw pliers to compress the end-fitting tabs.

5. Installation is the reverse of removal. Adjust the cable as necessary.

Fuel Tank

REMOVAL AND INSTALLATION

1. Jack up your vehicle and support it with jack stands.

2. Disconnect the negative battery terminal.

3. Remove the gas cap to relieve any pressure in the tank.

4. Disconnect the fuel supply line at the right front shockabsorber tower, and drain the fuel tank.

5. Remove the screws that hold the filler tube to the quarter panel.

6. Remove the right rear wheel and disconnect the wiring from the tank.

7. Remove the screws from the exhaust pipe to fuel tank shield, and allow this shield to rest on the exhaust pipe.

8. Support the tank with a jack and remove the tank strap bolts.

9. Lower the tank slightly, and carefully remove the filler tube from the tank.

10. Lower the fuel tank, disconnect the vapor separator rollover valve hose, and remove the fuel tank and insulator pad.

11. Installation is the reverse of removal.

Chassis Electrical 5

HEATER

Blower Motor

REMOVAL AND INSTALLATION

Without Air Conditioning

The blower motor is located under the instrument panel on the left side of the heater assembly.

1. Disconnect the negative battery terminal.
2. Disconnect the motor wiring.
3. Remove the left outlet duct if necessary.
4. Remove the motor retaining screws and the motor.
5. Installation is the reverse of removal.

Air Conditioned Cars

1. Disconnect the negative battery terminal.
2. Remove the three screws securing the glovebox to the instrument panel.
3. Disconnect the wiring from the blower and case.
4. Remove the blower vent tube from the case.
5. Loosen the recirculating door from its bracket and remove the actuator from the housing. Leave the vacuum lines attached.
6. Remove the seven screws attaching the recirculating housing to the A/C unit and remove the housing.
7. Remove the three mounting flange nuts and washers.
8. Remove the blower motor from the unit.
9. Installation is the reverse of removal. Replace any damaged sealer.

Heater Core

REMOVAL AND INSTALLATION

Without Air Conditioning

1. Remove the heater assembly.
2. Remove the padding from around the

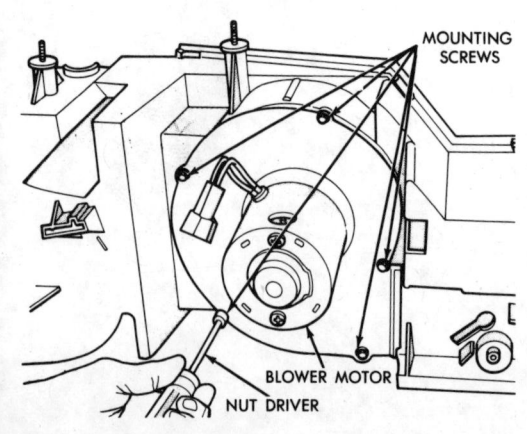

Removing blower motor

CHASSIS ELECTRICAL 73

heater core outlets and remove the upper core mounting screws.

3. Pry loose the retaining snaps from around the outer edge of the housing cover.

NOTE: *If a retaining snap should break, the housing cover has provisions for mounting screws.*

4. Remove the housing top cover.
5. Remove the bottom heater core mounting screw.
6. Slide the heater core out of the housing.
7. Installation is the reverse of removal.

Air Conditioned Cars

Removal of the Heater-Evaporator Unit is required for core removal. Two people will be required to perform the operation. Discharge, evacuation and recharge and leak testing of the refrigerant system is necessary. This work should only be performed by a trained technician. Have the system discharged before attempting removal. During installation, a small can of refrigerant oil will be necessary.

1. Disconnect the battery ground.
2. Drain the coolant.
3. Disconnect the temperature door cable from the heater-evaporator unit.
4. Disconnect the temperature door cable from the retaining clips.
5. Remove the glovebox.
6. Disconnect the vacuum harness from the control head.
7. Disconnect the blower motor lead and anti-diesel relay wire.
8. Remove the seven screws fastening the right trim bezel to the instrument panel. Starting at the right side, swing the bezel clear and remove it.
9. Remove the three screws on the bottom of the center distribution duct cover and slide the cover rearward and remove it.
10. Remove the center distribution duct.
11. Remove the defroster duct adaptor.
12. Remove the H-type expansion valve, located on the right side of the firewall:
    a. remove the 5/18 in. bolt in the center of the plumbing sealing plate.
    b. carefully pull the refrigerant lines toward the front of the car, taking care to avoid scratching the valve sealing surfaces.
    c. remove the two Allenhead capscrews and remove the valve.
13. Cap the pipe openings at once. Wrap the valve in a plastic bag.

14. Disconnect the hoses from the core tubes.
15. Disconnect the vacuum lines at the intake manifold and water valve.
16. Remove the unit-to-firewall retaining nuts.
17. Remove the panel support bracket.
18. Remove the right cowl lower panel.
19. Remove the instrument panel pivot bracket screw from the right side.
20. Remove the screws securing the lower instrument panel at the steering column.
21. Pull back the carpet from under the unit as far as possible.
22. Remove the nut from the evaporator-heater unit-to-plenum mounting brace and blower motor ground cable. While supporting the unit, remove the brace from its stud.
23. Lift the unit, pulling it rearward to allow clearance. These operations may require two people.
24. Slowly lower the unit taking care to keep the studs from hanging-up on the insulation.
25. When the unit reaches the floor, slide it rearward until it is out from under the instrument panel.
26. Remove the unit from the car.
27. Place the unit on a workbench. On the inside-the-car-side, remove the nut from the mode door actuator on the top cover and the two retaining clips from the front edge of the cover. To remove the mode door actuator, remove the two screws securing it to the cover.
28. Remove the screws attaching the cover to the assembly and lift off the cover. Lift the mode door out of the unit.
29. Remove the screw from the core retaining bracket and lift out the core.

To install:

30. Place the core in the unit and install the bracket.
31. Install the actuator arm.

CAUTION: *When installing the unit in the car, care must be taken that the vacuum lines to the engine compartment do not hang-up on the accelerator or become trapped between the unit and the firewall. If this happens, kinked lines will result and the unit will have to be removed to free them. Proper routing of these lines will require two people. The portion of the vacuum harness which is routed through the steering column support MUST be positioned BEFORE the distribution housing is installed. The harness MUST be routed*

74 CHASSIS ELECTRICAL

ABOVE the temperature control cable.

32. Place the unit on the floor as far under the panel as possible.
33. Raise the unit carefully, at the same time pull the lower instrument panel rearward as far as possible.
34. Position the unit in place and attach the brace to the stud.
35. Install the lower ground cable and attach the nut.
36. Install and tighten the unit-to-firewall nuts.
37. Reposition the carpet and install, but do not tighten the right instrument panel pivot bracket screw.
38. Place a piece of sheet metal or thin cardboard against the evaporator-heater assembly to center the assembly duct seal.
39. Position the center distributor duct in place making sure that the upper left tab comes in through the left center A/C outlet opening and that each air take-off is properly inserted in its respective outled.

NOTE: *Make sure that the radio wiring connector does not interfere with the duct.*

40. Install and tighten the screw securing the upper left tab of the center air distribution duct to the instrument panel.
41. Remove the sheet metal or cardboard from between the unit and the duct.

NOTE: *Make sure that the unit seal is properly aligned with the duct opening.*

42. Install and tighten the two lower screws fastening the center distribution duct to the instrument panel.
43. Install and tighten the screws securing the lower instrument panel at the steering column.
44. Install and tighten the nut securing the instrument panel to the support bracket.
45. Make sure that the seal on the unit is properly aligned and seated against the distribution duct assembly.
46. Tighten the instrument panel pivot bracket screw and install the right cowl lower trim.
47. Slide the distributor duct cover assembly onto the center distribution duct so that the notches lock into the tabs and the tabs slide over the rear and side ledges of the center duct assembly.
48. Install the three screws securing the ducting.
49. Install the right trim bezel.
50. Connect the vacuum harness to the control head.
51. Connect the blower lead and the anti-diesel wire.
52. Install the glovebox.
53. Connect the temperature door cable.
54. Install new O-rings on the evaporator plate and the plumbing plate. Coat the new O-rings with clean refrigerant oil.
55. Place the H-valve against the evaporator sealing plate surface and install the two through-bolts. Torque to 6–10 ft. lb.
56. Carefully hold the refrigerant line connector against the valve and install the bolt. Torque to 14–20 ft. lb.
57. Install the heater hoses at the core tubes.
58. Connect the vacuum lines at the manifold and water valve.
59. Install the condensate drain tube.
60. Have the system evacuated, charged and leak tested by a trained technician.

Heater Assembly

All Aries/Reliant cars use a "Blend-Air" type heater. Outside air enters the heater through the cowl opening and passes through a plenum chamber to the heater unit.

NOTE: *The air intake, located on the hood, must be kept free of ice, snow, and other obstructions for the heater to draw in sufficient outside air.*

A blend air door in the heater housing directs incoming air through the heater core and/or the heater core by-pass. The amount of blended air is determined by the setting of the temperature lever on the heater control panel.

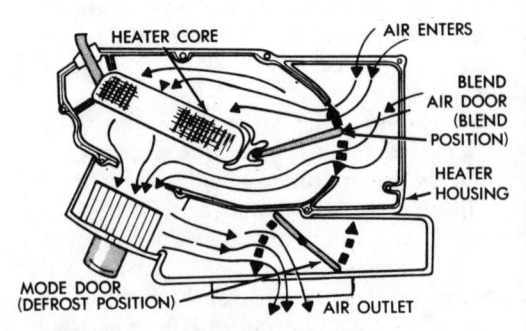

Blend air heater system—typical

REMOVAL AND INSTALLATION
Without Air Conditioning

1. Disconnect the negative battery cable and drain the radiator.

CHILTON'S
FUEL ECONOMY & TUNE-UP TIPS

Tune-Up • Spark Plug Diagnosis • Emission Controls
Fuel System • Cooling System • Tires and Wheels
General Maintenance

35 WAYS TO IMPROVE FUEL ECONOMY

CHILTON'S FUEL ECONOMY & TUNE-UP TIPS

Fuel economy is important to everyone, no matter what kind of vehicle you drive. The maintenance-minded motorist can save both money and fuel using these tips and the periodic maintenance and tune-up procedures in this Repair and Tune-Up Guide.

There are more than 130,000,000 cars and trucks registered for private use in the United States. Each travels an average of 10-12,000 miles per year, and, in total they consume close to 70 billion gallons of fuel each year. This represents nearly ⅔ of the oil imported by the United States each year. The Federal government's goal is to reduce consumption 10% by 1985. A variety of methods are either already in use or under serious consideration, and they all affect your driving and the cars you will drive. In addition to "down-sizing", the auto industry is using or investigating the use of electronic fuel delivery, electronic engine controls and alternative engines for use in smaller and lighter vehicles, among other alternatives to meet the federally mandated Corporate Average Fuel Economy (CAFE) of 27.5 mpg by 1985. The government, for its part, is considering rationing, mandatory driving curtailments and tax increases on motor vehicle fuel in an effort to reduce consumption. The government's goal of a 10% reduction could be realized — and further government regulation avoided — if every private vehicle could use just 1 less gallon of fuel per week.

How Much Can You Save?

Tests have proven that almost anyone can make at least a 10% reduction in fuel consumption through regular maintenance and tune-ups. When a major manufacturer of spark plugs sur-

TUNE-UP

1. Check the cylinder compression to be sure the engine will really benefit from a tune-up and that it is capable of producing good fuel economy. A tune-up will be wasted on an engine in poor mechanical condition.

2. Replace spark plugs regularly. New spark plugs alone can increase fuel economy 3%.

3. Be sure the spark plugs are the correct type (heat range) for your vehicle. See the Tune-Up Specifications.

Heat range refers to the spark plug's ability to conduct heat away from the firing end. It must conduct the heat away in an even pattern to avoid becoming a source of pre-ignition, yet it must also operate hot enough to burn off conductive deposits that could cause misfiring.

The heat range is usually indicated by a number on the spark plug, part of the manufacturer's designation for each individual spark plug. The numbers in bold-face indicate the heat range in each manufacturer's identification system.

Manufacturer	Typical Designation
AC	R **45** TS
Bosch (old)	WA **145** T30
Bosch (new)	HR **8** Y
Champion	RBL **15** Y
Fram/Autolite	**4**15
Mopar	P-**62** PR
Motorcraft	BRF-**4**2
NGK	BP **5** ES-15
Nippondenso	W **16** EP
Prestolite	14GR **5** 2A

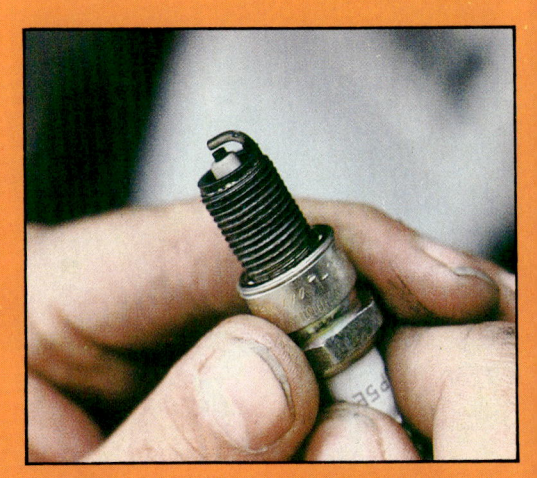

Periodically, check the spark plugs to be sure they are firing efficiently. They are excellent indicators of the internal condition of your engine.

On AC, Bosch (new), Champion, Fram/Autolite, Mopar, Motorcraft and Prestolite, a higher number indicates a hotter plug. On Bosch (old), NGK and Nippondenso, a higher number indicates a colder plug.

4. Make sure the spark plugs are properly gapped. See the Tune-Up Specifications in this book.

5. Be sure the spark plugs are firing efficiently. The illustrations on the next 2 pages show you how to "read" the firing end of the spark plug.

6. Check the ignition timing and set it to specifications. Tests show that almost all cars

veyed over 6,000 cars nationwide, they found that a tune-up, on cars that needed one, increased fuel economy over 11%. Replacing worn plugs alone, accounted for a 3% increase. The same test also revealed that 8 out of every 10 vehicles will have some maintenance deficiency that will directly affect fuel economy, emissions or performance. Most of this mileage-robbing neglect could be prevented with regular maintenance.

Modern engines require that all of the functioning systems operate properly for maximum efficiency. A malfunction anywhere wastes fuel. You can keep your vehicle running as efficiently and economically as possible, by being aware of your vehicles operating and performance characteristics. If your vehicle suddenly develops performance or fuel economy problems it could be due to one or more of the following:

PROBLEM	POSSIBLE CAUSE
Engine Idles Rough	Ignition timing, idle mixture, vacuum leak or something amiss in the emission control system.
Hesitates on Acceleration	Dirty carburetor or fuel filter, improper accelerator pump setting, ignition timing or fouled spark plugs.
Starts Hard or Fails to Start	Worn spark plugs, improperly set automatic choke, ice (or water) in fuel system.
Stalls Frequently	Automatic choke improperly adjusted and possible dirty air filter or fuel filter.
Performs Sluggishly	Worn spark plugs, dirty fuel or air filter, ignition timing or automatic choke out of adjustment.

Check spark plug wires on conventional point type ignition for cracks by bending them in a loop around your finger.

Be sure that spark plug wires leading to adjacent cylinders do not run too close together. (Photo courtesy Champion Spark Plug Co.)

have incorrect ignition timing by more than 2°.

7. If your vehicle does not have electronic ignition, check the points, rotor and cap as specified.

8. Check the spark plug wires (used with conventional point-type ignitions) for cracks and burned or broken insulation by bending them in a loop around your finger. Cracked wires decrease fuel efficiency by failing to deliver full voltage to the spark plugs. One misfiring spark plug can cost you as much as 2 mpg.

9. Check the routing of the plug wires. Misfiring can be the result of spark plug leads to adjacent cylinders running parallel to each other and too close together. One wire tends to pick up voltage from the other causing it to fire "out of time".

10. Check all electrical and ignition circuits for voltage drop and resistance.

11. Check the distributor mechanical and/or vacuum advance mechanisms for proper functioning. The vacuum advance can be checked by twisting the distributor plate in the opposite direction of rotation. It should spring back when released.

12. Check and adjust the valve clearance on engines with mechanical lifters. The clearance should be slightly loose rather than too tight.

SPARK PLUG DIAGNOSIS

Normal

APPEARANCE: This plug is typical of one operating normally. The insulator nose varies from a light tan to grayish color with slight electrode wear. The presence of slight deposits is normal on used plugs and will have no adverse effect on engine performance. The spark plug heat range is correct for the engine and the engine is running normally.
CAUSE: Properly running engine.
RECOMMENDATION: Before reinstalling this plug, the electrodes should be cleaned and filed square. Set the gap to specifications. If the plug has been in service for more than 10-12,000 miles, the entire set should probably be replaced with a fresh set of the same heat range.

Oil Deposits

APPEARANCE: The firing end of the plug is covered with a wet, oily coating.
CAUSE: The problem is poor oil control. On high mileage engines, oil is leaking past the rings or valve guides into the combustion chamber. A common cause is also a plugged PCV valve, and a ruptured fuel pump diaphragm can also cause this condition. Oil fouled plugs such as these are often found in new or recently overhauled engines, before normal oil control is achieved, and can be cleaned and reinstalled.
RECOMMENDATION: A hotter spark plug may temporarily relieve the problem, but the engine is probably in need of work.

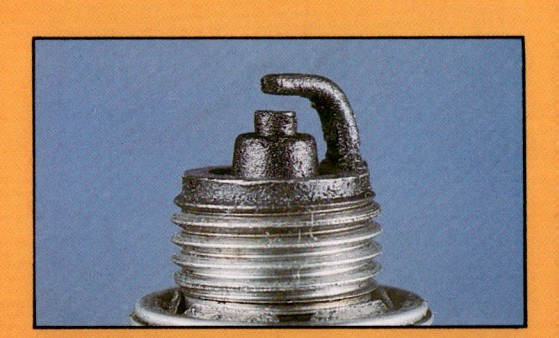

Incorrect Heat Range

APPEARANCE: The effects of high temperature on a spark plug are indicated by clean white, often blistered insulator. This can also be accompanied by excessive wear of the electrode, and the absence of deposits.
CAUSE: Check for the correct spark plug heat range. A plug which is too hot for the engine can result in overheating. A car operated mostly at high speeds can require a colder plug. Also check ignition timing, cooling system level, fuel mixture and leaking intake manifold.
RECOMMENDATION: If all ignition and engine adjustments are known to be correct, and no other malfunction exists, install spark plugs one heat range colder.

Carbon Deposits

APPEARANCE: Carbon fouling is easily identified by the presence of dry, soft, black, sooty deposits.
CAUSE: Changing the heat range can often lead to carbon fouling, as can prolonged slow, stop-and-start driving. If the heat range is correct, carbon fouling can be attributed to a rich fuel mixture, sticking choke, clogged air cleaner, worn breaker points, retarded timing or low compression. If only one or two plugs are carbon fouled, check for corroded or cracked wires on the affected plugs. Also look for cracks in the distributor cap between the towers of affected cylinders.
RECOMMENDATION: After the problem is corrected, these plugs can be cleaned and reinstalled if not worn severely.

Photos Courtesy Champion Spark Plug Co.

MMT Fouled

APPEARANCE: Spark plugs fouled by MMT (Methycyclopentadienyl Maganese Tricarbonyl) have reddish, rusty appearance on the insulator and side electrode.

CAUSE: MMT is an anti-knock additive in gasoline used to replace lead. During the combustion process, the MMT leaves a reddish deposit on the insulator and side electrode.

RECOMMENDATION: No engine malfunction is indicated and the deposits will not affect plug performance any more than lead deposits (see Ash Deposits). MMT fouled plugs can be cleaned, regapped and reinstalled.

High Speed Glazing

APPEARANCE: Glazing appears as shiny coating on the plug, either yellow or tan in color.

CAUSE: During hard, fast acceleration, plug temperatures rise suddenly. Deposits from normal combustion have no chance to fluff-off; instead, they melt on the insulator forming an electrically conductive coating which causes misfiring.

RECOMMENDATION: Glazed plugs are not easily cleaned. They should be replaced with a fresh set of plugs of the correct heat range. If the condition recurs, using plugs with a heat range one step colder may cure the problem.

Ash (Lead) Deposits

APPEARANCE: Ash deposits are characterized by light brown or white colored deposits crusted on the side or center electrodes. In some cases it may give the plug a rusty appearance.

CAUSE: Ash deposits are normally derived from oil or fuel additives burned during normal combustion. Normally they are harmless, though excessive amounts can cause misfiring. If deposits are excessive in short mileage, the valve guides may be worn.

RECOMMENDATION: Ash-fouled plugs can be cleaned, gapped and reinstalled.

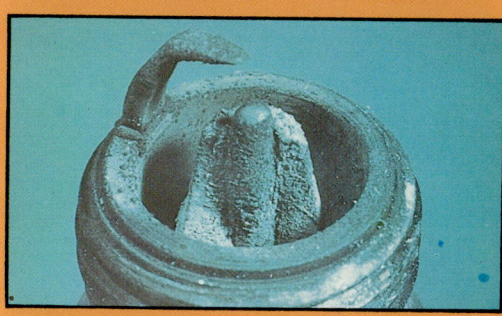

Detonation

APPEARANCE: Detonation is usually characterized by a broken plug insulator.

CAUSE: A portion of the fuel charge will begin to burn spontaneously, from the increased heat following ignition. The explosion that results applies extreme pressure to engine components, frequently damaging spark plugs and pistons.

Detonation can result by over-advanced ignition timing, inferior gasoline (low octane) lean air/fuel mixture, poor carburetion, engine lugging or an increase in compression ratio due to combustion chamber deposits or engine modification.

RECOMMENDATION: Replace the plugs after correcting the problem.

Photos Courtesy Fram Corporation

EMISSION CONTROLS

13. Be aware of the general condition of the emission control system. It contributes to reduced pollution and should be serviced regularly to maintain efficient engine operation.

14. Check all vacuum lines for dried, cracked or brittle conditions. Something as simple as a leaking vacuum hose can cause poor performance and loss of economy.

15. Avoid tampering with the emission control system. Attempting to improve fuel econ-

FUEL SYSTEM

Check the air filter with a light behind it. If you can see light through the filter it can be reused.

Extremely clogged filters should be discarded and replaced with a new one.

18. Replace the air filter regularly. A dirty air filter richens the air/fuel mixture and can increase fuel consumption as much as 10%. Tests show that ⅓ of all vehicles have air filters in need of replacement.

19. Replace the fuel filter at least as often as recommended.

20. Set the idle speed and carburetor mixture to specifications.

21. Check the automatic choke. A sticking or malfunctioning choke wastes gas.

22. During the summer months, adjust the automatic choke for a leaner mixture which will produce faster engine warm-ups.

COOLING SYSTEM

29. Be sure all accessory drive belts are in good condition. Check for cracks or wear.

30. Adjust all accessory drive belts to proper tension.

31. Check all hoses for swollen areas, worn spots, or loose clamps.

32. Check coolant level in the radiator or expansion tank.

33. Be sure the thermostat is operating properly. A stuck thermostat delays engine warm-up and a cold engine uses nearly twice as much fuel as a warm engine.

34. Drain and replace the engine coolant at least as often as recommended. Rust and scale

TIRES & WHEELS

38. Check the tire pressure often with a pencil type gauge. Tests by a major tire manufacturer show that 90% of all vehicles have at least 1 tire improperly inflated. Better mileage can be achieved by over-inflating tires, but never exceed the maximum inflation pressure on the side of the tire.

39. If possible, install radial tires. Radial tires deliver as much as ½ mpg more than bias belted tires.

40. Avoid installing super-wide tires. They only create extra rolling resistance and decrease fuel mileage. Stick to the manufacturer's recommendations.

41. Have the wheels properly balanced.

omy by tampering with emission controls is more likely to worsen fuel economy than improve it. Emission control changes on modern engines are not readily reversible.

16. Clean (or replace) the EGR valve and lines as recommended.

17. Be sure that all vacuum lines and hoses are reconnected properly after working under the hood. An unconnected or misrouted vacuum line can wreak havoc with engine performance.

23. Check for fuel leaks at the carburetor, fuel pump, fuel lines and fuel tank. Be sure all lines and connections are tight.

24. Periodically check the tightness of the carburetor and intake manifold attaching nuts and bolts. These are a common place for vacuum leaks to occur.

25. Clean the carburetor periodically and lubricate the linkage.

26. The condition of the tailpipe can be an excellent indicator of proper engine combustion. After a long drive at highway speeds, the inside of the tailpipe should be a light grey in color. Black or soot on the insides indicates an overly rich mixture.

27. Check the fuel pump pressure. The fuel pump may be supplying more fuel than the engine needs.

28. Use the proper grade of gasoline for your engine. Don't try to compensate for knocking or "pinging" by advancing the ignition timing. This practice will only increase plug temperature and the chances of detonation or pre-ignition with relatively little performance gain.

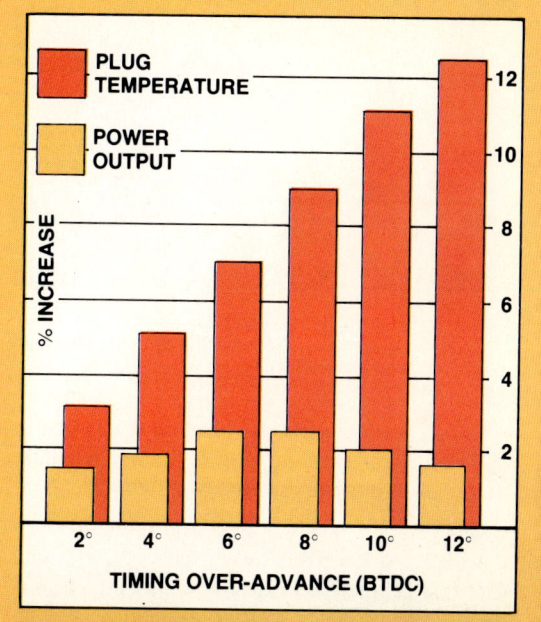

Increasing ignition timing past the specified setting results in a drastic increase in spark plug temperature with increased chance of detonation or preignition. Performance increase is considerably less. (Photo courtesy Champion Spark Plug Co.)

that form in the engine should be flushed out to allow the engine to operate at peak efficiency.

35. Clean the radiator of debris that can decrease cooling efficiency.

36. Install a flex-type or electric cooling fan, if you don't have a clutch type fan. Flex fans use curved plastic blades to push more air at low speeds when more cooling is needed; at high speeds the blades flatten out for less resistance. Electric fans only run when the engine temperature reaches a predetermined level.

37. Check the radiator cap for a worn or cracked gasket. If the cap does not seal properly, the cooling system will not function properly.

42. Be sure the front end is correctly aligned. A misaligned front end actually has wheels going in different directions. The increased drag can reduce fuel economy by .3 mpg.

43. Correctly adjust the wheel bearings. Wheel bearings that are adjusted too tight increase rolling resistance.

Check tire pressures regularly with a reliable pocket type gauge. Be sure to check the pressure on a cold tire.

GENERAL MAINTENANCE

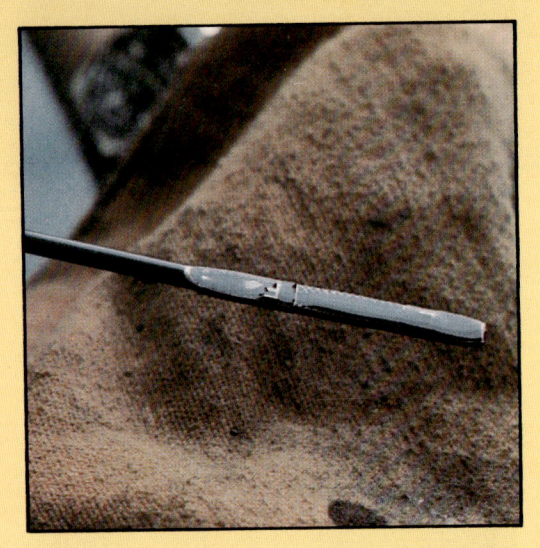

Check the fluid levels (particularly engine oil) on a regular basis. Be sure to check the oil for grit, water or other contamination.

A vacuum gauge is another excellent indicator of internal engine condition and can also be installed in the dash as a mileage indicator.

44. Periodically check the fluid levels in the engine, power steering pump, master cylinder, automatic transmission and drive axle.

45. Change the oil at the recommended interval and change the filter at every oil change. Dirty oil is thick and causes extra friction between moving parts, cutting efficiency and increasing wear. A worn engine requires more frequent tune-ups and gets progressively worse fuel economy. In general, use the lightest viscosity oil for the driving conditions you will encounter.

46. Use the recommended viscosity fluids in the transmission and axle.

47. Be sure the battery is fully charged for fast starts. A slow starting engine wastes fuel.

48. Be sure battery terminals are clean and tight.

49. Check the battery electrolyte level and add distilled water if necessary.

50. Check the exhaust system for crushed pipes, blockages and leaks.

51. Adjust the brakes. Dragging brakes or brakes that are not releasing create increased drag on the engine.

52. Install a vacuum gauge or miles-per-gallon gauge. These gauges visually indicate engine vacuum in the intake manifold. High vacuum = good mileage and low vacuum = poorer mileage. The gauge can also be an excellent indicator of internal engine conditions.

53. Be sure the clutch is properly adjusted. A slipping clutch wastes fuel.

54. Check and periodically lubricate the heat control valve in the exhaust manifold. A sticking or inoperative valve prevents engine warm-up and wastes gas.

55. Keep accurate records to check fuel economy over a period of time. A sudden drop in fuel economy may signal a need for tune-up or other maintenance.

CHASSIS ELECTRICAL 75

Heater assembly—typical

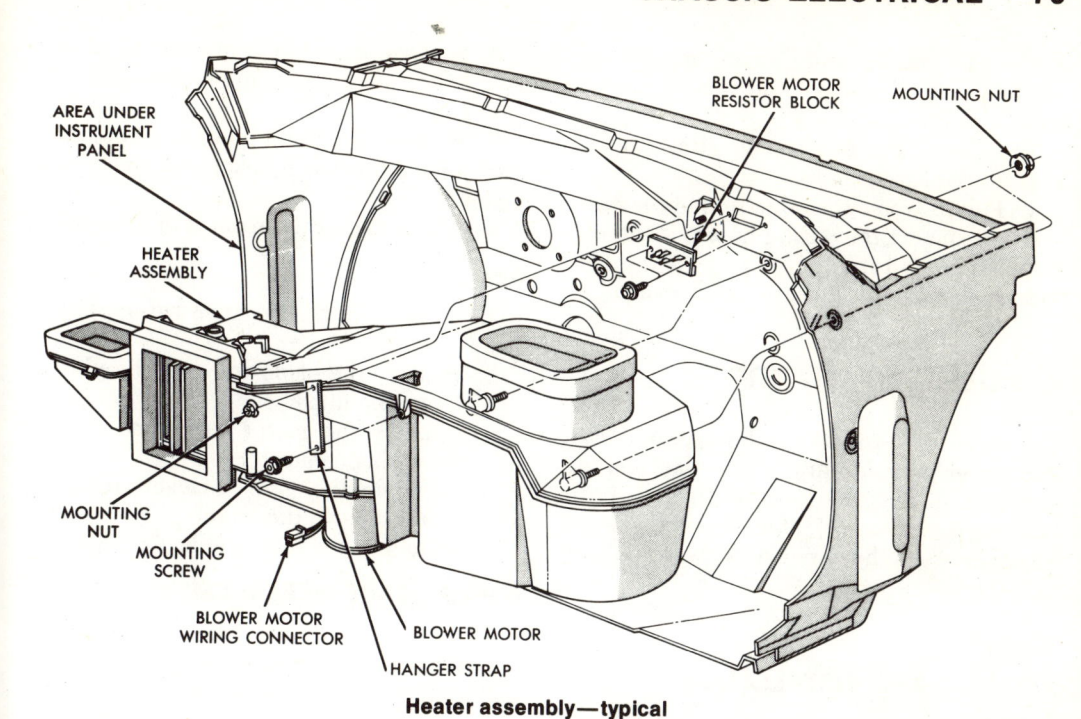

2. Disconnect the blower motor wiring connector.
3. Reach under the unit, depress the tab on the mode door and temperature control cables, pull the flags from the receivers, and remove the self-adjust clip from the crank arm.
4. Remove the glove box assembly.
5. Disconnect the heater hoses to the unit on the engine side and seal the heater core tube openings and hoses.
6. Through the glove box opening, remove the screw attaching the hanger strap to the heater assembly.
7. Remove the nut attaching the hanger strap to the dash panel and remove the hanger strap.
8. Remove the two nuts attaching the heater assembly to the dash panel. The nuts are on the engine side.
9. Pull out the bottom of the instrument panel and slide out the heater assembly.
10. Installation is the reverse of removal.

RADIO

AM, AM/FM monaural, or AM/FM stereo multiplex units are available. All radios are trimmed at the factory and should require no further adjustment. However, after repair or

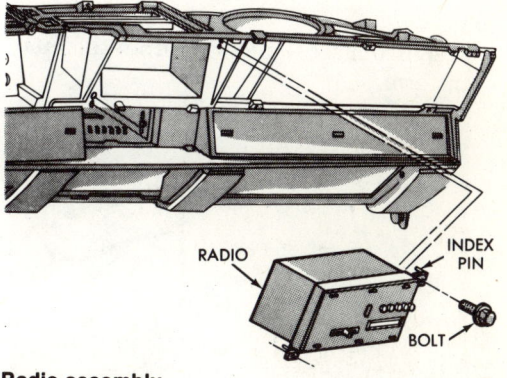

Radio assembly

if the antenna trim is to be verified, proceed as follows:
1. Turn radio on.
2. Manually tune the radio to a weak station between 1400 and 1600 KHz on AM.
3. Increase the volume and set the tone control to full treble (clockwise).
4. Viewing the radio from the front, the trimmer control is a slot-head located at the rear of the right side. Adjust it carefully by turning it back and forth with a screwdriver until maximum loudness is achieved.

REMOVAL AND INSTALLATION

1. Remove the center bezel.
2. If equipped with a mono-speaker, re-

76 CHASSIS ELECTRICAL

move the instrument panel top cover, speaker, and disconnect the wires from the radio.

3. Remove the two screws attaching the radio to the base panel.

4. Pull the radio thru the front of the base, then disconnect the wiring harness, antenna lead and ground strap.

5. Installation is the reverse of removal.

WINDSHIELD WIPERS

The windshield wipers can be operated with the wiper switch only when the ignition switch is in the Accessory or Ingition position. A circuit breaker, integral with the wiper switch protects the circuitry of the wiper system and the vehicle.

Motor

REMOVAL AND INSTALLATION
Front

1. Disconnect the negative battery terminal.

2. Disconnect the linkage from the motor crank arm.

3. Remove the wiper motor plastic cover.

4. Disconnect the wiring harness from the motor.

5. Remove the three mounting bolts from the motor mounting bracket and remove the motor.

6. Installation is the reverse of removal.

Rear

1. Disconnect the negative battery terminal.

2. Remove the blade and arm assembly.

3. Open the liftgate.

4. Remove the motor cover and disconnect the wiring connector.

5. Remove the four bracket retaining screws and remove the motor.

6. Installation is the reverse of removal.

WIPER BLADE REPLACEMENT

1. Lift the wiper arm away from the glass.

2. Depress the release lever on the bridge and remove the blade assembly from the arm.

3. Lift the tab and pinch the end bridge to release it from the center bridge.

4. Slide the end bridge from the blade element and the element from the opposite end bridge.

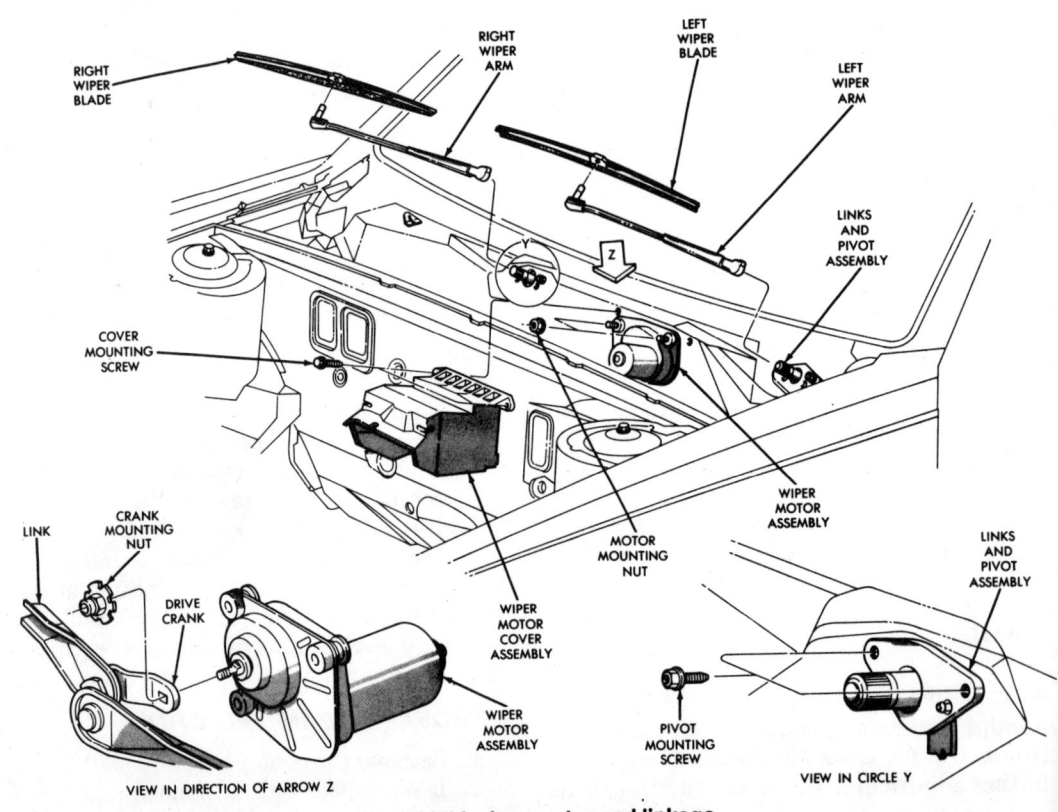

Windshield wiper motor and linkage

CHASSIS ELECTRICAL 77

5. Assembly is the reverse of removal. Make sure that the element locking tabs are securely locked in position.

Wiper Arm
REMOVAL AND INSTALLATION
Front

1. Lift the arm so that the latch can be pulled out to the holding position and then release the arm. The arm will remain off the windshield in this position.
2. Remove the arm off the pivot using a rocking motion.
3. When installing, the motor should be in the park position and the tips of the blades 1½" above the bottom of the windshield moulding.

Rear

1. To remove the rear wiper arm assembly the use of special tool C-3982 is necessary.
NOTE: *The use of a screwdriver is not recommended as it will distort and damage the arm.*
2. With the tool installed on the arm, lift the arm then remove it from the output shaft.
3. To install, the wiper motor should be in the park position.
4. Install the arm so that the tip of the blade is about 1.3 inches above the lower liftgate gasket.

Linkage
REMOVAL AND INSTALLATION

1. Put the windshield wipers in the park position.
2. Raise the hood and disconnect the negative battery terminal.
3. Remove the wiper arms and blades as previously described.
4. Disconnect the hoses from the tee connector.
5. Remove the pivot screws.
6. Remove the wiper motor plastic cover, and disconnect the wiring harness.
7. Remove the plastic screen from the cowl.
8. Remove the three motor mounting bolts.
9. Push the pivots down into the plenum chamber. Pull the motor out until it clears the mounting studs and then move it to the driver's side as far as it will go. Pull the right pivot and link out through the opening, then shift the motor to the right and remove the motor, the left link and pivot.
NOTE: *Do not rotate the motor output shaft from the park position.*
10. Installation is the reverse of removal.

INSTRUMENT CLUSTER
REMOVAL AND INSTALLATION

1. Disconnect the negative battery terminal.
2. Place the gearshift lever in position "1".
3. Remove the instrument panel trim strip.
4. Remove the left upper and lower cluster bezel screws.
5. Remove the right lower cluster bezel screw and retaining clip.
6. Remove the instrument cluster bezel by snapping the bezel off of the five retaining clips.
7. Remove the seven retaining screws and remove the upper right bezel.
8. Remove the four rear instrument panel top cover mounting screws.
9. Lift the rear edge of the panel top cover and remove the two screws attaching the upper trim strip retainer and cluster housing to the base panel.
10. Remove the trim strip retainer.
11. Remove the two screws attaching the cluster housing to the base panel of the lower cluster.
12. Lift the rearward edge of the panel top cover and slide the cluster housing rearward.
13. Disconnect the right printed circuit board connector from behind the cluster housing.
14. Disconnect the speedometer cable connector.
15. Disconnect the left printed circuit connector.
16. Remove the cluster assembly.
17. Installation is the reverse of removal.

Headlight Switch
REMOVAL AND INSTALLATION

1. Remove the three screws securing the headlamp switch mounting plate to the base panel.
2. Pull the switch and plate rearward and disconnect the wiring connector.
3. Depress the button on the switch and remove the knob and stem.
4. Snap out the escutcheon, then remove

78 CHASSIS ELECTRICAL

Instrument panel

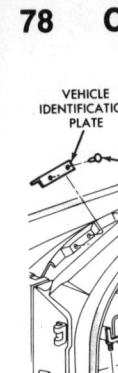

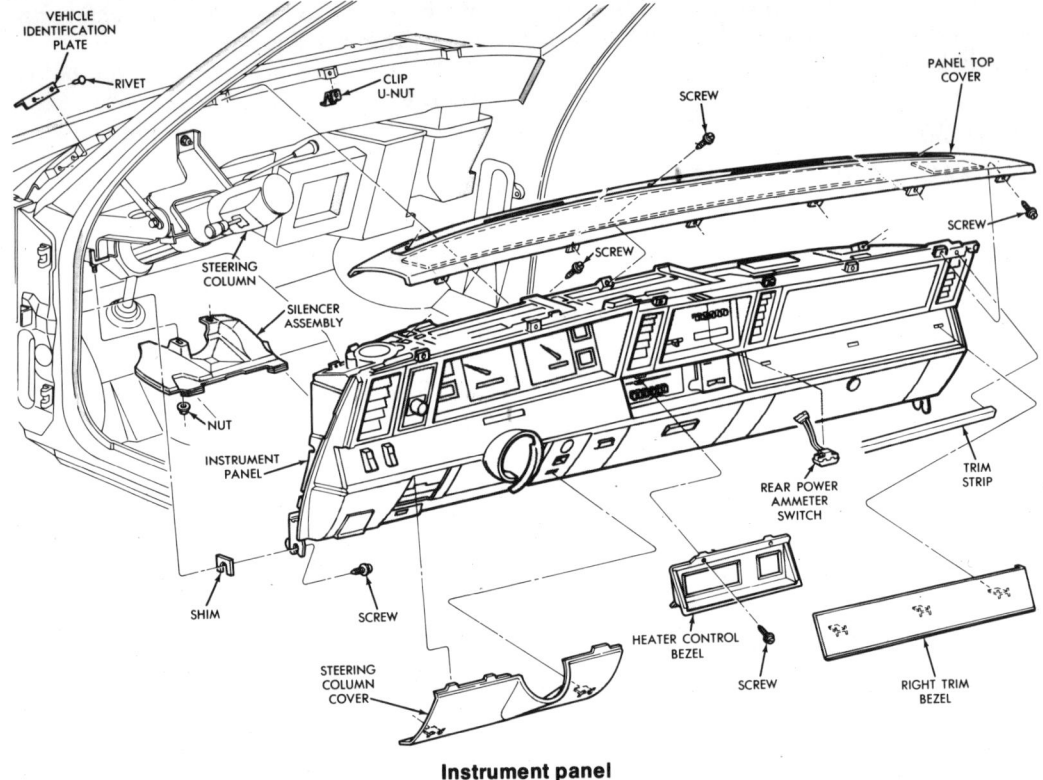

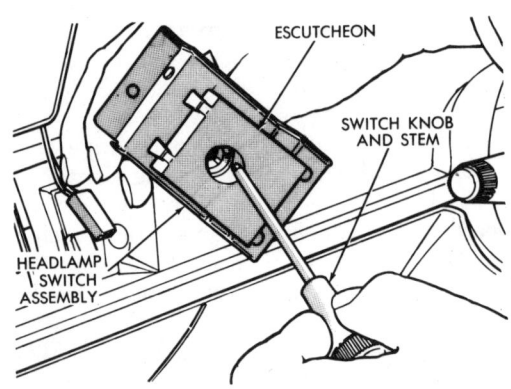

Headlight switch knob and stem

the nut that attaches the switch to the mounting plate.

5. Installation is the reverse of removal.

Speedometer Cable Replacement

1. Reach under the instrument panel and depress the spring clip retaining the cable to the speedometer head. Pull the cable back and away from the head.

2. If the core is broken, raise and support the vehicle and remove the cable retaining screw from the cable bracket. Carefully slide the cable out of the transaxle.

3. Coat the new core sparingly with speedometer cable lubricant and insert it in the cable. Install the cable at the transaxle, lower the car and install the cable at the speedometer head.

HEADLIGHTS

REMOVAL AND INSTALLATION

1. Remove the headlight bezel.
2. Unhook the spring from the headlight retaining ring if so equipped.
3. Unscrew the retaining ring and remove it.

NOTE: *Do not disturb the two long aiming screws.*

4. Unplug the old sealed beam.

Lightbulb Chart

Back Up Lamps	1156
Headlamps	6052
License Plate Lamp	168
Park and Turn Signal Lamp	2057 N.A.
Side Marker Lamps (Front)	168
Side Marker Lamps (Rear)*	168
Tail, Stop, and Turn Signal Lamp	2057

*Tail Lamp serves as Rear Side Marker on Wagon Models.
Halogen Headlamps Optional.
N.A. Amber Glass

HEADLIGHT SWITCH RHEOSTAT DIMMING

Air Conditioning Controls	#158
Ash Tray	#161
Clock Electronic (Note B)	
Gear Shift Selector Column (Note A)	#158
Gear Shift Selector Console	#158
Heated Rear Window Control	#158
Heater Controls	#158
Instrument Cluster Illumination	#194
Radio AM	#158
Radio AM-FM	#158
Radio AM-FM Stereo	#53
Radio CB	#1815
Radio 8 Track Stereo	#1815
Radio Cassette Stereo	#1815
Speedometer	#194
Switch Callouts	#158

NON-DIMMING

Battery Indicator	#194
Brake Indicator	#194
Cargo Lamp	#211-2
Dome Lamp	#211-2
Engine Indicator	#194
Fasten Seat Belts	#194
Gage Open (Note C)	#2382D
Glove Compartment	#1891
Heated Rear Window Indicator	L.E.D.
High Beam Indicator	#194
Ignition Switch Lamp	#1445
Map Lamp	#912
Oil Pressure Temperature Indicator	#194
Radio AM-FM Stereo or CB Indicator	#73
Transmission (Manual Reverse Indicator)	#158
Trunk Lamp	#1003
Turn Signal Indicator	#194
Underhood Lamp	#1003
Vanity Lamp	#194

NOTE: (A) Included in instrument cluster lighting.
(B) Electronic display serviced by authorized service dealer only.
(C) Part of housing assembly; bulb is not replaced individually.
(D) All bulbs are brass or glass wedge base. Aluminum bulbs are not approved and are not to be used.

CHASSIS ELECTRICAL

5. Connect the replacement bulb and install into the receptacle.
6. Install the retaining ring and connect the spring.
7. Install the headlight bezel.

FUSIBLE LINKS

CAUTION: *Do not replace blown fusible links with standard wire. Only fusible type wire with hypalon insulation can be used, or damage to the electrical system will occur.*

When a fusible link blows it is very important to find out why. They are placed in the electrical system for protection against dead shorts to ground, which can be caused by electrical component failure or various wiring failures.

CAUTION: *Do not just replace the fusible link to correct a problem.*

When replacing all fusible links, they are to be replaced with the same type of prefabricated link available from your Chrysler dealer.

REPLACEMENT

1. Cut the fusible link including the connection insulator from the main harness wire.
2. Remove 1 in. of insulation from both new fusible link, and the main harness, and wrap together.
3. Heat the splice with a soldering gun, and apply rosin type solder.

NOTE: *Do not use acid core solder.*

4. Allow the connection to cool, and wrap the new splice with at least 3 layers of electrical tape.
5. Fusible link locations are shown on the wiring diagram available from your Chrysler dealer.

WIRING DIAGRAMS

Wiring diagrams have been omitted from this book. As automobiles have become more complex, and available with longer and longer option lists, wiring diagrams have grown in size and complexity also. It has become virtually impossible to provide a readable reproduction in a reasonable number of pages.

Clutch and Transaxle

TRANSAXLE

REMOVAL AND INSTALLATION

1. Disconnect the negative battery terminal.
2. Jack up your vehicle and support it with jack stands.
3. Disconnect the shift linkage rods.
4. Disconnect the starter wires and remove the starter.
5. Disconnect the back-up light switch.
6. Disconnect the clutch cable.
7. Remove the bolt securing the speedometer adapter to the transaxle.
8. With the cable housing connected, carefully work the adapter and speedometer gear out of the transaxle.
    NOTE: *Only one, 16 tooth speedometer gear is available for your vehicle.*
9. Attach an engine lifting device, to the engine. Put a slight amount of tension on this device.
10. Remove the left wheel assembly.
11. Disconnect the right driveshaft and tie it out of the way.
12. Remove the left driveshaft.
13. Remove the left splash shield.
14. Remove the small dust cover at the bell housing.
15. Remove the large dust cover bolts at the bell housing.
16. Drain the fluid from the transaxle.
17. Place a transmission jack under the transaxle.
18. Remove the bolts from the left engine mount.
19. Remove the bolts attaching the transaxle to the engine.
20. Slide the transaxle assembly to the left and rear of the car until the mainshaft clears the clutch.
21. Remove the transaxle from beneath the car.
22. Installation is the reverse of removal.
    NOTE: *The A-412 manual transaxle uses SAE 80W-90 gear oil. The A-460 manual and all automatic transaxles use Dexron® II fluid only.*

Halfshaft

REMOVAL AND INSTALLATION

The driveshaft assemblies are three piece units. Each driveshaft has an inner sliding constant velocity (Tripod) joint bolted to the transaxle, and an outer constant velocity (Rzeppa) joint with a stub shaft splined into the hub. The connecting shafts for the C/V joints are unequal in length and construction. The left side is a short solid shaft and the right is longer and tubular.
    NOTE: *Driveshafts on Aries/Reliant models*

CLUTCH AND TRANSAXLE

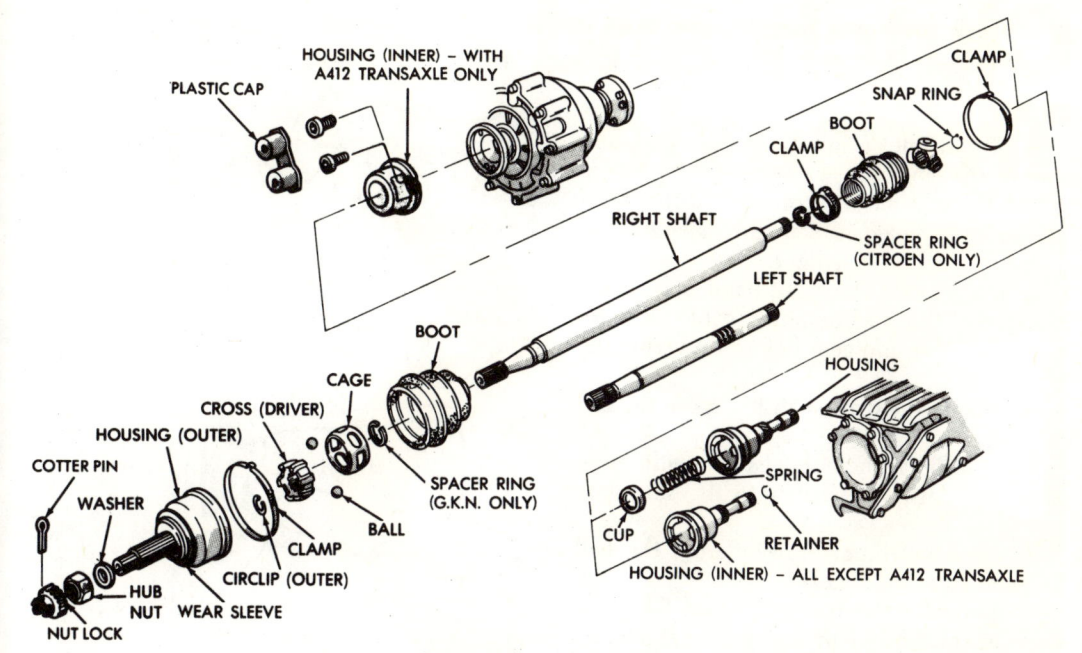

Driveshaft components

are interchangeable from manual to automatic transmission models.

Manual Transmission

1. With the vehicle on the floor and the brakes applied, loosen the hub nut.

NOTE: *The hub and driveshafts are splined together and retained by the hub nut which is torqued to at least 180 ft. lbs.*

2. Raise and support the vehicle and remove the hub nut and washer.

NOTE: *Always support both ends of the driveshaft during removal.*

3. Disconnect the lower control arm ball joint stud nut from the steering knuckle.

4. Remove the six 1/18 inch Allenhead screws which secure the CV joint to the transmission flange.

5. Holding the CV housing, push the outer joint and knuckle assembly outward while disengaging the inner housing from the flange face. Quickly turn the open end of the joint upward to retain as much lubricant as possible, then carefully pull the outer joint spline out of the hub. Cover the joint with a clean towel to prevent dirt contamination.

NOTE: *The outer joint and shaft must be supported during disengagement of the inner joint.*

6. Before installation, make sure that any lost lubricant is replaced. The only lubricant specified is Chrysler part number 4131389. No other lubricant of any type is to be used, as premature failure of the joint will result.

7. Clean the joint body and mating flange face.

8. Install the outer joint splined shaft into the hub. Do not secure with the nut and washer.

9. Early production vehicles were built with a cover plate between the hub and flange face. This cover is not necessary and should be discarded.

10. Position the inner joint in the transmission drive flange and secure it with *six* new screws. Torque the screws to 37–40 ft. lb.

11. Connect the lower control arm to the knuckle.

12. Install the outer joint and secure it with a *new* nut and washer. Torque the nut with the car on the ground and the brake set. Torque is 180 ft. lbs. Reinstall the cotter pin and locknut.

13. After attaching the driveshaft, if the inboard boot appears to be collapsed or deformed, vent the inner boot by inserting a round-tipped, small diameter rod between the boot and the shaft. As venting occurs, boot will return to its original shape.

Automatic Transmission

The inboard CV joints are retained by circlips in the differential side gears. The circlip

82 CLUTCH AND TRANSAXLE

tangs are located on a machined surface on the inner end of the stub shaft.

1. With the car on the ground, loosen the hub nut.
2. Drain the transaxle differential and remove the cover.
   NOTE: *Anytime the transaxle differential cover is removed, a new gasket should be formed from RTV sealant.*
3. To remove the right-hand driveshaft, disconnect the speedometer cable and remove the cable and gear before removing the driveshaft.
4. Rotate the driveshaft to expose the circlip tangs.
5. Compress the circlip with needle nose pliers and push the shaft into the side gear cavity.
6. Remove the clamp bolt from the ball stud and steering knuckle.
7. Separate the ball joint stud from the steering knuckle, by prying against the knuckle leg and control arm.
8. Separate the outer CV joint splined shaft from the hub by holding the CV housing and moving the hub away. Do not pry on the slinger or outer CV joint.
9. Support the shaft at the CV joints and remove the shaft. Do not pull on the shaft.
   NOTE: *Removal of the left shaft may be made easier by inserting the blade of a thin prybar between the differential pinion shaft and prying against the end face of the shaft.*
10. Installation is the reverse of removal. Be sure the circlip tangs are positioned against the flattened end of the shaft before installing the shaft. A quick thrust will lock the circlip in the groove. Tighten the hub nut with the wheels on the ground to 180 ft. lbs.

HALFSHAFT OVERHAUL

1. With the driveshaft assembly removed from the vehicle, remove the clamps and boot.
2. Depending on the unit (GKN or Citröen) separate the tripod assembly from the housing, as follows:

Citröen

Since the trunion ball rollers are not retained on bearing studs a retaining ring is used to prevent accidental tripod/housing separation, which would allow roller and needle bearings to fall away.

In the case of the spring loaded inner C/V joints, if it weren't for the retaining ring, the spring would automatically force the tripod

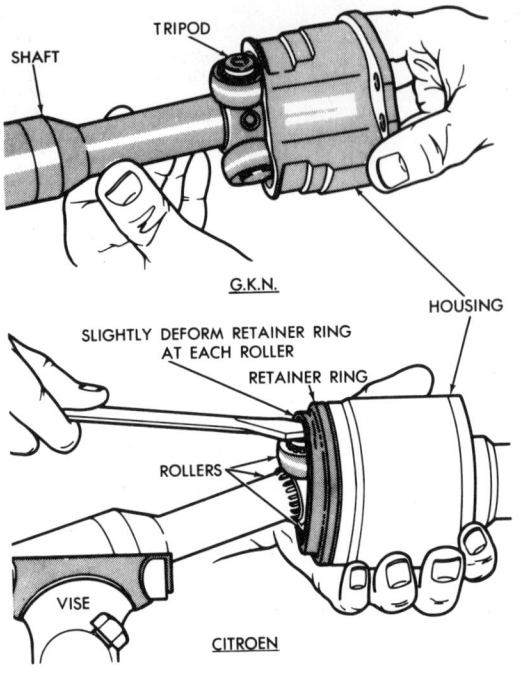

Separate tripod from housing

out of the housing whenever the shaft was not installed in the vehicle.

Separate the tripod from the housing by slightly deforming the retaining ring in 3 places, with a suitable tool.
   CAUTION: *Secure the rollers to the studs during separation. With the tripod out of the housing secure the assembly with tape.*

GKN

The non-spring loaded GKN inboard joint tripods will slide right out of the housing. There is no retaining ring to prevent their removal. Spring loaded GKN inboard C/V joints have tabs on the can cover that prevent the spring from forcing the tripod out of the housing. These tabs must be bent back with

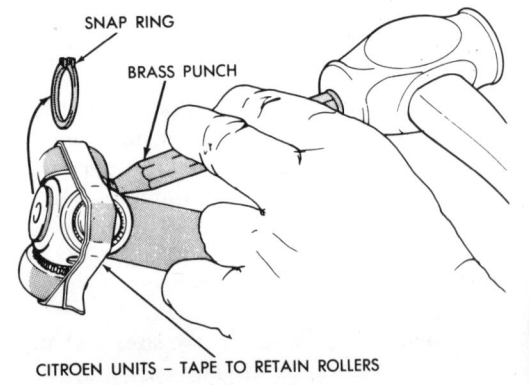

Remove snapring—then tripod

CLUTCH AND TRANSAXLE

a pair of pliers before the tripod can be removed. Under normal conditions it is not necessary to secure the GKN rollers to their studs during separation due to the presence of a retainer ring on the end of each stud. This retention force can easily be overcome if the rollers are pulled or impacted. It is also possible to pull the rollers off by removing or installing the tripod with the connecting shaft at too high an angle, relative to the housing.

Remove the snapring from the shaft end groove then remove the tripod with a brass punch.

DISASSEMBLY

1. Remove the boot clamps and discard them.
2. Wipe away the grease to expose the joint.
3. Support the shaft in a vice. Hold the outer joint, and using a plastic hammer, give a sharp tap to the top of the joint body to dislodge it from the internal circlip.
4. If the shaft is bent carefully pry the wear sleeve from the C/V joint machined ledge.
5. Remove the circlip from the shaft and discard it.

NOTE: *Replacement boot kits will contain this circlip.*

6. Unless the shaft is damaged do not remove the heavy spacer ring from the shaft.

NOTE: *If the shaft must be replaced, care must be taken that the new shaft is of the proper construction, depending on whether the inner joint is spring loaded or not.*

If the C/V joint was operating satisfactorily, and the grease does not appear contaminated, just replace the boot. If the outer joint is noisy or badly worn, replace the entire unit.

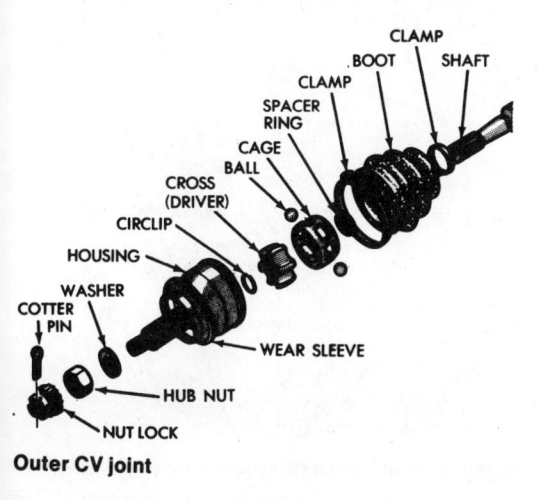

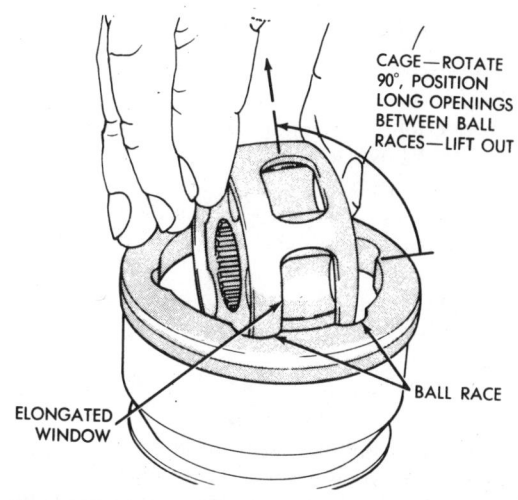

Removing cage and cross assembly from housing

The repair kit will include boot, clamps, retaining ring (circlip) and lubricant.

7. Wipe off the grease and mark the position of the inner cross, cage and housing with a dab of paint.
8. Hold the joint vertically in a vise. Do not crush the splines on the shaft.
9. Press down on one side of the inner race to tilt the cage and remove the balls from the opposite side.
10. If the joint is tight, use a hammer and brass drift pin to tap the inner race. Repeat this step until all balls have been removed.

CAUTION: *Do not hit the cage.*

11. Tilt the cage and inner race assembly vertically and position the two opposing, elongated cage windows in the area between the ball grooves. Pull the cage out of the housing.
12. Turn the inner cross 90° and align the race lands with an elongated hole in the cage. Remove the inner race.
13. Installation is the reverse of removal.

NOTE: *Spring loaded parts and non-spring loaded parts are not interchangeable.*

Outer CV joint

SHIFTER ADJUSTMENT
Model A-412

1. Place the transmission in neutral at the 3-4 position.
2. Loosen the shift tube clamp.
3. Place a ¾ inch spacer between the slider and blocker bracket.
4. Tighten the shift tube clamp remove the spacer.

84 CLUTCH AND TRANSAXLE

Model A-460

A new Chrysler designed manual transaxle (A-460) is used beginning with January 1981 productions. Models produced prior to January 1981 will continue to use the current manual transaxle.

The new transaxle uses a double ended pin that is used to lock the linkage in place prior to adjustment.

1. Remove the screw from the top and re-insert the other end, locking the linkage in place.
2. The linkage is locked in the Neutral detent between 1st and 2nd gears.
3. Align the marks on the linkage.
4. Remove the pin and replace it in its original location. Check the operation of the shift linkage.

CLUTCH

The clutch is a dry disc unit, with no adjustment for wear provided in the clutch itself. Adjustment is made through an adjustable sleeve in the pedal linkage.

REMOVAL AND INSTALLATION

A-412 Transaxle

NOTE: *Chrysler recommends the use of special tool L-4533 for disc alignment.*

1. Remove the transaxle.
2. Loosen the flywheel-to-pressure plate bolts diagonally, one or two turns at a time to avoid warpage.
3. Remove the flywheel and clutch disc from the pressure plate.
4. Remove the retaining ring and release plate.
5. Diagonally loosen the pressure plate-to-crankshaft bolts. Mark all parts for reassembly.
6. Remove the bolts, spacer and pressure plate.
7. The flywheel and pressure plate surfaces should be cleaned thoroughly with fine sandpaper.
8. Align marks and install the pressure plate, spacer and bolts. Coat the bolts with thread compound and torque them to 55 ft. lbs.
9. Install the release plate and retaining ring.
10. Using special tool L-4533 or its equivalent, install the clutch disc and flywheel on the pressure plate.

CAUTION: *Make certain that the drilled mark on the flywheel is at the top, so that the two dowels on the flywheel align with the proper holes in the pressure plate.*

11. Install the six flywheel bolts and tighten them to 15 ft. lbs.
12. Remove the aligning tool.
13. Install the transmission.
14. Adjust the freeplay.

A-460 Transaxle

NOTE: *Chrysler recommends the use of special tool #C4676 for disc alignment.*

1. Remove the transaxle.
2. Matchmark the clutch cover and flywheel for easy reinstallation.
3. Insert special tool C4676 or its equivalent to hold the clutch disc in place.
4. Loosen the cover attaching bolts. Do this procedure in a diagonal manner, a few turns at a time to prevent warping the cover.

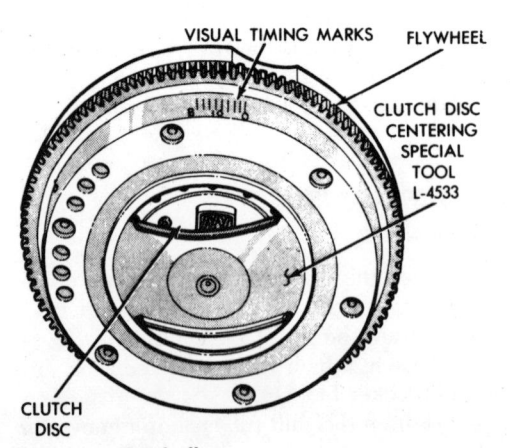

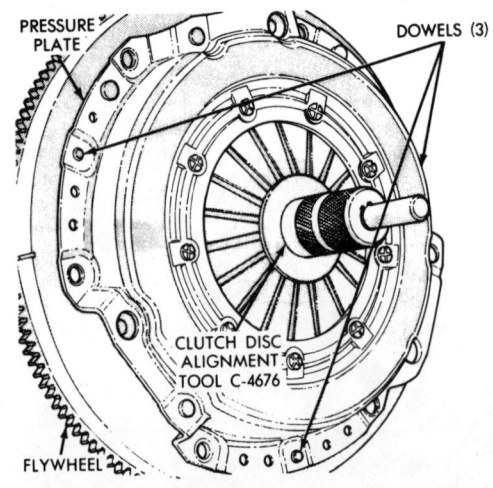

Centering clutch disc

A-460 manual transaxle clutch disc aligning tool

CLUTCH AND TRANSAXLE 85

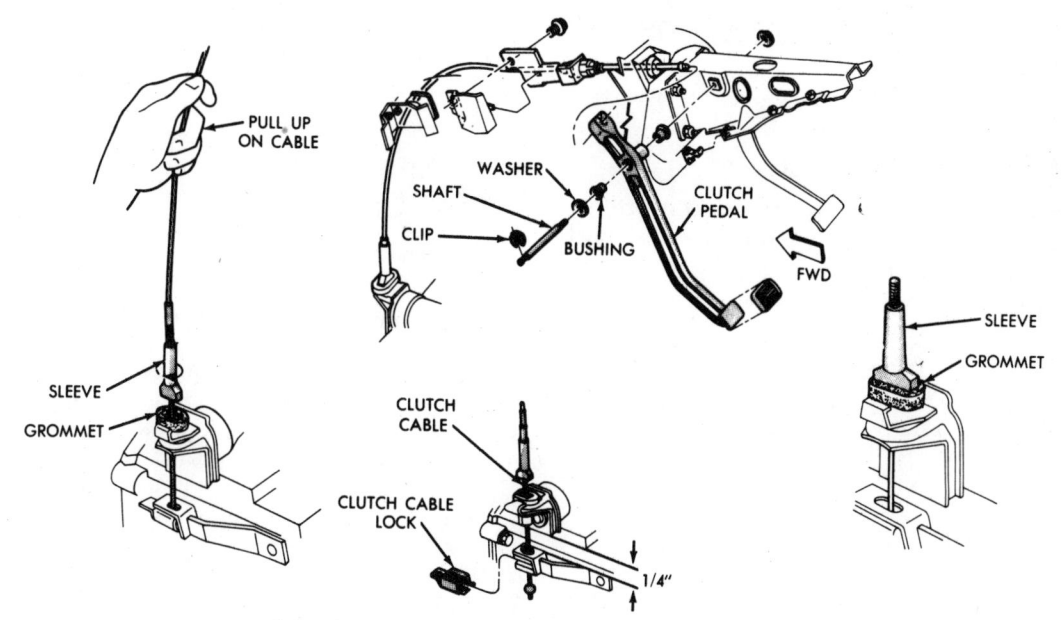

Adjusting clutch free play—A-412 manual transaxle

5. Remove the cover assembly and disc from the flywheel.
6. Remove the clutch release shaft and slide the release bearing off the input shaft seal retainer.
7. Remove the fork from the release bearing thrust plate.
8. Installation is the reverse of removal. Upon reinstallation tighten the clutch cover bolts to 21 ft. lbs.

FREEPLAY ADJUSTMENT
A-412 Transaxle

NOTE: *The A-460 Transaxle is equipped with a self-adjusting clutch release mechanism.*

1. Pull up on the clutch cable.
2. While holding the cable up, rotate the adjusting sleeve downward until a snug contact is made against the grommet.

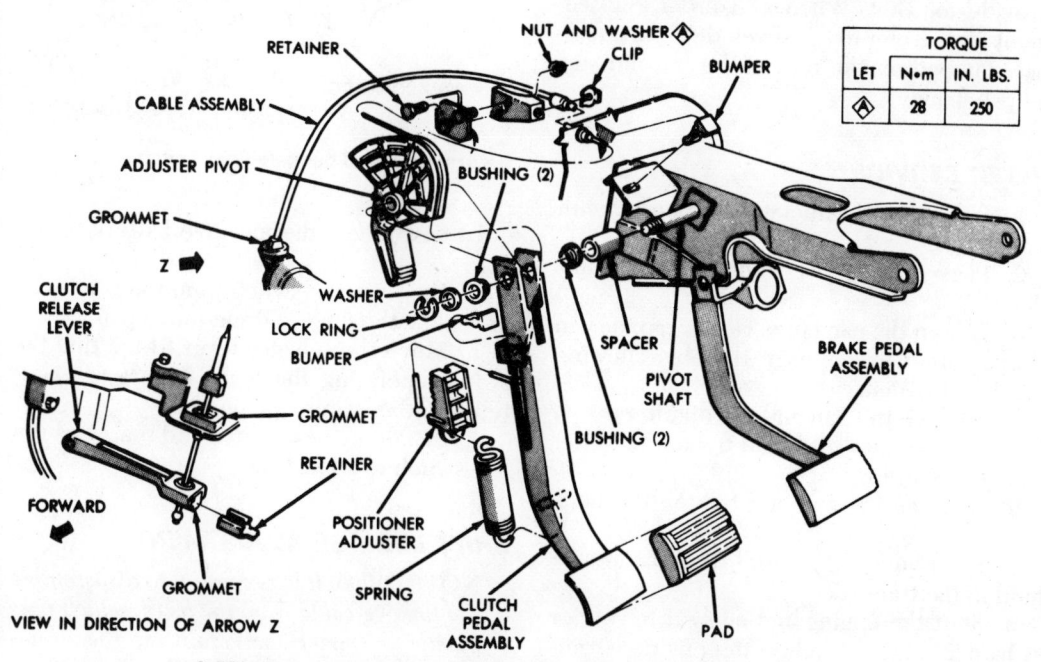

TORQUE		
LET	N•m	IN. LBS.
◇	28	250

A-460 manual transaxle self-adjusting clutch release mechanism

86 CLUTCH AND TRANSAXLE

3. Rotate the sleeve slightly to allow the end of the sleeve to seat in the rectangular hole in the grommet.

Automatic Transaxle

The transaxle combines a torque converter, a fully automatic 3 speed transmission, final drive gearing and a differential, into a compact front wheel drive system.

Automatic transaxle

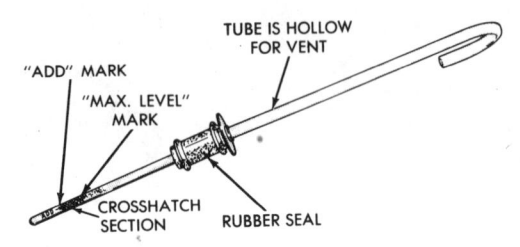

Dipstick and transmission vent

Transaxle operation requirements are different for each vehicle and engine combination. Some internal parts will be different to provide for this. When you order replacement parts, refer to the seven digit part number stamped on the rear of the transmission oil pan flange.

FILTER SERVICE

1. Jack up your vehicle and support it with jack stands.
2. Place a drain pan under the transmission.
3. Loosen the pan bolts. Gently tap the pan at one corner to loosen it, thereby, allowing the fluid to drain.
4. Remove the pan and the oil filter.
5. Install a new filter and tighten the filter bolts to 40 in. lbs.
6. Reinstall the pan and tighten the bolts to 14 ft. lbs.
7. Put 4 quarts of Dexron II® transmission fluid in the transaxle.
8. Start the engine and allow it to run for at least 2 minutes. While the engine is running, hold your foot on the service brake, apply the emergency brake and shift the transmission through all gears.
9. Check the fluid in the neutral or park position, and add more if necessary. Recheck the fluid after it has reached normal operating temperature. The fluid level should be between the "Max" and "Add" lines on the dipstick.

NEUTRAL SAFETY/BACK-UP LIGHT SWITCH

The neutral safety switch is the center terminal of the three terminal switch, located on the transaxle. The back-up light switch uses the two outside terminals. The center terminal provides a ground for the starter solenoid circuit through the selector lever in the Park and Neutral positions only.

NOTE: *No adjustments are possible on this switch.*

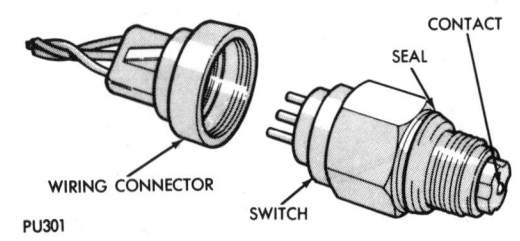

Neutral start and back-up light switch

1. Disconnect the negative battery terminal.
2. Unscrew the switch from the transaxle, and allow the fluid to drain into a pan.
3. Move the selector lever to see that the switch operating the lever fingers are centered in the switch opening.
4. Install the new switch and seal. Tighten the switch to 24 ft. lbs.

SHIFT LINKAGE ADJUSTMENT

NOTE: *When it is necessary to disassemble the linkage cable from the lever, which uses plastic grommets as retainers, the grommets should be replaced with new ones.*

CLUTCH AND TRANSAXLE

Gearshift linkage

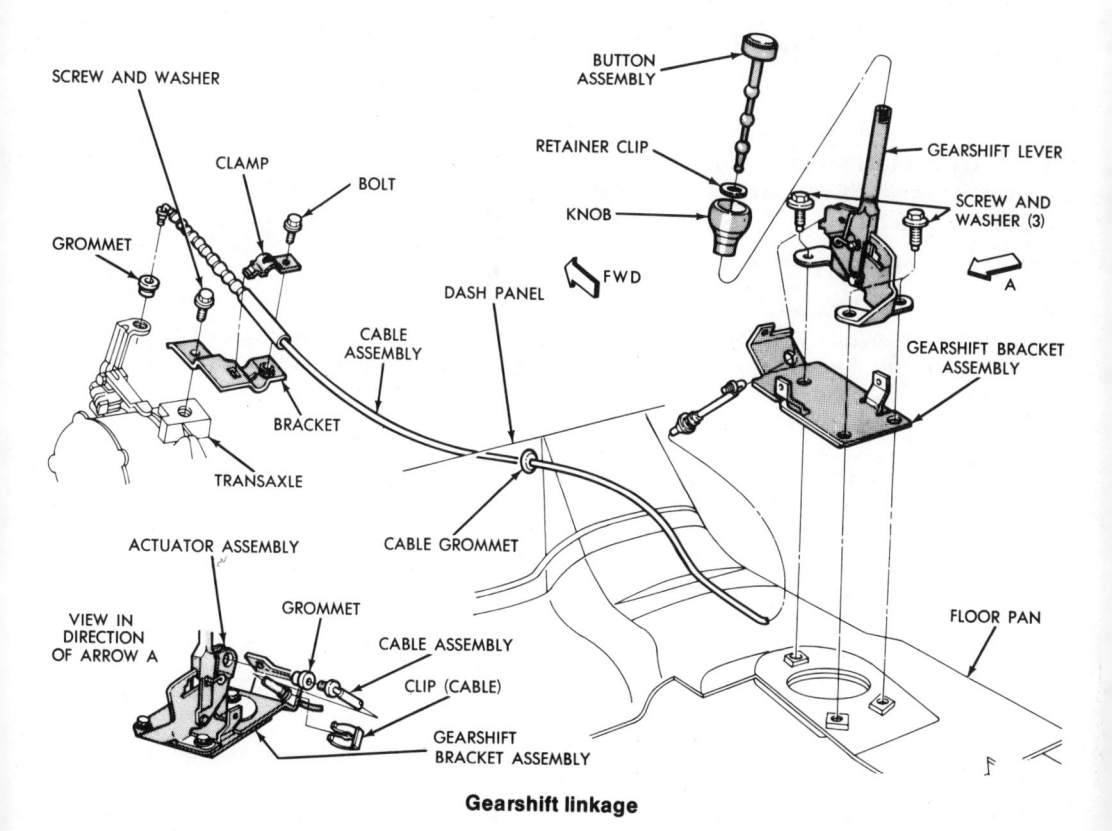

1. Place the gearshift lever in the Park position.
2. While maintaining a slight pressure on the shift lever, tighten the locknut bolt to 90 in. lbs. The shift lever should now be properly adjusted.
3. Check the adjustment as follows:
   a. The detent position for Neutral and Drive should be within the limits of the hand lever gate stops.
   b. The engine should start only in the Park or Neutral positions.

THROTTLE CABLE ADJUSTMENT

NOTE: *This adjustment should be performed while the engine is at normal operating temperature. Make sure that the carburetor is not on fast idle by disconnecting the choke.*

1. Loosen the adjustment bracket lock screw.
2. To insure proper adjustment, the bracket must be free to slide on its slot.
3. Hold the throttle lever firmly rearward against its internal stop and tighten the adjusting bracket lock to 105 in. lbs. (8¾ ft. lb.)
4. Reconnect the choke. Test the cable operation by moving the throttle lever forward and slowly releasing it to confirm it will return fully rearward.

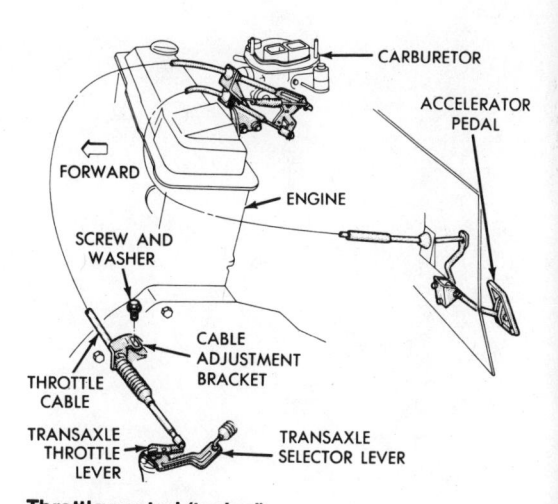

Throttle control (typical)

FRONT BAND ADJUSTMENT

The kickdown band adjusting screw is located on the left side (top front) of the transaxle case.

1. Loosen the locknut and back off the nut approximately 5 turns. Test the adjusting screw for free turning in the transaxle case.

CLUTCH AND TRANSAXLE

2. Using special tool #C-3380-A or its equivalent, tighten the adjusting screw to 72 in. lbs.

3. Back off the adjusting screw 3 turns (A-404) 2¾ turns (A-413 and A-470). Hold the adjusting screw in this position and tighten the locknut to 35 in. lbs.

REAR BAND ADJUSTMENT

NOTE: *The A-404 transaxle has no adjustment for the rear band. Before attempting adjustment, the low-reverse (rear) band should be checked for end gap.*

1. Remove the oil pan and pressurize the low-reverse servo with 30 psi of air pressure.

2. Measure the gap between the band ends. If the gap is less than .080 in., the band has worn excessively and should be replaced. Band replacement is best left to a qualified repair facility.

3. Loosen and back off the locknut approximately 5 turns.

4. Tighten the adjusting screw to 41 in. lbs.

5. Back off the adjusting screw 3½ turns.

6. Tighten the locknut to 20 ft. lbs.

Suspension and Steering

7

FRONT SUSPENSION

A MacPherson Type front suspension, with vertical shock absorbers attached to the upper fender reinforcement and the steering knuckle, is used. Lower control arms, attached inboard to a cross-member and outboard to the steering knuckle through a ball joint, provide lower steering knuckle position. During steering manuevers, the upper strut and steering knuckle turn as an assembly.

Strut Damper
REMOVAL AND INSTALLATION

1. Jack up your vehicle and support it with jack stands.
2. Remove the tire and wheel assembly.
3. Remove the cam adjusting bolt, through bolt, and brake hose bracket screw.
4. Remove the strut mounting nuts and the strut.
5. Installation is the reverse of removal.
NOTE: *If the original strut is to be reinstalled mark the adjusting bolt prior to removal.*
The following torques are necessary for reinstallation: Strut mounting nuts 20 ft. lbs.; Brake hose bracket screw 10 ft. lbs.; Cam bolts 45 ft. lbs. plus ¼ turn; and the wheel nuts to 80 ft. lbs.

Ball Joints

The lower front suspension ball joints operate with no free play. The ball joint housing is pressed into the lower control arm with the joint stud retained in the steering knuckle with a (clamp) bolt.

INSPECTION

With the weight of the vehicle resting on the ground, grasp the ball joint grease fitting, and attempt to move it. If the ball joint is worn the grease fitting will move easily. If movement is noted, replacement of the ball joint is recommended.

REMOVAL AND INSTALLATION

1. Pry off the seal.
2. Position a receiving cup, special tool #C-4699-2 or its equivalent to support the lower control arm.
3. Install a 1¹/₁₆ inch deep socket over the stud and against the joint upper housing.
4. Press the joint assembly from the arm.
5. To install, position the ball joint housing into the control arm cavity.
6. Position the assembly in a press with

90 SUSPENSION AND STEERING

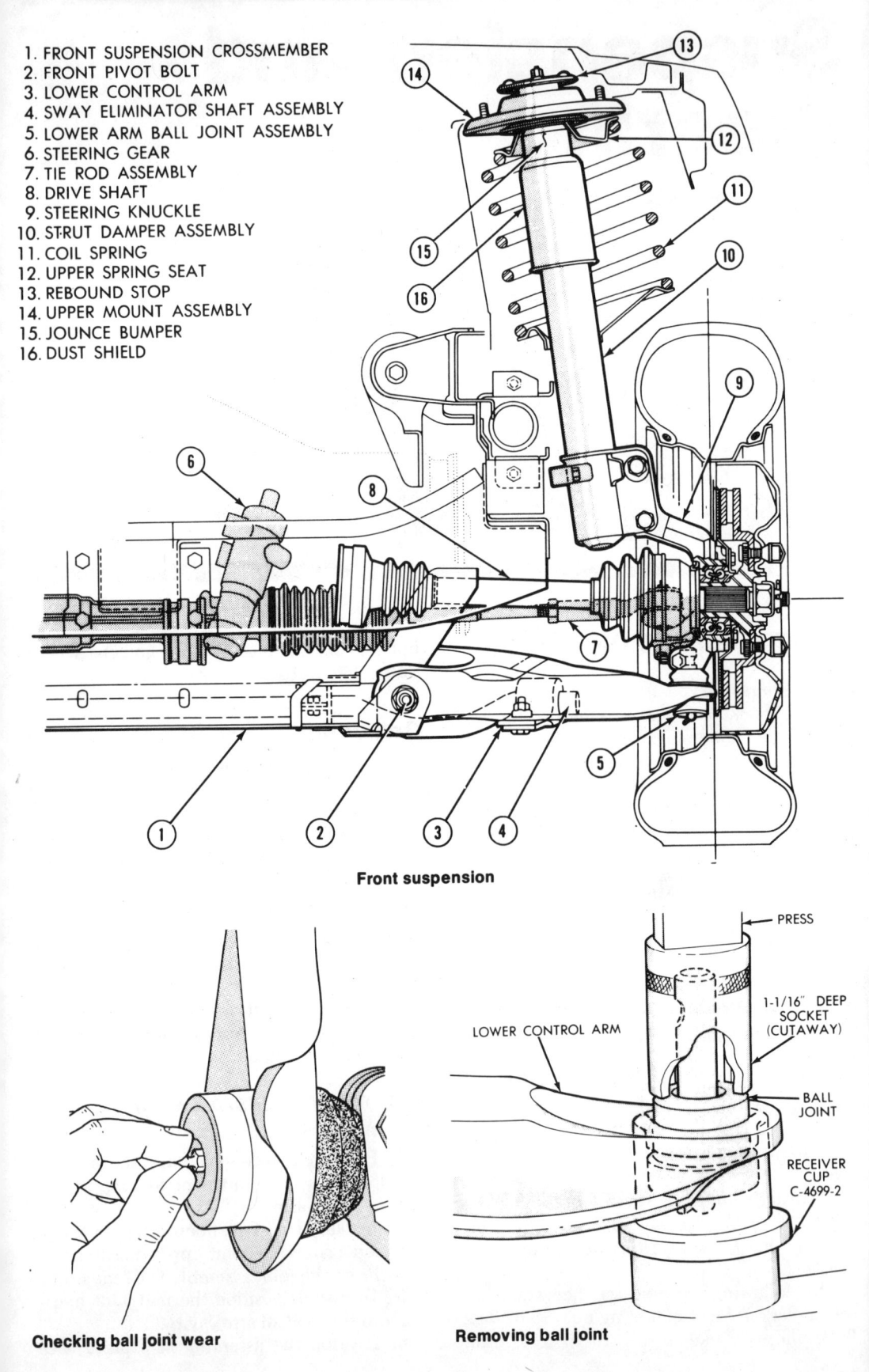

1. FRONT SUSPENSION CROSSMEMBER
2. FRONT PIVOT BOLT
3. LOWER CONTROL ARM
4. SWAY ELIMINATOR SHAFT ASSEMBLY
5. LOWER ARM BALL JOINT ASSEMBLY
6. STEERING GEAR
7. TIE ROD ASSEMBLY
8. DRIVE SHAFT
9. STEERING KNUCKLE
10. STRUT DAMPER ASSEMBLY
11. COIL SPRING
12. UPPER SPRING SEAT
13. REBOUND STOP
14. UPPER MOUNT ASSEMBLY
15. JOUNCE BUMPER
16. DUST SHIELD

Front suspension

Checking ball joint wear

Removing ball joint

SUSPENSION AND STEERING

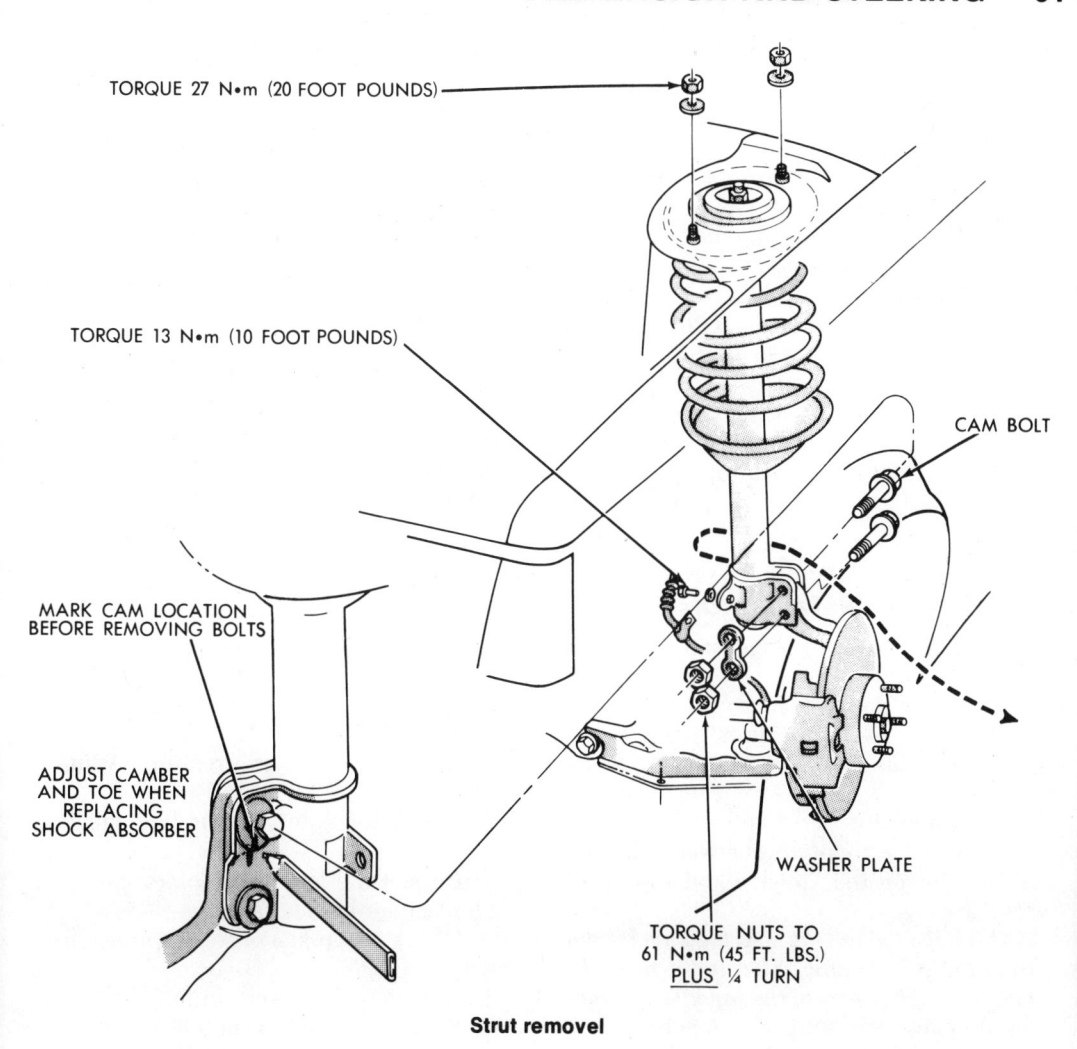

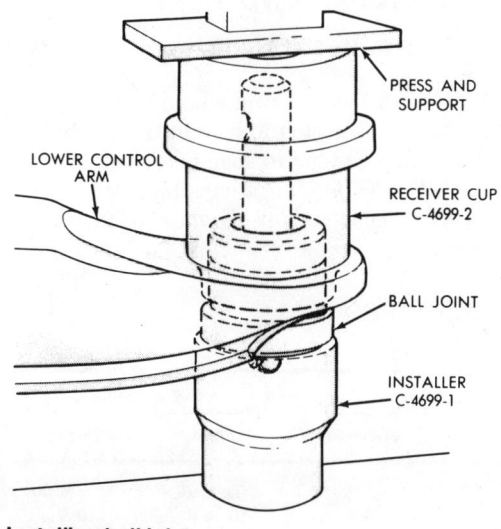

Strut removal

Installing ball joint

special tool #C-4699-1 or its equivalent, supporting the control arm.

7. Align the ball joint assembly, then press it until the housing ledge stops against the control arm cavity down flange.

8. To install a new seal, support the ball joint housing with tool #C-4699-2 and place a new seal over the stud, against the housing.

9. With a 1½ inch socket, press the seal onto the joint housing with the seat against the control arm.

Spring

REMOVAL AND INSTALLATION

1. Remove the struts as previously outlined.
2. Compress the spring, using a reliable coil spring compressor.

92 SUSPENSION AND STEERING

3. Hold the strut rod and remove the rod nut.
4. Remove the retainers and bushings.
5. Remove the spring.

NOTE: *Springs are not interchangeable from side to side.*

CAUTION: *When removing the spring from the compressor, open the compressor evenly and not more than 9¼ inches.*

6. Assembly is the reverse of disassembly.

NOTE: *Torque rod nut to 55 ft. lbs. before removing the spring compressor. Be sure the lower coil end of the spring is seated in the recess. Use a "crow's foot" adaptor to tighten the nut while holding the rod with an open end wrench.*

Lower Control Arm

REMOVAL AND INSTALLATION

1. Jack up your vehicle and support it with jack stands.
2. Remove the front inner pivot through bolt, the rear stub strut nut, retainer and bushing, and the ball joint-to-steering knuckle clamp bolt.
3. Separate the ball joint stud from the steering knuckle by prying between the ball stud retainer on the knuckle and the lower control arm.

CAUTION: *Pulling the steering knuckle out from the vehicle after releasing it from the ball joint can separate the inner C/V joint.*

4. Remove the sway bar-to-control arm nut and reinforcement and rotate the control arm over the sway bar. Remove the rear stub strut bushing, sleeve and retainer.

NOTE: *The substitution of fasteners other than those of the grade originally used is not recommended.*

5. Install the retainer, bushing and sleeve on the stub strut.
6. Position the control arm over the sway bar and install the rear stub strut and front pivot into the crossmember.
7. Install the front pivot bolt and loosely install the nut.
8. Install the stub strut bushing and retainer and loosely assemble the nut.
9. Position the sway bar bracket and stud through the control arm and install the retainer nut. Tighten the nut to 10 ft. lb.
10. Install the ball joint stud into the steering knuckle and install the clamp bolt. Torque the clamp bolt to 50 ft. lb.

Front End Alignment

Front wheel alignment is the proper adjustment of all the inter-related suspension angles affecting the running and steering of the front wheels.

There are six basic factors which are the foundation of front wheel alignment, height, caster camber, toe-in, steering axis inclination, and toe-out on turns. Of these basic factors, only camber and toe are mechanically adjustable.

CAMBER ADJUSTMENT

1. Check the tire air pressure. Adjust if necessary.
2. Check the front wheels for radial run out.
3. Inspect the lower ball joints and steering linkage for looseness.
4. Check for broken or weak springs, front and rear.
5. Loosen the cam and through bolts.
6. Rotate the upper cam bolt to move the wheel in or out to the specified camber.
7. Tighten the bolts to 45 ft. lbs. plus ¼ turn.

TOE-IN ADJUSTMENT

1. Follow steps 1–4 from the previous procedure.
2. Center the steering wheel and hold it.
3. Loosen the tie rod lock nuts. Rotate the rods to align the toe to specifications.

CAUTION: *Do not twist the tie rod to steering gear rubber boots during alignment.*

Wheel Alignment Specifications
(Caster is not adjustable)

Year	Front Camber Range (deg.)	Front Camber Preferred	Rear Camber Range (deg.)	Rear Camber Preferred	Toe-Out (in.) Front	Toe-Out (in.) Rear
'81–'82	¼N to ¾P	5/16P	1N-0	½N	7/32 out to 1/8 in	3/16 out to 3/16 in

SUSPENSION AND STEERING 93

Alignment—camber/toe

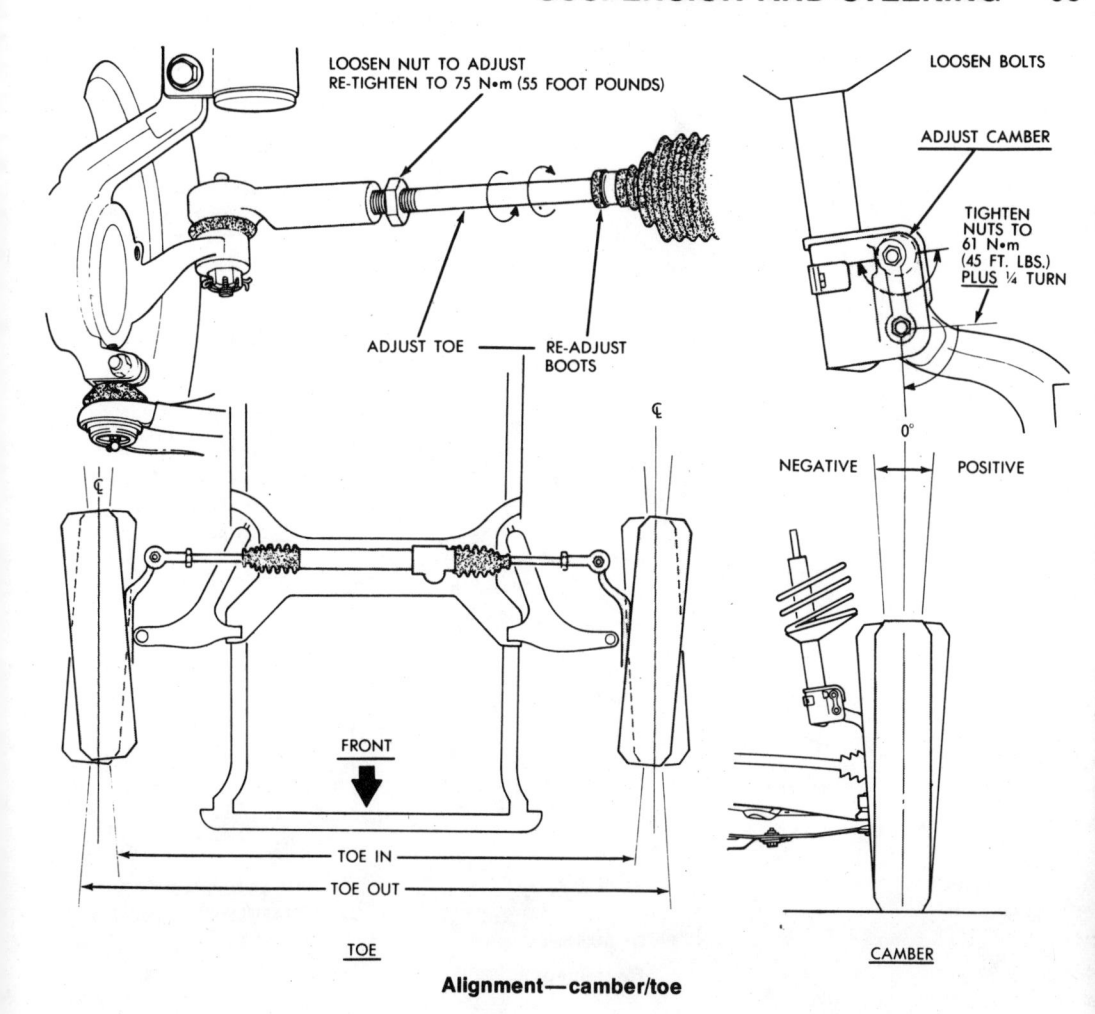

4. Tighten the tie rod lock nuts to 55 ft. lbs.
5. A the steering gear to tie rod boots at the tie rod.

REAR SUSPENSION

Aries/Reliant use a flexible beam axle with trailing links and coil springs. One shock absorber on each side is mounted outside the coil spring and attached to the body and the beam axle. Wheel spindles are bolted to the outer ends of the axle.

Springs

REMOVAL AND INSTALLATION

1. Jack up your vehicle and support it with jack stands.
2. Support the rear axle with a floor jack.
3. Remove the bottom bolt from both rear shock absorbers.
4. Lower the axle assembly until the spring and upper isolator can be removed.
5. Remove the spring and isolator.
NOTE: *Do not stretch the brake hoses.*
6. Installation is the reverse of removal.

Shock Absorbers

TESTING

Shock absorbers require replacement if the car fails to recover quickly after hitting a large bump or if it sways excessively following a directional change.

A good way to test the shock absorbers is to intermittently apply downward pressure to the side of the car until it is moving up and down for almost its full suspension travel. Release it and observe its recovery. If the car bounces once or twice after having been released and then comes to a rest, the shocks are alright. If the car continues to bounce, the shocks will probably require replacement.

94 SUSPENSION AND STEERING

TORQUE		
Ⓐ	54 N•m	40 FT. LBS.
Ⓑ	108 N•m	80 FT. LBS.
Ⓒ	61 N•m	45 FT. LBS.
Ⓓ	8 N•m	70 IN. LBS.

Rear suspension

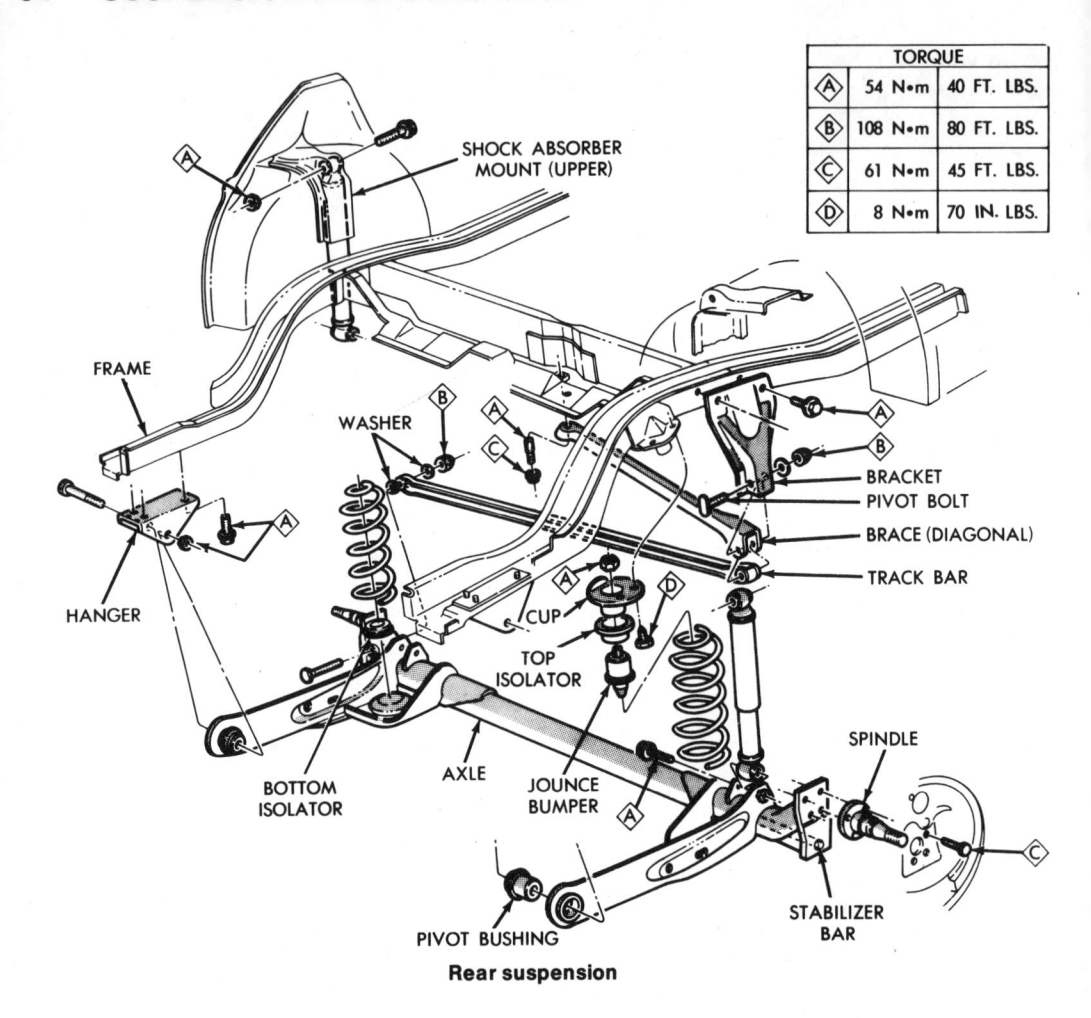

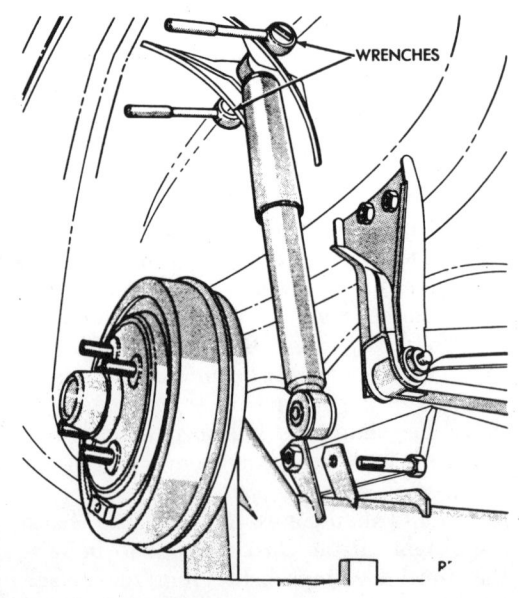

Rear shock absorbers

REMOVAL AND INSTALLATION

1. Jack up your vehicle and support it with jack stands.
2. Support the rear axle with a floor jack.
3. Remove the top and bottom shock absorber bolts.
4. Remove the shock absorbers.
5. Installation is the reverse of removal.

Rear Axle Alignment

The Aries/Reliant are equipped with a rear suspension, using wheel spindles, thereby, making it possible to align the camber and toe of the rear wheels.

Alignment adjustment, if required, is made by adding shims (Part #5205114 or equivalent) between the spindle mounting surface and axle mounting plate.

Because of the specialized equipment needed to perform this procedure it is best

SUSPENSION AND STEERING

left to your Chrysler dealer or a reliable repair facility.

STEERING

The manual steering system consists of a tube which contains the toothed rack, a pinion, the rack slipper, and the rack slipper spring. Steering effort is transmitted to the steering arms by the tie rods which are coupled to the ends of the rack, and tie rod ends. The connection between the ends of the rack and the tie rod is protected by a bellows type oil seal which retains the gear lubricant.

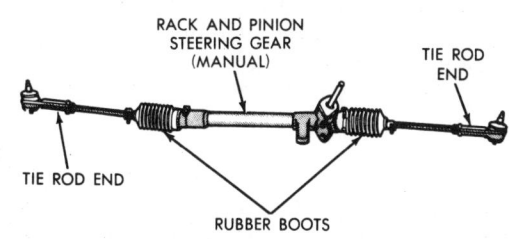

Manual steering gear

The power steering system consists of four major parts: the power gear, power steering pump, pressure hose and the return hose. As with the manual system, the turning of the steering wheel is converted into linear travel through the meshing of the helical pinion teeth with the rack teeth. Power assist is provided by an open center, rotary type, three-way control valve which directs fluid to either side of the rack control piston.

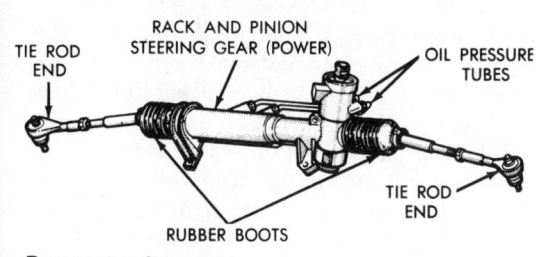

Power steering gear

Steering Wheel
REMOVAL AND INSTALLATION

1. Remove the horn button and horn switch.
2. Remove the steering wheel nut.
3. Using a steering wheel puller, remove the steering wheel.
4. Align the master serration in the wheel

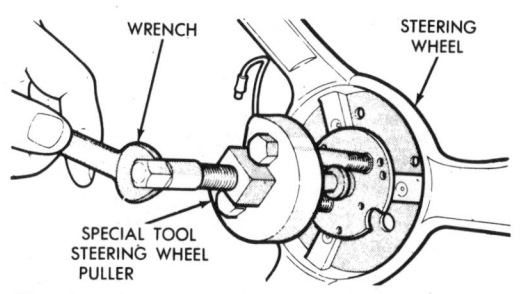

Steering wheel removal

hub with the missing tooth on the shaft. Torque the shaft nut to 60 ft. lbs. 1981 models, 45 ft. lbs. 1982 models.

CAUTION: *Do not torque the nut against the steering column lock or damage will occur.*

5. Replace the horn switch and button.

Turn Signal Switch
REMOVAL AND INSTALLATION
Without Tilt Wheel

1. Disconnect the negative battery terminal.
2. Remove the steering wheel as described earlier.
3. On vehicles equipped with intermittent wipe or intermittent wipe with speed control, remove the two screws that attach the turn signal lever cover to the lock housing and remove the turn signal lever cover.
4. Remove the wash/wipe switch assembly.
5. Pull the hider up the control stalk and remove the two screws that attach the control stalk sleeve to the wash/wipe switch.
6. Rotate the control stalk shaft to the full clockwise position and remove the shaft from the switch by pulling straight out of the switch.
7. Remove the turn signal switch and upper bearing retainer screws. Remove the retainer and lift the switch up and out.
8. Installation is the reverse of removal.

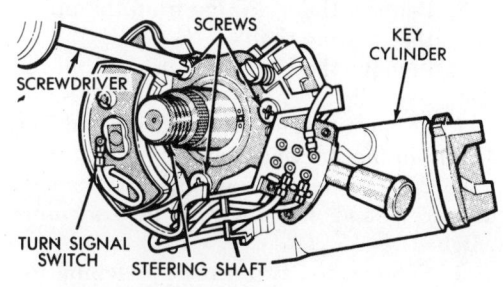

Turn signal switch removal

SUSPENSION AND STEERING

With Tilt Wheel

1. Disconnect the negative battery terminal.
2. Remove the steering wheel as previously described.
3. Remove the tilt lever and push the hazard warning knob in and unscrew it to remove it.
4. Remove the ignition key lamp assembly.
5. Pull the knob off the wash/wipe switch assembly.
6. Pull the hider up the stalk and remove the two screws that attach the sleeve to the wash/wipe switch and remove the sleeve.
7. Rotate the shaft in the wiper switch to the full clockwise position and remove the shaft by pulling straight out of the wash/wipe switch.
8. Remove the plastic cover from the lock plate. Depress the lock plate with tool C-4156 and pry the retaining ring out of the groove. Remove the lock plate, canceling cam and upper bearing spring.
9. Remove the switch actuator screw and arm.
10. Remove the three turn signal switch attaching screws and place the shift bowl in low position. Wrap a piece of tape around the connector and wires to prevent snagging then remove the switch and wires.
11. Installation is the reverse of removal.

Ignition Switch and Keylock
REMOVAL AND INSTALLATION
Without Tilt Wheel

1. Follow the turn signal switch removal procedure previously described.
2. Unclip the horn and key light ground wires.
3. Remove the retaining screw and move the ignition key lamp assembly out of the way.
4. Remove the four screws that hold the bearing housing to the lock housing.
5. Remove the snap ring from the upper end of the steering shaft.
6. Remove the bearing housing from the shaft.
7. Remove the lock plate spring and lock plate from the steering shaft.
8. Remove the ignition key, then remove the screw and lift out the buzzer/chime switch.
9. Remove the two screws attaching the ignition switch to the column jacket.
10. Remove the ignition switch by rotating the switch 90 degrees on the rod then sliding off the rod.
11. Remove the two mounting screws from the dimmer switch and disengage the switch from the actuator rod.
12. Remove the two screws that mount the bellcrank and slide the bellcrank up in the lock housing until it can be disconnected from the ignition switch actuator rod.
13. To remove the lock cylinder and lock levers place the cylinder in the lock position and remove the key.
14. Insert a small diameter screwdriver or similar tool into the lock cylinder release holes and push into the release spring loaded lock retainers. At the same time pull the lock cylinder out of the housing bore.
15. Grasp the lock lever and spring assembly and pull straight out of the housing.
16. If necessary the lock housing may be removed from the column jacket by removing the hex head retaining screws.
17. Installation is the reverse of removal. If the lock housing was removed tighten the lock housing screws to 90 inch pounds.
18. To install the dimmer switch, firmly seat the push rod into the switch. Compress the switch until two .093 inch drill shanks can be inserted into the alignment holes. Reposition the upper end of the push rod in the pocket of the wash/wipe switch. With a light rearward pressure on the switch, install the two screws.
19. Grease and assemble the two lock levers, lock lever spring and pin.
20. Install the lock lever assembly in the lock housing. Seat the pin firmly into the bottom of the slots and make sure the lock lever spring leg is firmly in place in the lock casting notch.
21. Install the ignition switch actuator rod from the bottom through the oblong hole in the lock housing and attach it to the bellcrank. Position the bellcrank assembly into the lock housing while pulling the ignition switch rod down the column, install the bellcrank onto its mounting surface. The gearshift lever should be in the park position.
22. Place the ignition switch on the ignition switch actuator rod and rotate it 90 degrees to lock the rod into position.
23. To install the ignition lock, turn the key to the lock position and remove the key. Insert the cylinder far enough into the housing to contact the switch actuator. Insert the key and press inward and rotate the cylinder.

SUSPENSION AND STEERING

When the parts align the cylinder will move inward and lock into the housing.

24. With the key cylinder in the lock position and the ignition switch in the lock position (second detent from top) tighten the ignition switch mounting screws.
25. Feed the buzzer/chime switch wires behind the wiring post and down through the space between the housing and the jacket. Remove the ignition key and position the switch in the housing and tighten the mounting screws. The ignition key should be removed.
26. Install the lock plate on the steering shaft.
27. Install the upper bearing spring, then the upper bearing housing.
28. Install the upper bearing snap ring on the steering shaft, locking the assembly in place.
29. Install the four screws attaching the bearing housing to the lock housing.
30. Install the key lamp and turn signal switch, following the procedure given previously.

Lock Cylinder

REMOVAL AND INSTALLATION
With Tilt Wheel

1. Remove the turn signal switch as previously described.
2. Place the lock cylinder in the lock position.
3. Insert a thin tool into the slot next to the switch mounting screwing boss (right hand slot) and depress the spring latch at the bottom of the slot and remove the lock.
4. Installation is the reverse of removal. Turn the ignition lock to the "Lock" position and remove the key. Insert the cylinder until the spring loaded retainer snaps into place.

Ignition Switch

REMOVAL AND INSTALLATION
With Tilt Wheel

Due to the complexity of the ignition switch removal procedure and the necessity of special tools it is recommended that the switch be replaced by a qualified repair shop.

Tie Rod Ends

REMOVAL AND INSTALLATION

1. Jack up your car and support it with jack stands.
2. Loosen the jam nut which connects the tie rod end to the rack.
3. Mark the tie rod position on the threads.
4. Remove the tie rod cotter pin and nut.
5. Using a puller, remove the tie rod from the steering knuckle.
6. Unscrew the tie rod end from the rack.
7. Install a new tie rod end, and retighten the jam nut.
8. Recheck the wheel alignment.

Brakes

08

BRAKES

A conventional front disc/rear drum setup is used. The front discs are single piston caliper types; the rear drums are activated by a conventional top mounted wheel cylinder. Disc brakes require no adjustments, the drum brakes are self adjusting by means of the parking brake cable. The system is diagonally balanced, that is, the front left and right rear are on one system and the front right and left rear on the other. No proportioning valve is used. Power brakes are optional.

Master Cylinder

REMOVAL AND INSTALLATION

With Power Brakes

1. Disconnect the primary and secondary brake lines from the master cylinder. Plug the openings.
2. Remove the nuts attaching the cylinder to the power brake booster.
3. Slide the master cylinder straight out, away from the booster.
4. Installation is the reverse of removal.
5. Remember to bleed the brake system.

With Non-Power Brakes

1. Disconnect the primary and secondary brake lines and install plugs in the master cylinder openings.
2. Disconnect the stoplight switch mounting bracket from under the instrument panel. Pull the stop light switch out of the way to prevent switch damage.
3. Pull the brake pedal backward to disengage the pushrod from the master cylinder piston.

NOTE: *This will destroy the grommet.*

4. Remove the master cylinder-to-firewall nuts.
5. Slide the master cylinder out and away from the firewall. Be sure to remove all pieces of the broken grommet.
6. Install the boot on the pushrod.
7. Install a new grommet on the pushrod.
8. Apply a soap and water solution to the grommet and slide it firmly into position in the primary piston socket. Move the pushrod from side to side to make sure it's seated.
9. From the engine side, press the pushrod through the master cylinder mounting plate and align the mounting studs with the holes in the cylinder.
10. Install the nuts and torque them to 250 in. lbs.
11. From under the instrument panel, place the pushrod on the pin on the pedal and install a new retaining clip.

CAUTION: *Be sure to lubricate the pin.*

BRAKES

Master cylinder assembly

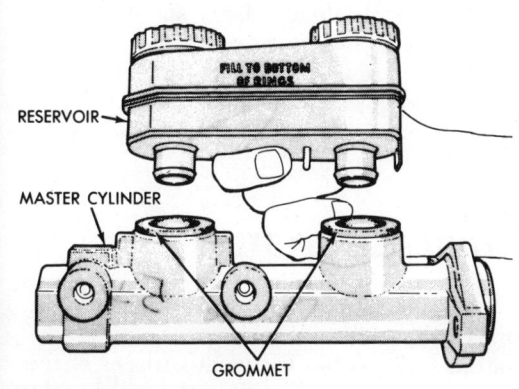

Removing the reservoir

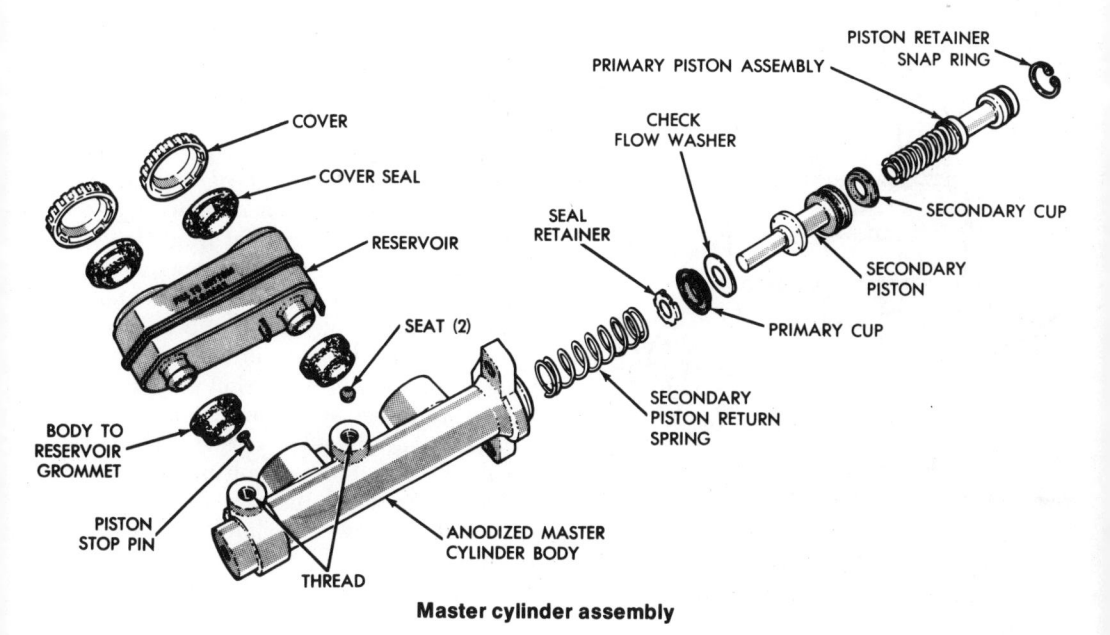

12. Install the brake lines on the master cylinder.
13. Bleed the system.

OVERHAUL

1. Remove the master cylinder as previously outlined.
2. Clean the housing and reservoir.
3. Remove the caps and empty the brake fluid.
4. Remove the reservoir by rocking it from side to side.
5. Remove the housing-to-reservoir grommets.
6. Use needle-nose pliers to remove the secondary piston stop pin from inside the master cylinder housing.
7. Remove the snapring from the outer end of the cylinder bore.
8. Slide the piston out of the cylinder bore.
9. Gently tap the end of the master cylinder on the bench to remove the secondary piston.

NOTE: *If the piston sticks in the bore use air pressure to force the piston out. New cups must be installed, if air pressure is used to force the piston out.*

10. Remove the rubber cups from the pistons, after noting the position of the cup lips.

NOTE: *Do not remove the primary cup of the primary piston. If the cup is damaged the entire piston assembly must be replaced.*

11. If the brass tube seats are not reusable, remove them with an Easy-out®, and insert new ones.
12. Wash the cylinder bore with clean brake fluid. Check for scoring, pitting or scratches. If any of these conditions exist replace the master cylinder. Replace the pistons if they are corroded. Replace the cups and seals. Discard all used rubber parts. Upon installation, coat all components with clean brake fluid.
13. Installation is the reverse of removal.

BLEEDING

1. Place the master cylinder in a vise.
2. Connect two lines to the fluid outlet orifices, and into the reservoir.
3. Fill the reservoir with brake fluid.
4. Using a wooden dowel, depress the pushrod slowly, allowing the pistons to return. Do this several times until the air bubbles are all expelled.

BRAKES

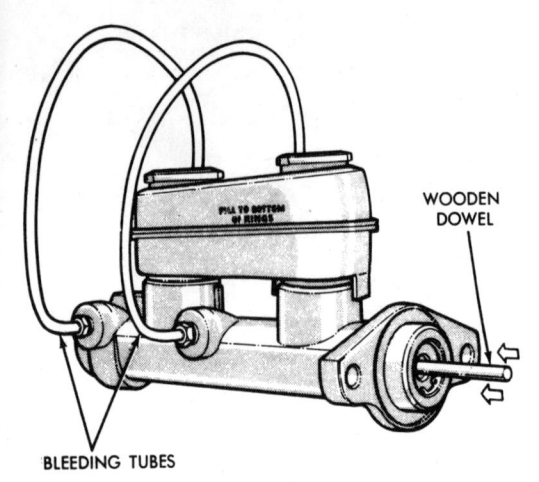

Bleeding the master cylinder

5. Remove the bleeding tubes from the master cylinder, plug the outlets and install the caps.

NOTE: *It is not necessary to bleed the entire system after replacing the master cylinder, provided the master cylinder has been bled and filled upon installation.*

Brake Booster

REMOVAL AND INSTALLATION

1. Remove the brake lines from the master cylinder.
2. Remove the nuts attaching the master cylinder to the brake booster, and remove the master cylinder.
3. Disconnect the vacuum line to the brake booster.
4. Underneath the instrument panel, remove the retainer clip from the brake pedal pin. Discard the retainer clip.
5. Remove the four power booster attaching nuts.
6. Remove the booster from the car.
7. Installation is the reverse of removal.

NOTE: *Remember to bleed the brake system.*

CAUTION: *The power brake booster is not repairable. Do not attempt to disassemble it.*

Tighten the brake booster mounting bolts to 21 ft. lb., the master cylinder bolts 14–20 ft. lbs.

Bleeding

The purpose of bleeding the brakes is to expel air trapped in the hydraulic system. The system must be bled whenever the pedal feels spongy, indicating that compressible air has entered the system. It must also be bled whenever the system has been opened or repaired. You will need a helper for this job.

CAUTION: *Never reuse brake fluid which has been bled from the brake system.*

1. The sequence for bleeding is right rear, left front, left rear and right front. If the car has power brakes, remove the vacuum by applying the brakes several times. Do not run the engine while bleeding the brakes.
2. Clean all the bleeder screws. You may want to give each one a shot of penetrating solvent to loosen it up; seizure is a common problem with bleeder screws, which then break off, sometimes requiring replacement of the part to which they are attached.
3. Fill the master cylinder with DOT 3 brake fluid.

NOTE: *Brake fluid absorbs moisture from the air. Don't leave the master cylinder or the fluid container uncovered any longer than necessary. Be careful handling the fluid—it eats paint.*

Check the level of the fluid often when bleeding, and refill the reservoirs as necessary. Don't let them run dry, or you will have to repeat the process.

4. Attach a length of clear vinyl tubing to the bleeder screw on the wheel cylinder. Insert the other end of the tube into a clear, clean jar half filled with brake fluid.
5. Have your assistant slowly depress the brake pedal. As this is done, open the bleeder screw ⅓–½ of a turn, and allow the fluid to run through the tube. Then close the bleeder screw before the pedal reaches the end of its travel. Have your assistant slowly release the pedal. Repeat this process until no air bubbles appear in the expelled fluid.
6. Repeat the procedure on the other three brakes, checking the level of fluid in the master cylinder reservoir often.

After you're done, there should be no sponginess in the brake pedal feel. If there is, either there is still air in the line, in which case the process should be repeated, or there is a leak somewhere, which of course must be corrected before the car is moved.

HYDRAULIC SYSTEM

A hydraulic system is used to actuate the brakes. The system transports the power required to force the frictional surfaces of the braking system together from the pedal to the individual braking units at each wheel. A hydraulic system is used for three reasons. First, fluid under pressure can be carried to all parts of the automobile by small hoses—some of which are flexible—without taking up a significant amount of room or posing routing problems. Second, liquid is noncompressible; a hydraulic system can transport force without modifying or reducing that force. Third, a great mechanical advantage can be given to the brake pedal end of the system, and the foot pressure required to actuate the brakes can be reduced by making the surface area of the master cylinder pistons smaller than that of any of the pistons in the wheel cylinders or calipers.

The master cylinder consists of a fluid reservoir and a double cylinder and piston assembly. Double type master cylinders are designed to separate the front and rear braking systems hydraulically in case of a leak.

Steel lines carry the brake fluid to a point on the vehicle's frame near each of the vehicle's wheels. The fluid is then carried to the slave cylinders by flexible tubes in order to allow for suspension and steering movements.

In drum brake systems, the slave cylinders are called wheel cylinders. Each wheel cylinder contains two pistons, one at either end, which push outward in opposite directions. In disc brake systems, the slave cylinders are part of the calipers. One or four cylinders are used to force the brake pads against the disc, but all cylinders contain one piston only. All slave cylinder pistons employ some type of seal, usually made of rubber, to minimize the leakage of fluid around the piston. A rubber dust boot seals the outer end of the cylinder against dust and dirt. The boot fits around the outer end of the piston on disc brake calipers, and around the brake actuating rod on wheel cylinders.

The hydraulic system operates as follows: When at rest, the entire system, from the pistons in the master cylinder to those in the wheel cylinders or calipers, is full of brake fluid. Upon application of the brake pedal, fluid trapped in front of the master cylinder pistons is forced through the lines to the slave cylinders. Here, it forces the pistons outward, in the case of drum brakes, and inward toward the disc, in the case of disc brakes. The motion of the pistons is opposed by return springs mounted outside the cylinders in drum brakes, and by internal springs or spring seals in disc brakes.

Upon release of the brake pedal, a spring located inside the master cylinder immediately returns the master cylinder pistons to the normal position. The pistons contain check valves and the master cylinder has compensating ports drilled in it. These are uncovered as the pistons reach their normal position. The piston check valves allow fluid to flow toward the wheel cylinders or calipers as the pistons withdraw. Then, as the return springs force the brake pads or shoes into the released position, the excess fluid returns to the master cylinder fluid reservoir through the compensating ports. It is during the time the pedal is in the released position that any fluid that has leaked out of the system will be replaced through the compensating ports.

Dual circuit master cylinders employ two pistons, located one behind the other, in the same cylinder. The primary piston is actuated directly by mechanical linkage from the brake pedal. The secondary piston is actuated by fluid trapped between the two pistons. If a leak develops in front of the secondary piston, it moves forward until it bottoms against the front of the master cylinder, and the fluid trapped between the pistons will operate the rear brakes. If the rear brakes develop a leak, the primary piston will move forward until direct contact with the secondary piston takes place, and it will force the secondary piston to actuate the front brakes. In either case, the brake pedal moves farther when the brakes are applied, and less braking power is available.

All dual-circuit systems use a distributor switch to warn the driver when only half of the brake system is operational. This switch is located in a valve body which is mounted on the master cylinder. A hydraulic piston receives pressure from both circuits, each circuit's pressure being applied to one end of the piston. When the pressures are in balance, the piston remains stationary. When one circuit has a leak, however, the greater pressure in that circuit during application of the brakes will push the piston to one side, closing the distributor switch and activating the brake warning light.

In disc brake systems, this valve body also contains a metering valve and, in some cases, a proportioning valve. The metering valve keeps pressure from traveling to the disc brakes on the front wheels until the brake shoes on the rear wheels have contacted the drums, ensuring that the front brakes will never be used alone. The proportioning valve

BRAKES

throttles the pressure to the rear brakes so as to avoid rear wheel lock-up during very hard braking.

These valves may be tested by removing the lines to the front and rear brake systems and installing special brake pressure testing gauges. Front and rear system pressures are then compared as the pedal is gradually depressed. Specifications vary with the manufacturer and design of the brake system.

Brake system warning lights may be tested by depressing the brake pedal and holding it while opening one of the wheel cylinder bleeder screws. If this does not cause the light to go on, substitute a new lamp, make continuity checks, and, finally, replace the switch as necessary.

The hydraulic system may be checked for leaks by applying pressure to the pedal gradually and steadily. If the pedal sinks very slowly to the floor, the system has a leak. This is not to be confused with a springy or spongy feel due to the compression of air within the lines. If the system leaks, there will be a gradual change in the position of the pedal with a constant pressure.

Check for leaks along all lines and at wheel cylinders. If no external leaks are apparent, the problem is inside the master cylinder.

FRONT DISC BRAKES

Disc Brake Pads

INSPECTION

1. Jack up your vehicle and support it with jack stands.

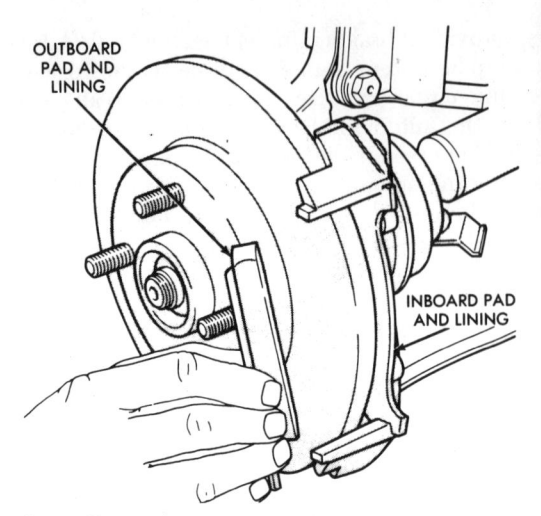

Outer disc pad

2. Remove the front wheels.
3. Remove the calipers.
4. Measure the thickness of the pad and lining assembly.
5. If the pads are worn to a thickness of approximately 5/16 inch they should be replaced.

NOTE: *Always replace the pads on both front wheels for proper braking.*

6. If the brake pads are to be reused make sure they are installed in exactly the same position from which they were removed.

CALIPER OVERHAUL

1. Remove the caliper as previously outlined leaving the brake line connected.
2. Carefully have your helper depress the

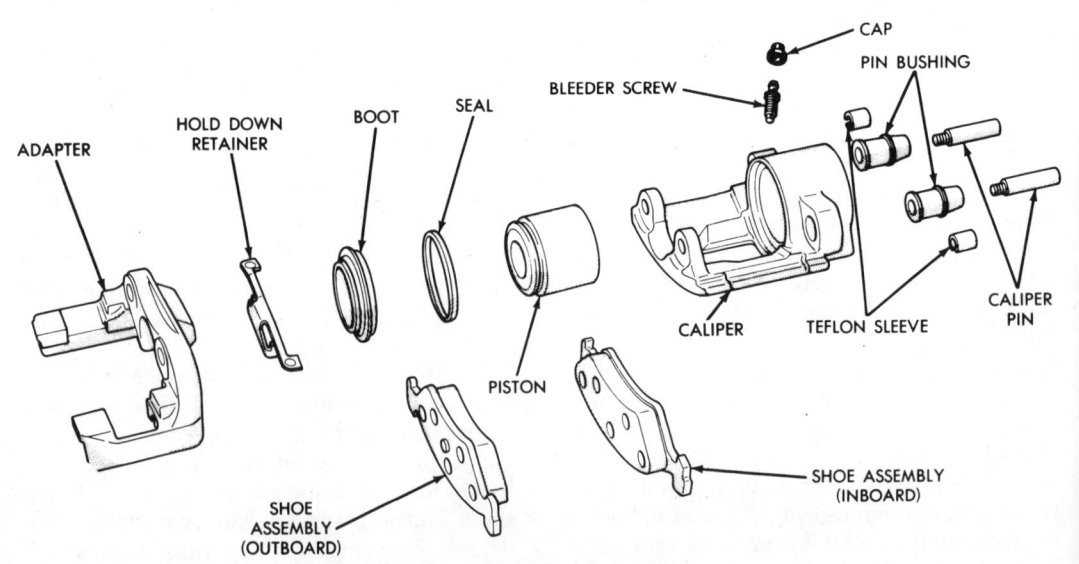

Exploded view—disc brake caliper

BRAKES 103

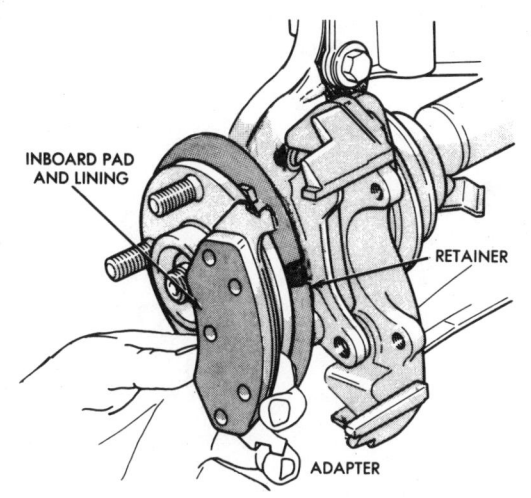

Inner disc pad

brake pedal to hydraulically push the piston out of the bore.

CAUTION: *Under no condition should air pressure be used to remove the piston. Personal injury could result from this practice.*

3. Disconnect the brake line from the caliper.

4. Place the caliper in a vise.

CAUTION: *Excessive vise pressure will cause bore distortion and piston binding.*

5. Remove the dust boot and discard it.

6. Use a plastic rod to work the piston seal out of its groove in the piston bore. Discard the old seal.

NOTE: *Do not use a metal tool for this procedure, because of the possibility of scratching the piston bore, or damaging the edges of the seal.*

7. Remove the bushings from the caliper by pressing them out, using a suitable tool. Discard the old bushings.

8. Clean all parts using alcohol and blow dry with compressed air.

NOTE: *Whenever a caliper has been disassembled, a new boot and seal must be installed.*

9. Inspect the piston bore for scoring or pitting. Bores with light scratches can be cleaned up. If the bore is scratched beyond repair, the caliper should be replaced.

10. Dip the new piston seal in clean brake fluid and install in the bore groove.

CAUTION: *Never use an old piston seal.*

11. Coat the new piston with clean brake fluid, leaving a generous amount inside the boot.

12. Position the dust boot over the piston.

13. Install the piston into the bore, pushing it past the piston seal until it bottoms in the bore.

CAUTION: *Force must be applied uniformly to avoid cocking the piston.*

14. Position the dust boot in the counterbore.

15. Using tool #C-4689 and C-4171 or their equivalents install the dust boot.

16. Remove the Teflon® sleeves from the guide pin bushings before installing the bushings into the caliper. After the new bushings are install in the caliper, reinstall the Teflon® sleeves into the bushings.

17. Be sure the flanges extend over the caliper casting evenly on both sides.

18. When reinstalling the calipers use new seal washers.

19. Bleed the brake system.

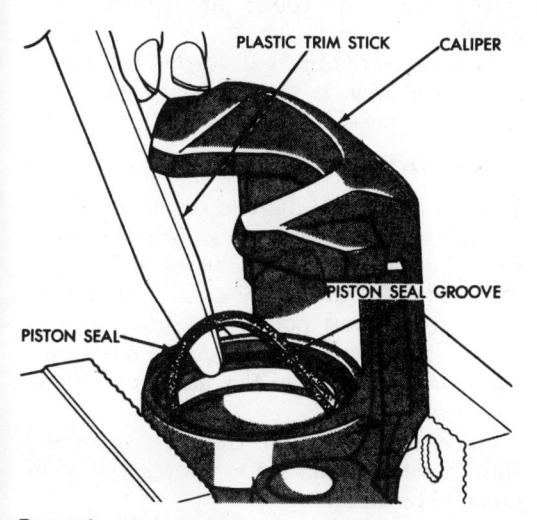

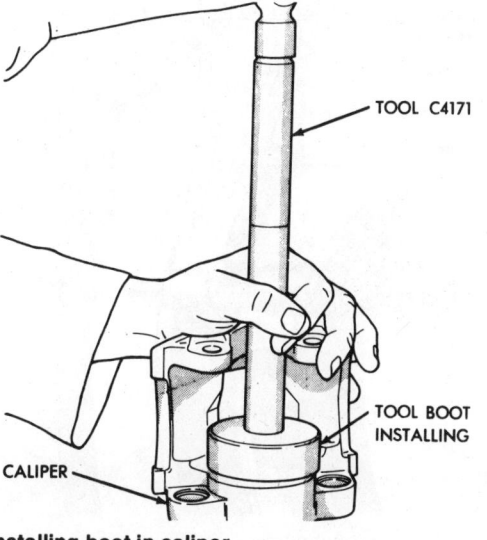

Removing piston seal

Installing boot in caliper

BRAKES

Brake Disc

REMOVAL AND INSTALLATION

1. Jack up your car and support it with jack stands.
2. Remove the front wheels.
3. Remove the caliper as previously outlined, and tie it out of the way with wire. Do not disconnect the brake line.
4. Remove the brake disc from the drive flange studs.
5. Installation is the reverse of removal.

NOTE: *If the disc needs to be resurfaced have this work performed by a qualified repair facility.*

Inspection

Light scoring is acceptable. Heavy scoring or warping will necessitate refinishing or replacement of the disc. The brake disc must be replaced if cracks or burned marks are evident.

Check the thickness of the disc. Measure the thickness at 12 equally spaced points 1 inch from the edge of the disc. If thickness varies more than 0.0005 in. the disc should be refinished, provided equal amounts are out from each side and the thickness does not fall below .882 in.

Check the run-out of the disc. Total run-out of the disc installed on the car should not exceed 0.0005 in. The disc can be resurfaced to correct minor variations as long as equal amounts are cut from each side and the thickness is at least .882 in. after resurfacing.

Check the run-out of the hub (disc removed). It should not be more than 0.002 in. If so, the hub should be replaced.

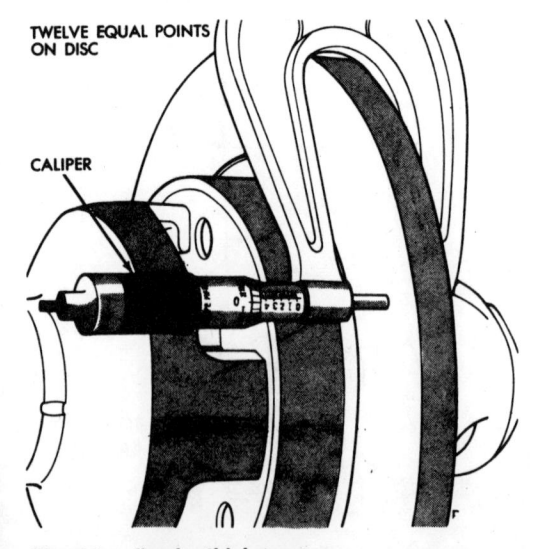

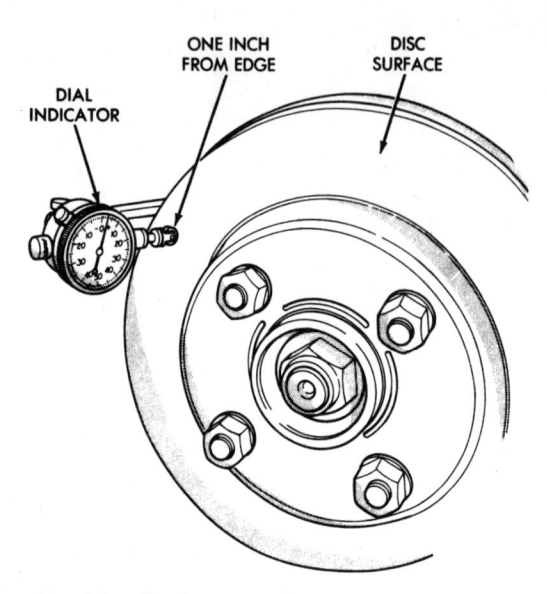

Checking disc for run-out

Checking disc for thickness

REAR DRUM BRAKES

Brake Drums

REMOVAL AND INSTALLATION

1. Jack up your car and support it with jack stands.
2. Remove the rear wheels.
3. Insert a brake spoon and release the brake shoe drag by moving up on the left side and down on the right side.
5. Remove the grease cap.
6. Remove the cotter pin, locknut, and washer.
7. Remove the brake drum and bearings.
8. Installation is the reverse of removal. Adjust the wheel bearings.

INSPECTION

Measure drum run-out and diameter. If the drum is not to specifications, have the drum resurfaced. The run-out should not exceed .006 inch. The diameter variation (ovalness) of the drum must not exceed .0025 inch in 30° or .0035 inch in 360°. All brake drums will show markings of the maximum allowable diameter.

Once the drum is off, clean the shoes and springs with a damp rag to remove the accumulated brake dust.

NOTE: *Avoid exposure to brake dust.*

Brake dust contains asbestos, a known cancer causing agent.

Grease on the shoes can be removed with alcohol or fine sandpaper.

After cleaning, examine the brake shoes for glazed, oily, loose, cracked or improperly worn linings. Light glazing is common and can be removed with fine sandpaper. Linings that are worn improperly or below 1/16" above rivet heads or brake shoe should be replaced. The NHSTA advises states with inspection programs to fail vehicles with brake linings less than 1/32". A good "eyeball" test is to replace the linings when the thickness is the same as or less than the thickness of the metal backing plate (shoe).

Wheel cylinders are a vital part of the brake system and should be inspected carefully. Gently pull back the rubber boots; if any fluid is visible, it's time to replace or rebuild the wheel cylinders. Boots that are distorted, cracked or otherwise damaged, also point to the need for service. Check the flexible brake lines for cracks, chafing or wear.

Check the brake shoe retracting and hold-down springs; they should not be worn or distorted. Be sure that the adjuster mechanism moves freely. The points on the backing plate where the shoes slide should be shiny and free of rust. Rust in these areas suggests that the brake shoes are not moving properly.

Brake Shoes

REMOVAL AND INSTALLATION

NOTE: *If you are not thoroughly familiar with the procedures involved in brake replacement, disassemble and assemble one side at a time, leaving the other wheel intact, as a reference.*

1. Remove the brake drum. See the procedure earlier in this chapter.
2. Unhook the parking brake cable from the secondary (trailing) shoe.
3. Remove the shoe-to-anchor springs (retracting springs). They can be gripped and unhooked with a pair of pliers.
4. Remove the shoe hold down springs: compress them slightly and slide them off of the hold down pins.
5. Remove the adjuster screw assembly by spreading the shoes apart. The adjuster nut must be fully backed off.
6. Raise the parking brake lever. Pull the secondary (trailing) shoe away from the backing plate so pull-back spring tension is released.
7. Remove the secondary (trailing) shoe and disengage the spring end from the backing plate.
8. Raise the primary (leading) shoe to release spring tension. Remove the shoe and disengage the spring end from the backing plate.
9. Inspect the brakes (see procedures under Brake Drum Inspection).
10. Lubricate the six shoe contact areas on the brake backing plate and the web end of the brake shoe which contacts the anchor plate. Use a multi-purpose lubricant or a high temperature brake grease made for this purpose.
11. Chrysler recommends that the rear wheel bearings be cleaned and repacked whenever the brakes are renewed. Be sure to install a new bearing seal.

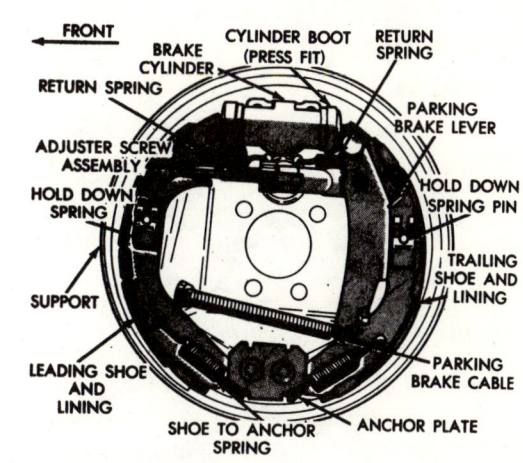

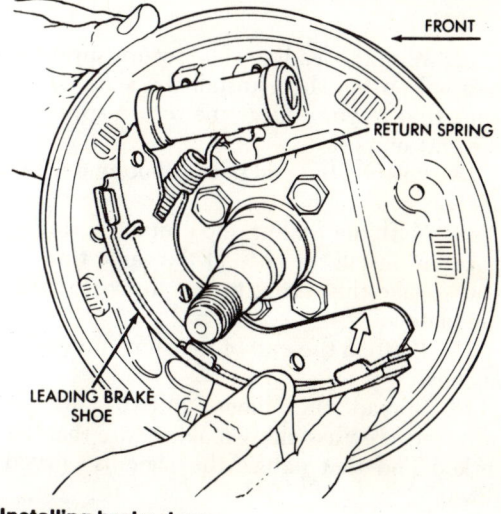

Left rear wheel brake

Installing brake drum

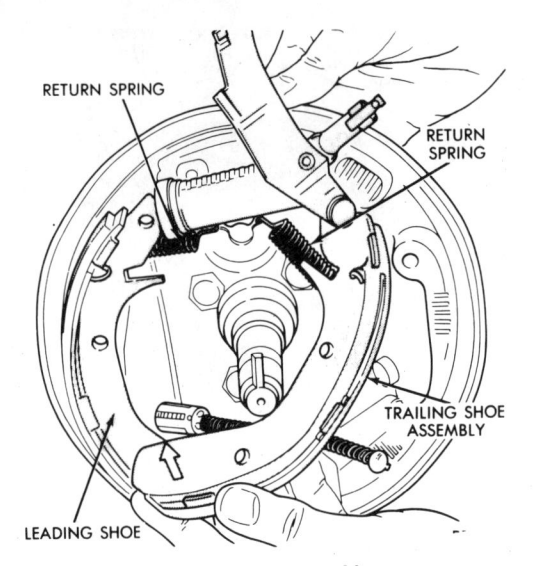

BRAKES

Installing trailing brake shoe and lever

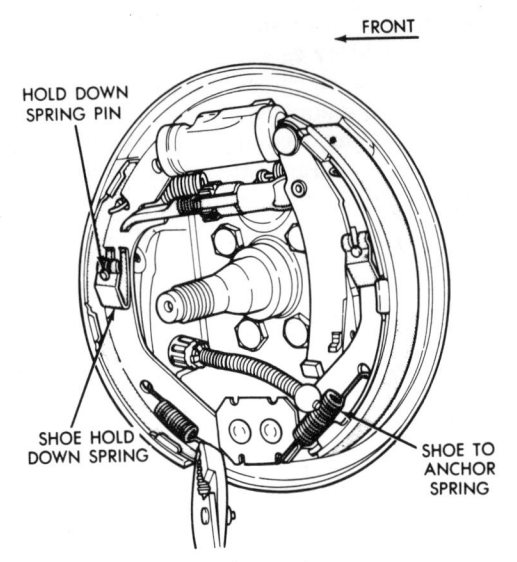

Installing shoe-to-anchor springs

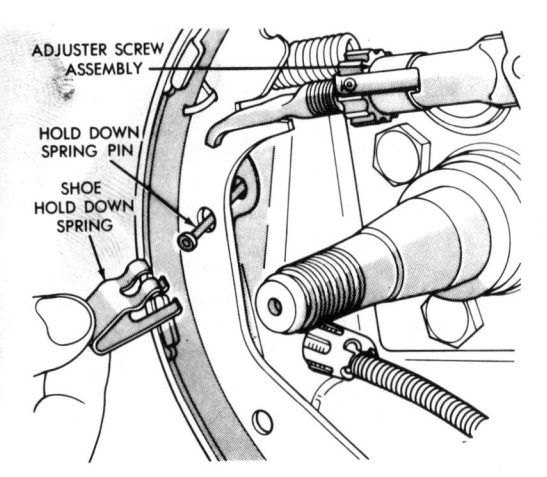

Installing shoe hold-down spring

12. With the leading shoe return spring in position on the shoe, install the shoe at the same time as you engage the return spring in the end support.
13. Position the end of the shoe under the anchor.
14. With the trailing shoe return spring in position, install the shoe at the same time as you engage the spring in the support (backing plate).
15. Position the end of the shoe under the anchor.
16. Spread the shoes and install the adjuster screw assembly making sure that the forked end that enters the shoe is curved down.

17. Insert the shoe hold down spring pins and install the hold down springs.
18. Install the shoe-to-anchor springs.
19. Install the parking brake cable onto the parking brake lever.
20. Replace the brake drum and tighten the nut to 240–300 in. lbs. while rotating the wheel.
21. Back off the nut enough to release the bearing preload and position the locknut with one pair of slots aligned with the cotter pin hole.
22. Install the cotter pin. The end play should be 0.001–0.003 in.
23. Install the grease cap.

Wheel Cylinders

REMOVAL AND INSTALLATION

1. Jack up your vehicle and support it with jack stands.
2. Remove the brake drums as previously outlined.
3. Visually inspect the wheel cylinder boots for signs of excessive leakage. Replace any boots that are torn or broken.

NOTE: *A slight amount of fluid on the boots may not be a leak but may be a preservative fluid used at the factory.*

4. If a leak has been discovered, remove the brake shoes and check for contamination. Replace the linings if they are soaked with grease or brake fluid.

BRAKES

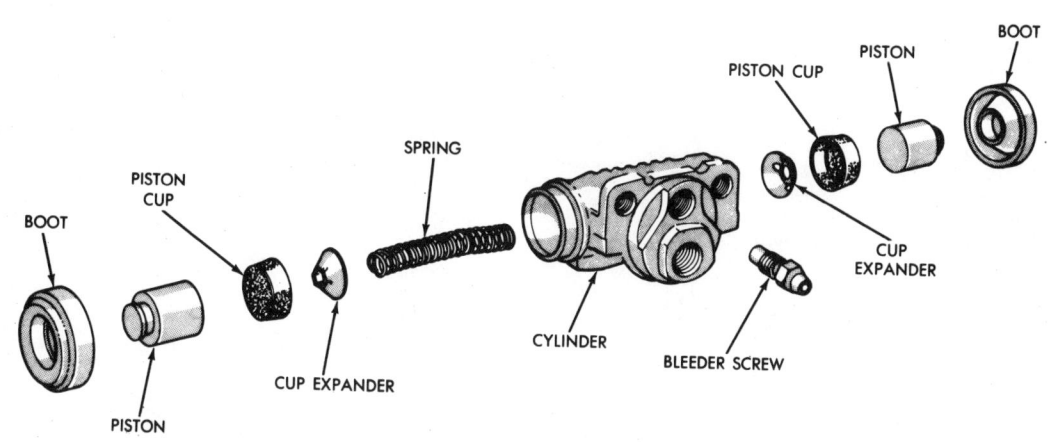

Rear wheel cylinder

5. Disconnect the brake line from the wheel cylinder.
6. Remove the wheel cylinder attaching bolts, then pull the wheel cylinder out of its support.
7. Installation is the reverse of removal.
8. Bleed the brake system.

OVERHAUL

1. Pry the boots away from the cylinder and remove the boots and piston as an assembly.
2. Disengage the boot from the piston.
3. Slide the piston into the cylinder bore and press inward to remove the other boot and piston. Also remove the spring with it the cup expanders.
4. Wash all parts (except rubber parts) in clean brake fluid thoroughly. Do not use a rag; lint will adhere to the bore.
5. Inspect the cylinder bores. Light scoring can usually be cleaned up with crocus cloth. Black stains are caused by the piston cups and are no cause of concern. Bad scoring or pitting means that the wheel cylinder should be replaced.
6. Dip the pistons and new cups in clean brake fluid prior to assembly.
7. Coat the wheel cylinder bore with clean brake fluid.
8. Install the expansion spring with the cup expanders.
9. Install the cups in each end of the cylinder with the open ends facing each other.
10. Assemble new boots on the piston and slide them into the cylinder bore.
11. Press the boot over the wheel cylinder until seated.
12. Install the wheel cylinder.

PARKING BRAKE

Cable
ADJUSTMENT

NOTE: *The service brakes must be properly adjusted before adjusting the parking brake.*

1. Release the parking brake lever, then back off the parking brake cable adjuster so there is slack in the cable.
2. Clean and lubricate the adjuster threads.
3. Use a brake spoon to turn the star-wheel adjuster until there is light shoe-to-drum contact. Back off the adjuster until the wheel rotates freely with no brake drag.
4. Tighten the parking brake adjuster until a slight drag is felt while rotating the wheels.
5. Loosen the cable adjusting nut until the rear wheels can be rotated freely, then back the cable adjuster nut off 2 full turns.
6. Test the parking brake. The rear wheels should rotate freely without dragging.

REMOVAL AND INSTALLATION
Front Cable

1. Jack up your car and support it with jack stands.
2. Loosen the cable adjusting nut and disengage the cable from the connectors.
3. Lift the floor mat for access to the floor pan.
4. Remove the floor pan seal panel.
5. Pull the cable end forward and disconnect it from the clevis.
6. Pull the cable assembly through the hole.

108 BRAKES

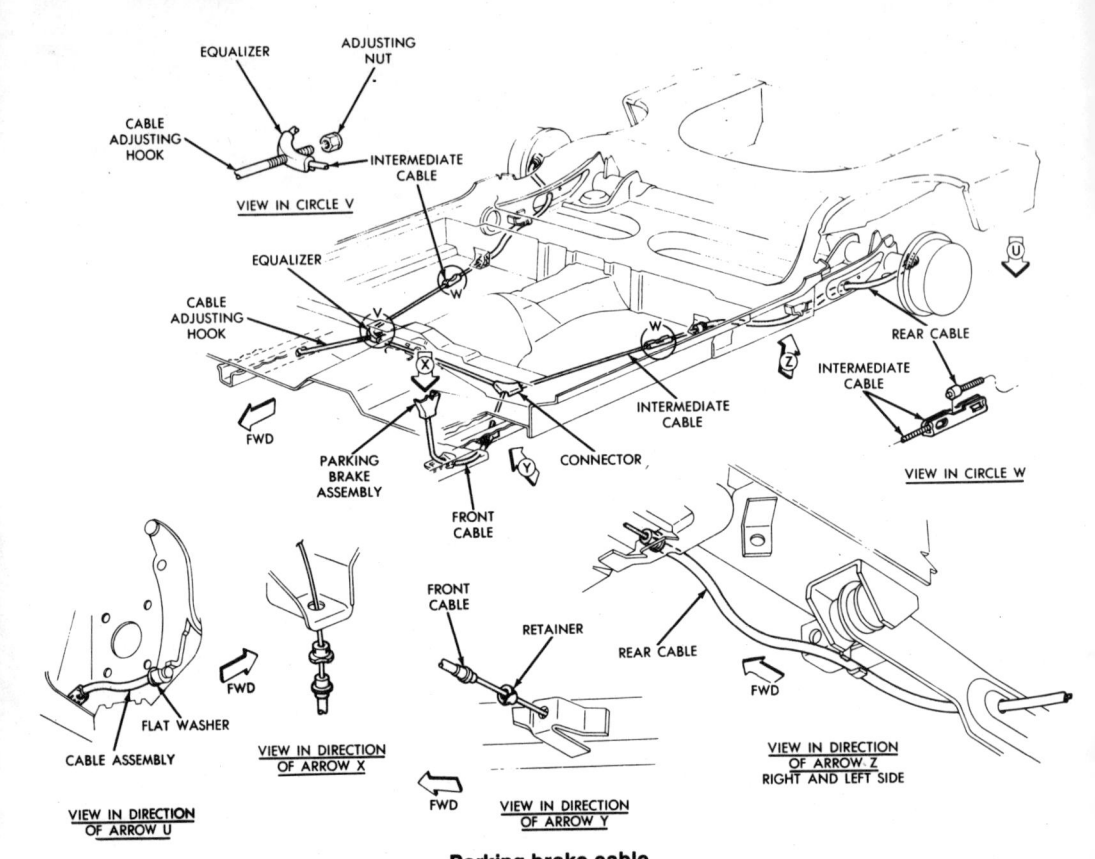

Parking brake cable

7. Installation is the reverse of removal.
8. Adjust the service and parking brake.

Rear Cable

1. Jack up your vehicle and support it with jack stands.
2. Remove the rear wheels.
3. Remove the brake drums.
4. Back off the cable adjuster to provide slack in the cable.
5. Compress the retainers on the end of the cable and remove the cable from the chassis mount. A worm gear type hose clamp can be used for this procedure.
6. Disconnect the cable from the brake shoe lever.
7. Use another hose clamp to assist in removing the cable housing from the support clamp. Remove the hose clamp when the cable has been removed.
8. Pull the brake cable from the rear axle.
9. Installation is the reverse of removal.
10. Adjust the service and parking brakes.

Brake Specifications

All measurements given are (in.) unless noted

Model	Lug Nut Torque (ft/lb)	Master Cylinder Bore	Brake Disc Minimum Thickness	Brake Disc Maximum Run-Out	Brake Drum Diameter	Brake Drum Max. Machine O/S	Brake Drum Max. Wear Limit	Minimum Lining Thickness Front	Minimum Lining Thickness Rear
1981–82	85	.875	.882	.005	7.87	①	①	.300	.710

① See figure stamped on the drum.
NOTE: Minimum lining thickness is as recommended by the manufacturer. Because of variations in state inspection regulations, the minimum allowable thickness may be different than recommended by the manufacturer.

Rear Wheel Bearings

The rear wheel bearings should be inspected and relubricated whenever the rear brakes are serviced or at least every 30,000 miles. Repack the bearings with high temperature multi-purpose grease.

Check the lubricant to see if it is contaminated. If it contains dirt or has a milky appearance indicating the presence of water, the bearings should be cleaned and repacked.

Clean the bearings in kerosene, mineral spirits or other suitable cleaning fluid. Do not dry them by spinning the bearings. Allow them to air dry.

1. Raise and support the car with the rear wheels off the floor.
2. Remove the wheel grease cap, cotter pin, nut-lock and bearing adjusting nut.
3. Remove the thrust washer and bearing.
4. Remove the drum from the spindle.
5. Thoroughly clean the old lubricant from the bearings and hub cavity. Inspect the bearing rollers for pitting or other signs of wear. Light discoloration is normal.
6. Repack the bearings with high temperature multi-purpose EP grease and add a small amount of new grease to the hub cavity. Be sure to force the lubricant between all rollers in the bearing.
7. Install the drum on the spindle after coating the polished spindle surfaces with wheel bearing lubricant.
8. Install the outer bearing cone, thrust washer and adjusting nut.
9. Tighten the adjusting nut to 20–25 ft. lbs. while rotating the wheel.
10. Back off the adjusting nut to completely release the preload from the bearing.
11. Tighten the adjusting nut finger-tight.
12. Position the nut-lock with one pair of slots in line with the cotter pin hole. Install the cotter pin.
13. Clean and install the grease cap and wheel.
14. Lower the car.

Body 9

You can repair most minor auto body damage yourself. Minor damage usually falls into one of several categories: (1) small scratches and dings in the paint that can be repaired without the use of body filler, (2) deep scratches and dents that require body filler, but do not require pulling, or hammering metal back into shape and (3) rust-out repairs. The repair sequences illustrated in this chapter are typical of these types of repairs. If you want to get involved in more complicated repairs including pulling or hammering sheet metal back into shape, you will probably need more detailed instructions. Chilton's *Minor Auto Body Repair, 2nd Edition* is a comprehensive guide to repairing auto body damage yourself.

TOOLS AND SUPPLIES

The list of tools and equipment you may need to fix minor body damage ranges from very basic hand tools to a wide assortment of specialized body tools. Most minor scratches, dings and rust holes can be fixed using an electric drill, wire wheel or grinder attachment, half-round plastic file, sanding block, various grades of sandpaper (#36, which is coarse through #600, which is fine) in both wet and dry types, auto body plastic, primer, touch-up paint, spreaders, newspaper and masking tape.

Most manufacturers of auto body repair products began supplying materials to professionals. Their knowledge of the best, most-used products has been translated into body repair kits for the do-it-yourselfer. Kits are available from a number of manufacturers and contain the necessary materials in the required amounts for the repair identified on the package.

Kits are available for a wide variety of uses, including:

- Rusted out metal
- All purpose kit for dents and holes
- Dents and deep scratches
- Fiberglass repair kit
- Epoxy kit for restyling.

Kits offer the advantage of buying what you need for the job. There is little waste and little chance of materials going bad from not being used. The same manufacturers also merchandise all of the individual products used—spreaders, dent pullers, fiberglass cloth, polyester resin, cream hardener, body filler, body files, sandpaper, sanding discs and holders, primer, spray paint, etc.

CAUTION: *Most of the products you will be using contain harmful chemicals, so be extremely careful. Always read the complete label before opening the containers. When* you put them away for future use, be sure they are out of children's reach!

Most auto body repair kits contain all the materials you need to do the job right in the kit. So, if you have a small rust spot or dent you want to fix, check the contents of the kit before you run out and buy any additional tools.

ALIGNING BODY PANELS

Doors

There are several methods of adjusting doors. Your vehicle will probably use one of those illustrated.

Whenever a door is removed and is to be reinstalled, you should matchmark the position of the hinges on the door pillars. The holes of the hinges and/or the hinge attaching points are usually oversize to permit alignment of doors. The striker plate is also moveable, through oversize holes, permitting up-and-down, in-and-out and fore-and-aft movement. Fore-and-aft movement is made by adding or subtracting shims from behind the striker and pillar post. The striker should be adjusted so that the door closes fully and remains closed, yet enters the lock freely.

DOOR HINGES

Don't try to cover up poor door adjustment with a striker plate adjustment. The gap on each side of the door should be equal and uniform and there should be no metal-to-metal contact as the door is opened or closed.

1. Determine which hinge bolts must be loosened to move the door in the desired direction.
2. Loosen the hinge bolt(s) just enough to allow the door to be moved with a padded pry bar.
3. Move the door a small amount and check the fit, after tightening the bolts. Be sure that there is no bind or interference with adjacent panels.
4. Repeat this until the door is properly positioned, and tighten all the bolts securely.

Hood, Trunk or Tailgate

As with doors, the outline of hinges should be scribed before removal. The hood and trunk can be aligned by loosening the hinge bolts in their slotted mounting holes and moving the hood or trunk lid as necessary.

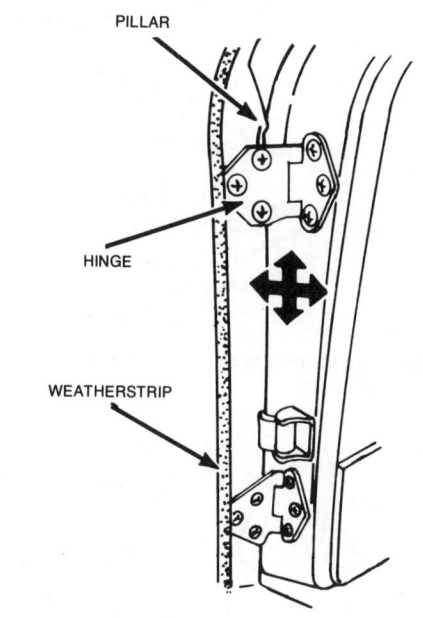

Door hinge adjustment

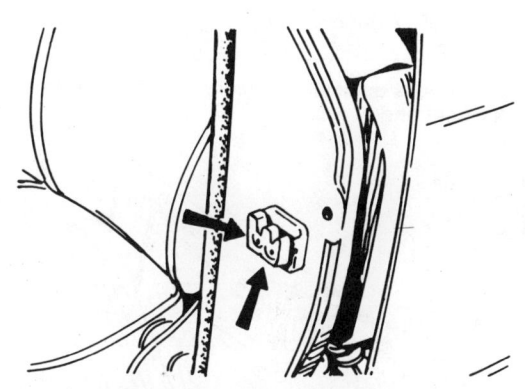

Move the door striker as indicated by arrows

Striker plate and lower block

112 BODY

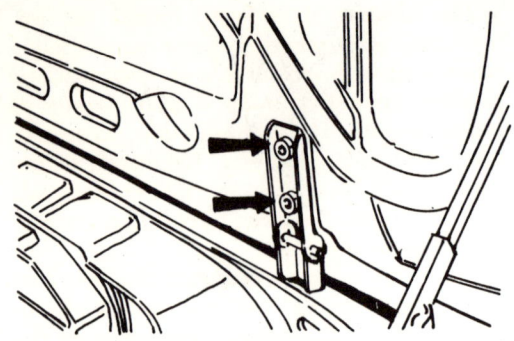

Loosen the hinge boots to permit fore-and-aft and horizontal adjustment

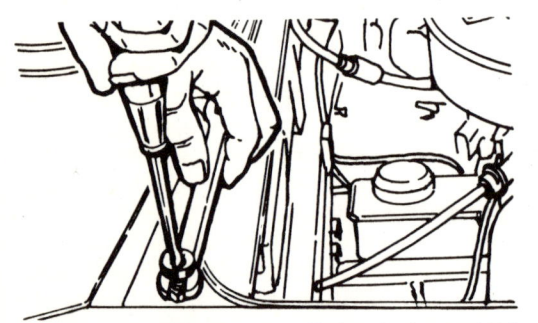

The hood is adjusted vertically by stop-screws at the front and/or rear

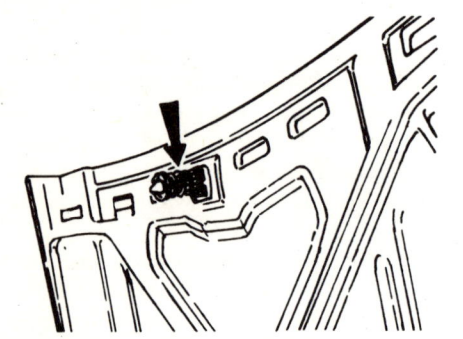

The hood pin can be adjusted for proper lock engagement

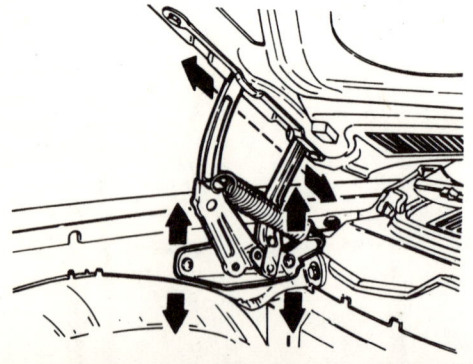

The height of the hood at the rear is adjusted by loosening the bolts that attach the hinge to the body and moving the hood up or down

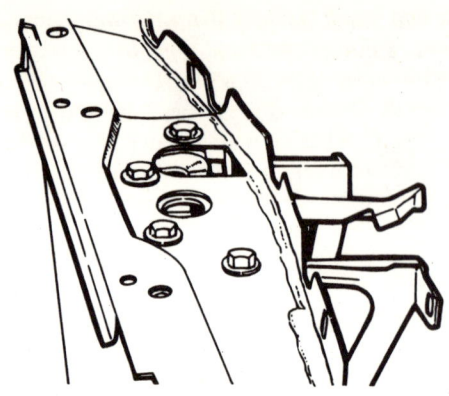

The base of the hood lock can also be repositioned slightly to give more positive lock engagement

The hood and trunk have adjustable catch locations to regulate lock engagement. Bumpers at the front and/or rear of the hood provide a vertical adjustment and the hood lockpin can be adjusted for proper engagement.

The tailgate on the station wagon can be adjusted by loosening the hinge bolts in their slotted mounting holes and moving the tailgate on its hinges. The latchplate and latch striker at the bottom of the tailgate opening can be adjusted to stop rattle. An adjustable bumper is located on each side.

RUST, UNDERCOATING, AND RUSTPROOFING

Rust

Rust is an electrochemical process. It works on ferrous metals (iron and steel) from the inside out due to exposure of unprotected surfaces to air and moisture. The possibility of rust exists practically nationwide—anywhere humidity, industrial pollution or chemical salts are present, rust can form. In coastal areas, the problem is high humidity and salt air; in snowy areas, the problem is chemical salt (de-icer) used to keep the roads clear, and in industrial areas, sulphur dioxide is present in the air from industrial pollution and is changed to sulphuric acid when it rains. The rusting process is accelerated by high temperatures, especially in snowy areas, when vehicles are driven over slushy roads and then left overnight in a heated garage.

Automotive styling also can be a contributor to rust formation. Spot welding of panels creates small pockets that trap moisture and form an environment for rust formation. Fortunately, auto manufacturers have been working hard to increase the corrosion protection of their products. Galvanized sheet metal enjoys much wider use, along with the increased use of plastic and various rust retardant coatings. Manufacturers are also designing out areas in the body where rust-forming moisture can collect.

To prevent rust, you must stop it before it gets started. On new vehicles, there are two ways to accomplish this.

First, the car or truck should be treated with a commercial rustproofing compound. There are many different brands of franchised rustproofers, but most processes involve spraying a waxy "self-healing" compound under the chassis, inside rocker panels, inside doors and fender liners and similar places where rust is likely to form. Prices for a quality rustproofing job range from $100–$250, depending on the area, the brand name and the size of the vehicle.

Ideally, the vehicle should be rustproofed as soon as possible following the purchase. The surfaces of the car or truck have begun to oxidize and deteriorate during shipping. In addition, the car may have sat on a dealer's lot or on a lot at the factory, and once the rust has progressed past the stage of light, powdery surface oxidation rustproofing is not likely to be worthwhile. Professional rustproofers feel that once rust has formed, rustproofing will simply seal in moisture already present. Most franchised rustproofing operations offer a 3–5 year warranty against rust-through, but will not support that warranty if the rustproofing is not applied within three months of the date of manufacture.

Undercoating should not be mistaken for rustproofing. Undercoating is a black, tar-like substance that is applied to the underside of a vehicle. Its basic function is to deaden noises that are transmitted from under the car. It simply cannot get into the crevices and seams where moisture tends to collect. In fact, it may clog up drainage holes and ventilation passages. Some undercoatings also tend to crack or peel with age and only create more moisture and corrosion attracting pockets.

The second thing you should do immediately after purchasing the car is apply a paint sealant. A sealant is a petroleum based product marketed under a wide variety of brand names. It has the same protective properties as a good wax, but bonds to the paint with a chemically inert layer that seals it from the air. If air can't get at the surface, oxidation cannot start.

The paint sealant kit consists of a base coat and a conditioning coat that should be applied every 6–8 months, depending on the manufacturer. The base coat must be applied before waxing, or the wax must first be removed.

Third, keep a garden hose handy for your car in winter. Use it a few times on nice days during the winter for underneath areas, and it will pay big dividends when spring arrives. Spraying under the fenders and other areas which even car washes don't reach will help remove road salt, dirt and other build-ups which help breed rust. Adjust the nozzle to a high-force spray. An old brush will help break up residue, permitting it to be washed away more easily.

It's a somewhat messy job, but worth it in the long run because rust often starts in those hidden areas.

At the same time, wash grime off the door sills and, more importantly, the under portions of the doors, plus the tailgate if you have a station wagon or truck. Applying a coat of wax to those areas at least once before and once during winter will help fend off rust.

When applying the wax to the under parts of the doors, you will note small drain holes. These holes often are plugged with undercoating or dirt. Make sure they are cleaned out to prevent water build-up inside the doors. A small punch or penknife will do the job.

Water from the high-pressure sprays in car washes sometimes can get into the housings for parking and taillights, so take a close look. If they contain water merely loosen the retaining screws and the water should run out.

114 BODY

Repairing Scratches and Small Dents

Step 1. This dent (arrow) is typical of a deep scratch or minor dent. If deep enough, the dent or scratch can be pulled out or hammered out from behind. In this case no straightening is necessary

Step 2. Using an 80-grit grinding disc on an electric drill grind the paint from the surrounding area down to bare metal. This will provide a rough surface for the body filler to grab

Step 3. The area should look like this when you're finished grinding

BODY 115

Step 4. Mix the body filler and cream hardener according to the directions

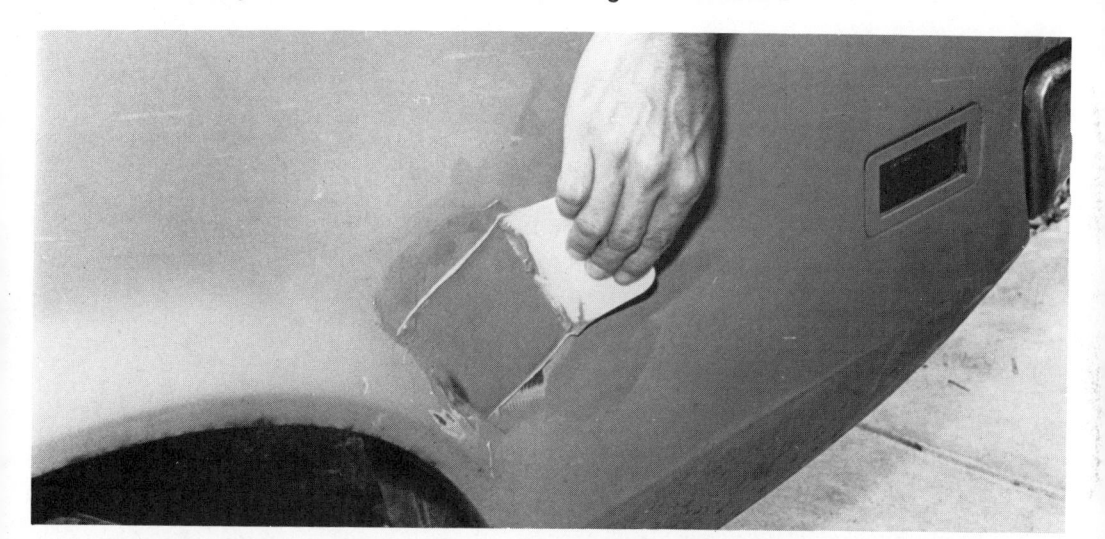

Step 5. Spread the body filler evenly over the entire area. Be sure to cover the area completely

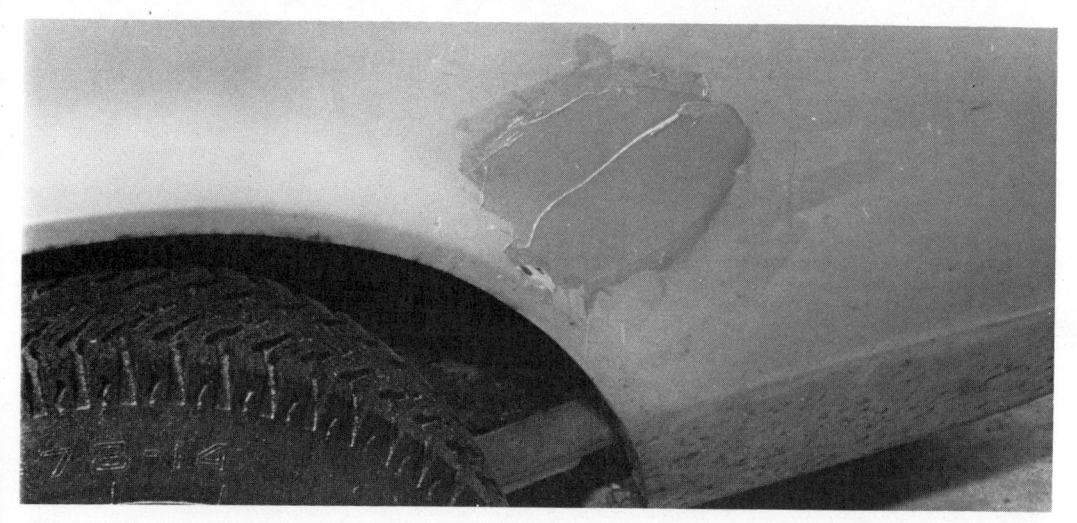

Step 6. Let the body filler dry until the surface can just be scratched with your fingernail

116 BODY

Step 7. Knock the high spots from the body filler with a body file

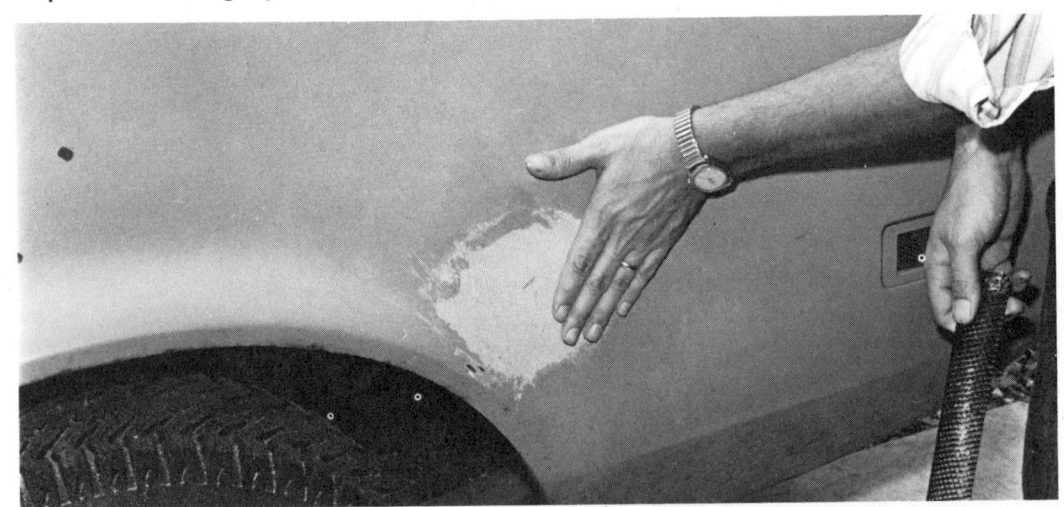

Step 8. Check frequently with the palm of your hand for high and low spots. If you wind up with low spots, you may have to apply another layer of filler

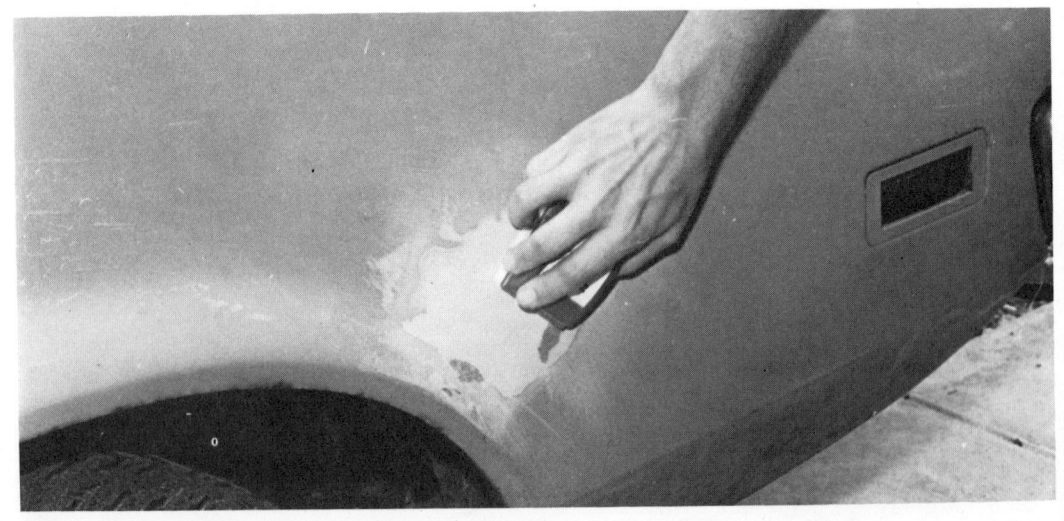

Step 9. Block sand the entire area with 320 grit paper

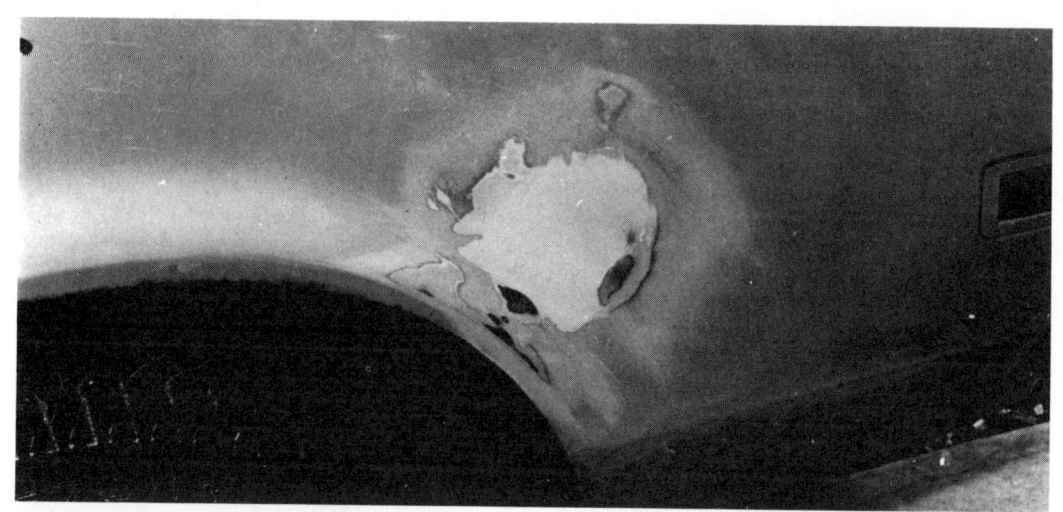

BODY 117

Step 10. When you're finished, the repair should look like this. Note the sand marks extending 2—3 inches out from the repaired area

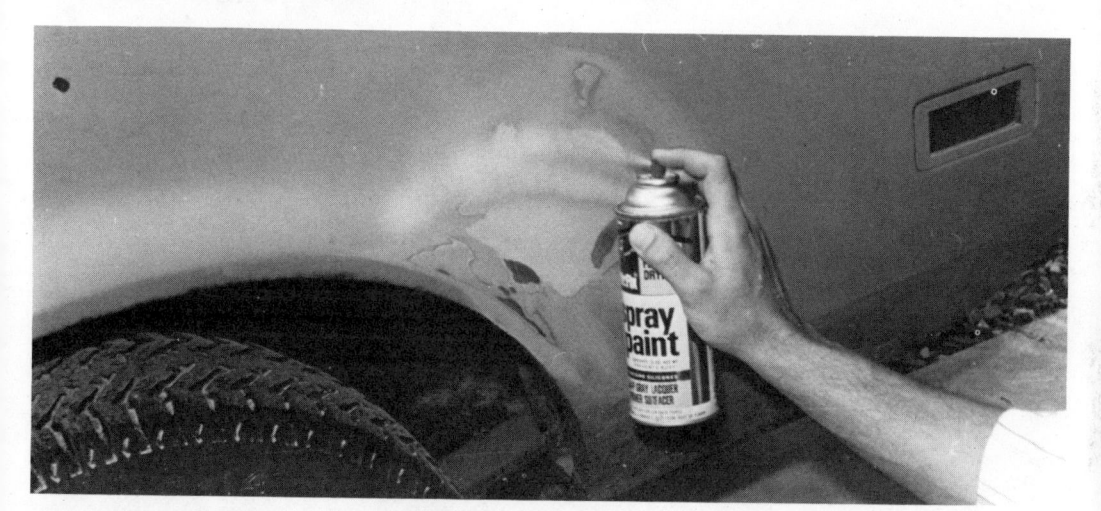

Step 11. Prime the entire area with automotive primer

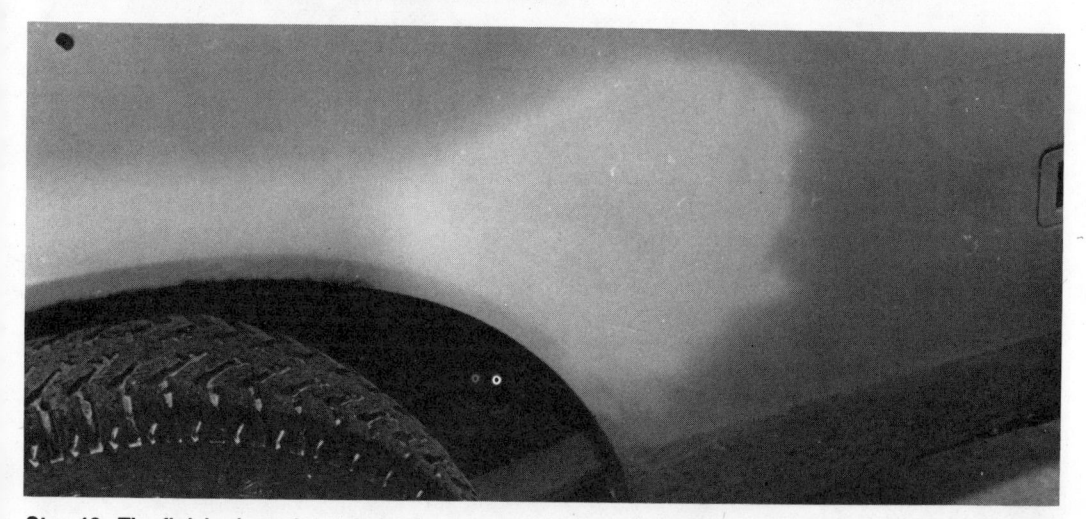

Step 12. The finished repair ready for the final paint coat. Note that the primer has covered the sanding marks (see Step 10). A repair of this size should be able to be spotpainted with good results

BODY

REPAIRING RUST HOLES

One thing you have to remember about rust: even if you grind away all the rusted metal in a panel, and repair the area with any of the kits available, *eventually* the rust will return. There are two reasons for this. One, rust is a chemical reaction that causes pressure under the repair from the inside out. That's how the blisters form. Two, the back side of the panel (and the repair) is wide open to moisture, and unpainted body filler acts like a sponge. That's why the best solution to rust problems is to remove the rusted panel and install a new one or have the rusted area cut out and a new piece of sheet metal welded in its place. The trouble with welding is the expense; sometimes it will cost more than the car or truck is worth.

One of the better solutions to do-it-yourself rust repair is the process using a fiberglass cloth repair kit (shown here). This will give a strong repair that resists cracking and moisture and is relatively easy to use. It can be used on large or small holes and also can be applied over contoured surfaces.

Step 1. Rust areas such as this are common and are easily fixed

Step 2. Grind away all traces of rust with a 24-grit grinding disc. Be sure to grind back 3—4 inches from the edge of the hole down to bare metal and be sure all traces of rust are removed

BODY 119

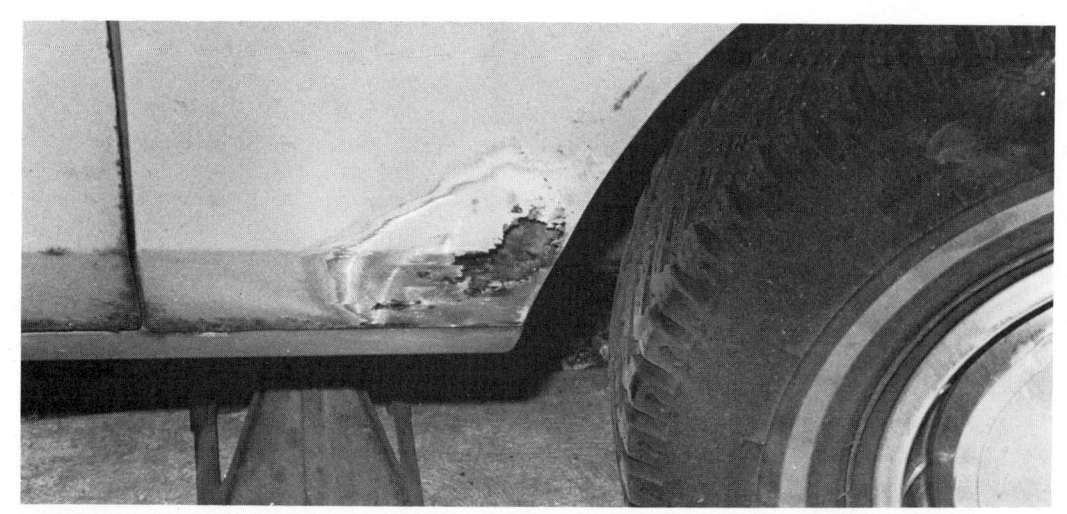

Step 3. Be sure all rust is removed from the edges of the metal. The edges must be ground back to un-rusted metal

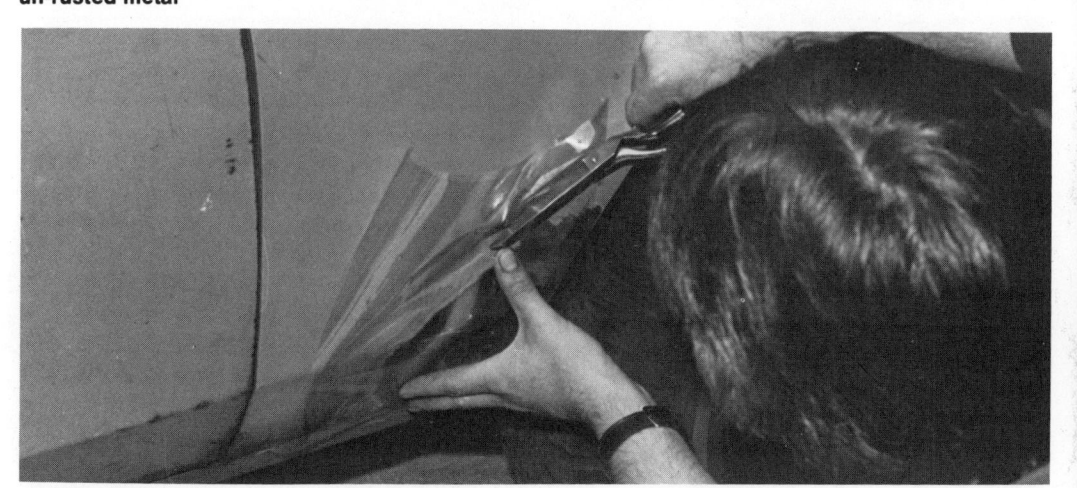

Step 4. If you are going to use release film, cut a piece about 2" larger than the area you have sanded. Place the film over the repair and mark the sanded area on the film. Avoid any unnecessary wrinkling of the film

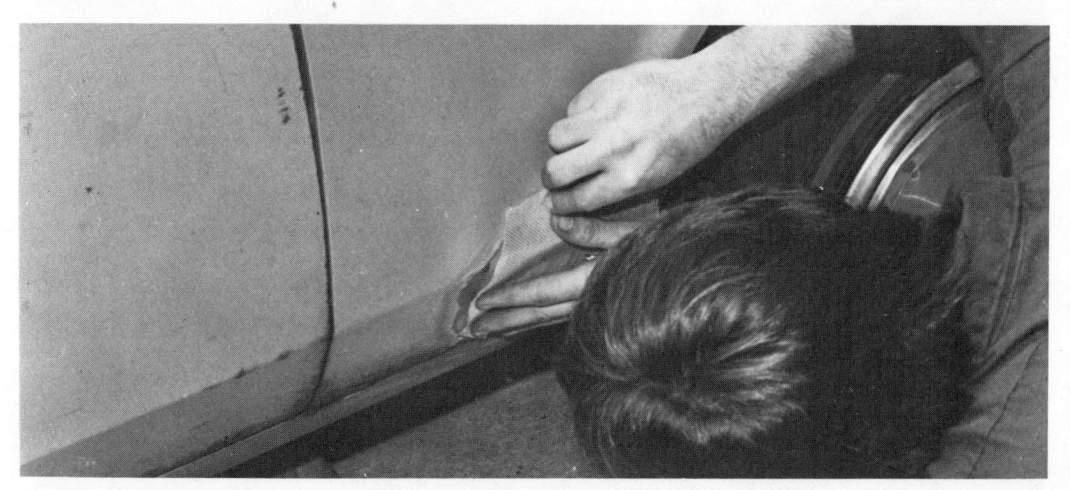

Step 5. Cut 2 pieces of fiberglass matte. One piece should be about 1" smaller than the sanded area and the second piece should be 1" smaller than the first. Use sharp scissors to avoid loose ends

120   BODY

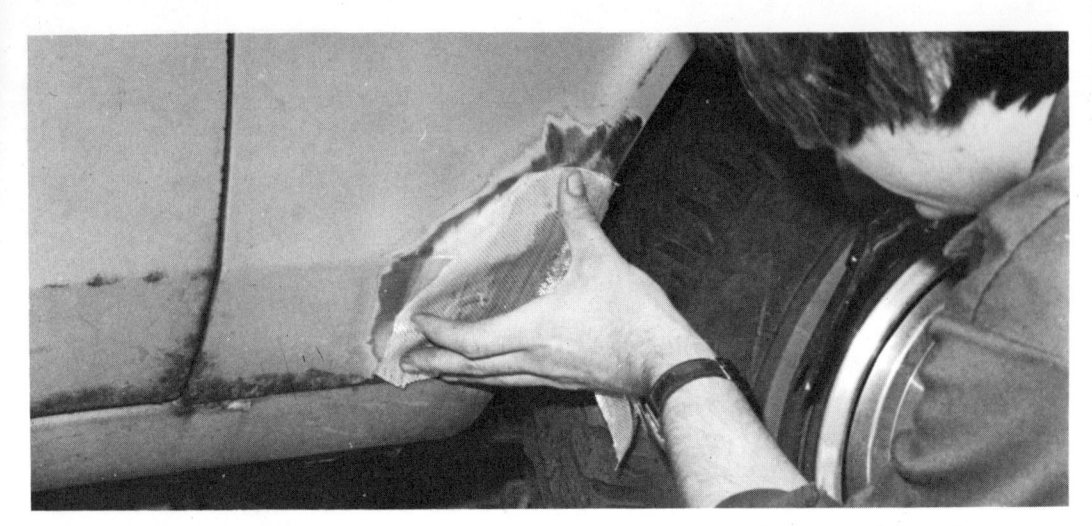

Step 6. Check the dimensions of the release film and cloth by holding them up to the repair area

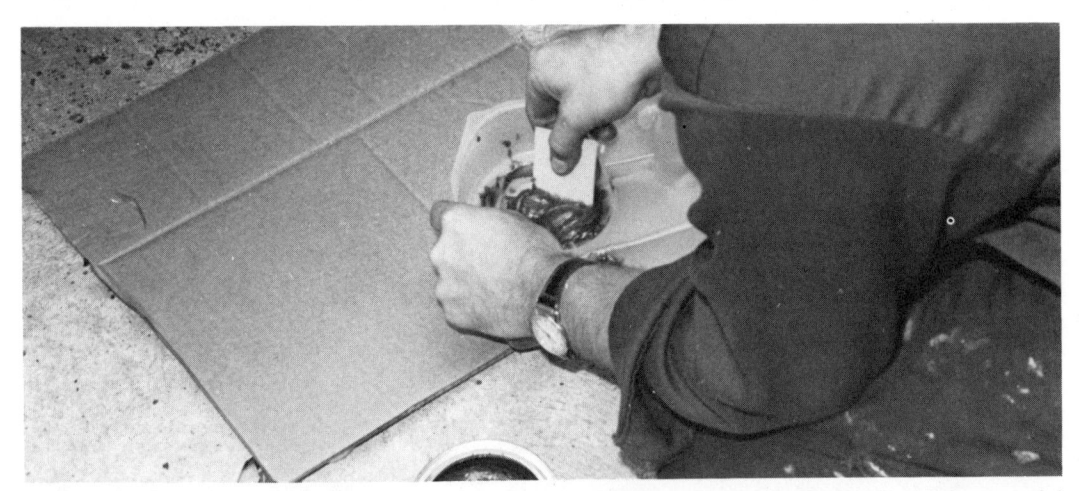

Step 7. Mix enough repair jelly and cream hardener in the mixing tray to saturate the fiberglass material or fill the repair area. Follow the directions on the container

Step 8. Lay the release sheet on a flat surface and spread an even layer of filler, large enough to cover the repair. Lay the smaller piece of fiberglass cloth in the center of the sheet and spread another layer of repair jelly over the fiberglass cloth. Repeat the operation for the larger piece of cloth. If the fiberglass cloth is not used, spread the repair jelly on the release film, concentrated in the middle of the repair

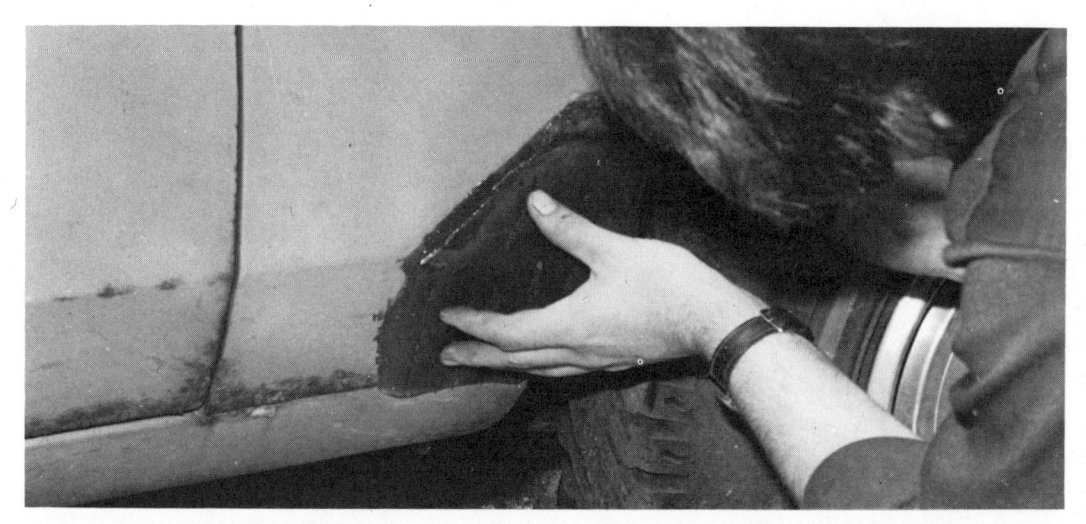

Step 9. Place the repair material over the repair area, with the release film facing outward

Step 10. Use a spreader and work from the center outward to smooth the material, following the body contours. Be sure to remove all air bubbles

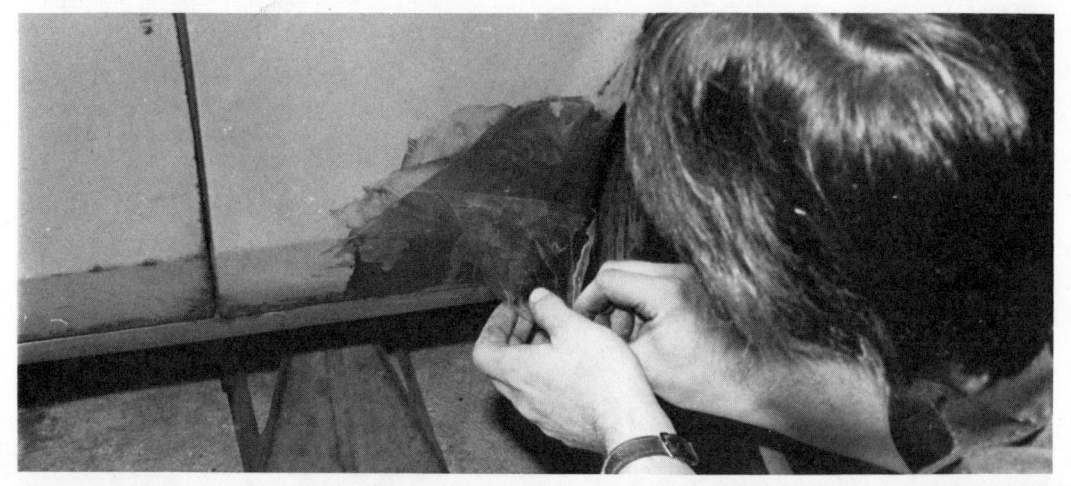

Step 11. Wait until the repair has dried tack-free and peel off the release sheet. The ideal working temperature is 65—90° F. Cooler or warmer temperatures or high humidity may require additional curing time

122 BODY

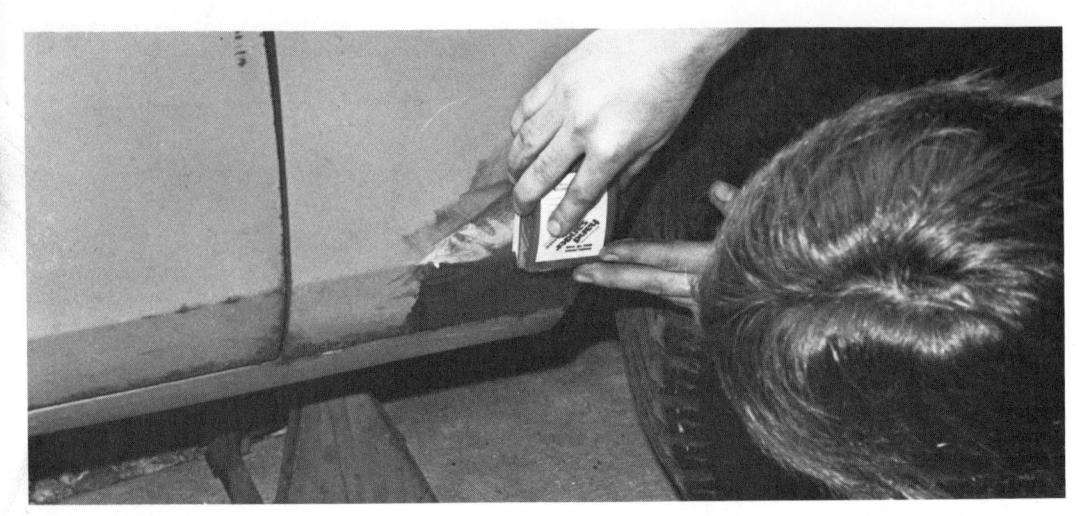

Step 12. Sand and feather-edge the entire area. The initial sanding can be done with a sanding disc on an electric drill if care is used. Finish the sanding with a block sander

Step 13. When the area is sanded smooth, mix some topcoat and hardener and apply it directly with a spreader. This will give a smooth finish and prevent the glass matte from showing through the paint

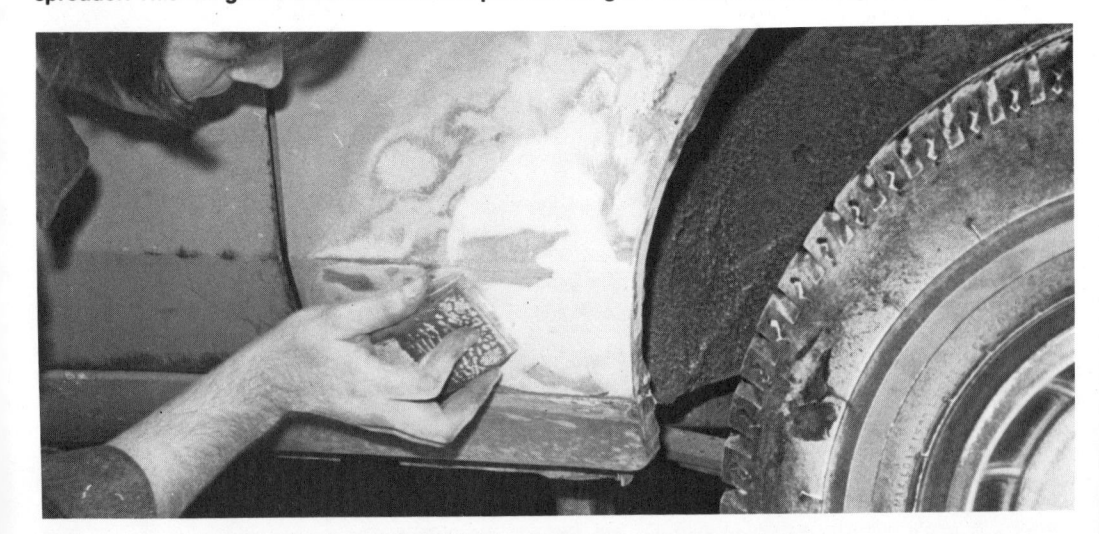

Step 14. Block sand the topcoat with finishing sandpaper

Step 15. To finish this repair, grind out the surface rust along the top edge of the rocker panel

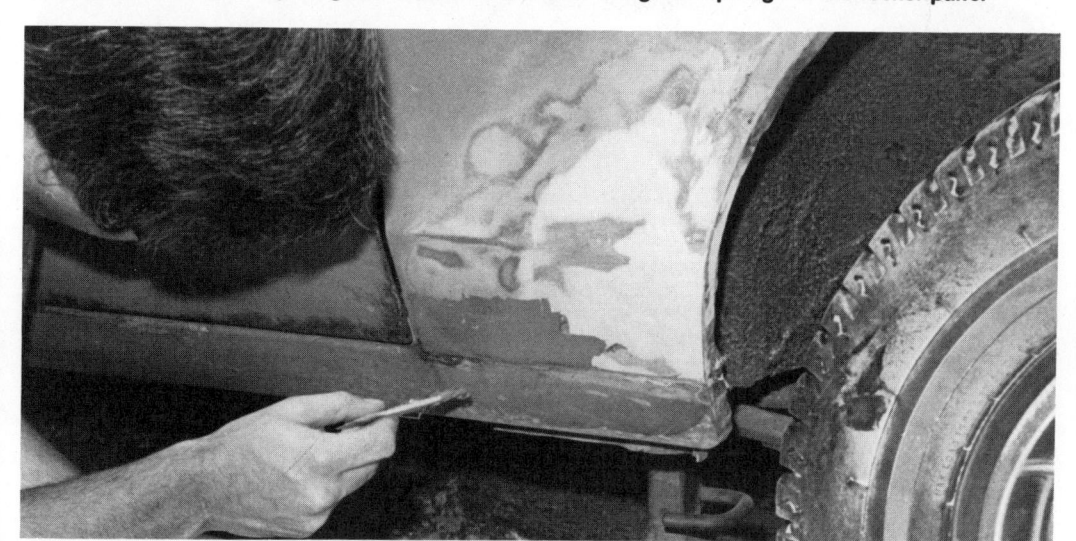

Step 16. Mix some more repair jelly and cream hardener and apply it directly over the surface

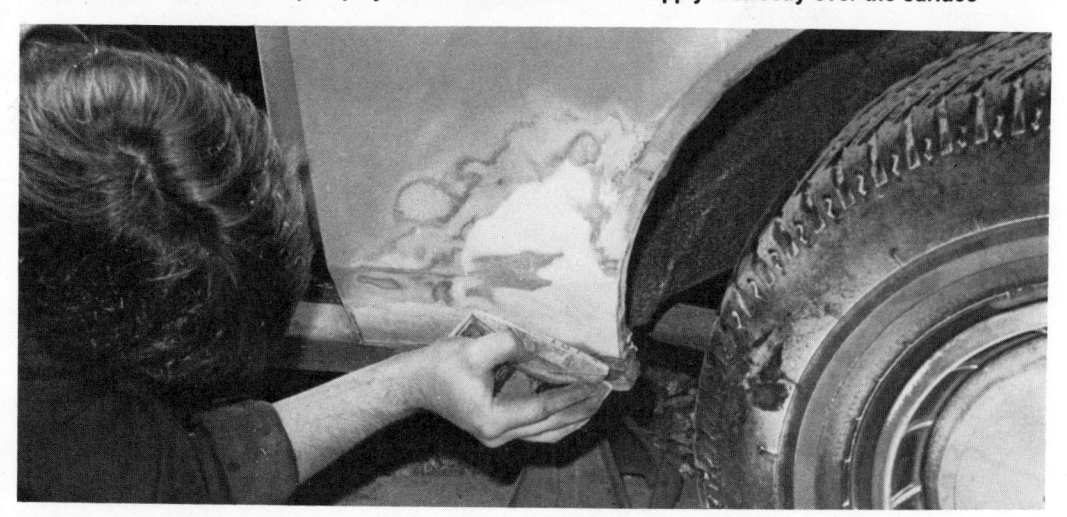

Step 17. When it dries tack-free, block sand the surface smooth

Step 18. If necessary, mask off adjacent panels and spray the entire repair with primer. You are now ready for a color coat

AUTO BODY CARE

There are hundreds—maybe thousands—of products on the market, all designed to protect or aid your car's finish in some manner. There are as many different products as there are ways to use them, but they all have one thing in common—the surface must be clean.

Washing

The primary ingredient for washing your car is water, preferably "soft" water. In many areas of the country, the local water supply is "hard" containing many minerals. The little rings or film that is left on your car's surface after it has dried is the result of "hard" water.

Since you usually can't change the local water supply, the next best thing is to dry the surface before it has a chance to dry itself.

Into the water you usually add soap. Don't use detergents or common, coarse soaps. Your car's paint never truly dries out, but is always evaporating residual oils into the air. Harsh detergents will remove these oils, causing the paint to dry faster than normal. Instead use warm water and a non-detergent soap made especially for waxed surfaces or a liquid soap made for waxed surfaces or a liquid soap made for washing dishes by hand.

Other products that can be used on painted surfaces include baking soda or plain soda water for stubborn dirt.

Wash the car completely, starting at the top, and rinse it completely clean. Abrasive grit should be loaded off under water pressure; scrubbing grit off will scratch the finish. The best washing tool is a sponge, cleaning mitt or soft towel. Whichever you choose, replace it often as each tends to absorb grease and dirt.

Other ways to get a better wash include:
• Don't wash your car in the sun or when the finish is hot.
• Use water pressure to remove caked-on dirt.
• Remove tree-sap and bird effluence immediately. Such substances will eat through wax, polish and paint.

One of the best implements to dry your car is a turkish towel or an old, soft bath towel. Anything with a deep nap will hold any dirt in suspension and not grind it into the paint. Harder cloths will only grind the grit into the paint making more scratches. Always start drying at the top, followed by the hood and trunk and sides. You'll find there's always more dirt near the rocker panels and wheelwells which will wind up on the rest of the car if you dry these areas first.

BODY   125

Cleaners, Waxes and Polishes

Before going any farther you should know the function of various products.

Cleaners—remove the top layer of dead pigment or paint.

Rubbing or polishing compounds—used to remove stubborn dirt, get rid of minor scratches, smooth away imperfections and partially restore badly weathered paint.

Polishes—contain no abrasives or waxes; they shine the paint by adding oils to the paint.

Waxes—are a protective coating for the polish.

CLEANERS AND COMPOUNDS

Before you apply any wax, you'll have to remove oxidation, road film and other types of pollutants that washing alone will not remove.

The paint on your car never dries completely. There are always residual oils evaporating from the paint into the air. When enough oils are present in the paint, it has a healthy shine (gloss). When too many oils evaporate the paint takes on a whitish cast known as oxidation. The idea of polishing and waxing is to keep enough oil present in the painted surface to prevent oxidation; but when it occurs, the only recourse is to remove the top layer of "dead" paint, exposing the healthy paint underneath.

Products to remove oxidation and road film are sold under a variety of generic names—polishes, cleaner, rubbing compound, cleaner/polish, polish/cleaner, self-polishing wax, pre-wax cleaner, finish restorer and many more. Regardless of name there are two types of cleaners—abrasive cleaners (sometimes called polishing or rubbing compounds) that remove oxidation by grinding away the top layer of "dead" paint, or chemical cleaners that dissolve the "dead" pigment, allowing it to be wiped away.

Abrasive cleaners, by their nature, leave thousands of minute scratches in the finish, which must be polished out later. These should only be used in extreme cases, but are usually the only thing to use on badly oxidized paint finishes. Chemical cleaners are much milder but are not strong enough for severe cases of oxidation or weathered paint.

The most popular cleaners are liquid or paste abrasive polishing and rubbing compounds. Polishing compounds have a finer abrasive grit for medium duty work. Rubbing compounds are a coarser abrasive and for heavy duty work. Unless you are familiar with how to use compounds, be very careful. Excessive rubbing with any type of compound or cleaner can grind right through the paint to primer or bare metal. Follow the directions on the container—depending on type, the cleaner may or may not be OK for your paint. For example, some cleaners are not formulated for acrylic lacquer finishes.

When a small area needs compounding or heavy polishing, it's best to do the job by hand. Some people prefer a powered buffer for large areas. Avoid cutting through the paint along styling edges on the body. Small, hand operations where the compound is applied and rubbed using cloth folded into a thick ball allow you to work in straight lines along such edges.

To avoid cutting through on the edges when using a power buffer, try masking tape. Just cover the edge with tape while using power. Then finish the job by hand with the tape removed. Even then work carefully. The paint tends to be a lot thinner along the sharp ridges stamped into the panels.

Whether compounding by machine or by hand, only work on a small area and apply the compound sparingly. If the materials are spread too thin, or allowed to sit too long, they dry out. Once dry they lose the ability to deliver a smooth, clean finish. Also, dried out polish tends to cause the buffer to stick in one spot. This in turn can burn or cut through the finish.

WAXES AND POLISHES

Your car's finish can be protected in a number of ways. A cleaner/wax or polish/cleaner followed by wax or variations of each all provide good results. The two-step approach (polish followed by wax) is probably slightly better but consumes more time and effort. Properly fed with oils, your paint should never need cleaning, but despite the best polishing job, it won't last unless it's protected with wax. Without wax, polish must be renewed at least once a month to prevent oxidation. Years ago (some still swear by it today), the best wax was made from the Brazilian palm, the Carnuba, favored for its vegetable base and high melting point. However, modern synthetic waxes are harder, which means they protect against moisture better, and chemically inert silicone is used for a long lasting protection. The only problem with silicone wax is that it penetrates all layers of paint. To repaint or touch up a panel or car protected by silicone wax, you have to completely strip the finish to avoid "fisheyes."

Under normal conditions, silicone waxes will last 4-6 months, but you have to be careful of wax build-up from too much waxing. Too thick a coat of wax is just as bad as no wax at all; it stops the paint from breathing.

Combination cleaners/waxes have become popular lately because they remove the old layer of wax plus light oxidation, while putting on a fresh coat of wax at the same time. Some cleaners/waxes contain abrasive cleaners which require caution, although many cleaner/waxes use a chemical cleaner.

Applying Wax or Polish

You may view polishing and waxing your car as a pleasant way to spend an afternoon, or as a boring chore, but it has to be done to keep the paint on your car. Caring for the paint doesn't require special tools, but you should follow a few rules.

1. Use a good quality wax.
2. Before applying any wax or polish, be sure the surface is completely clean. Just because the car looks clean, doesn't mean it's ready for polish or wax.
3. If the finish on your car is weathered, dull, or oxidized, it will probably have to be compounded to remove the old or oxidized paint. If the paint is simply dulled from lack of care, one of the non-abrasive cleaners known as polishing compounds will do the trick. If the paint is severely scratched or really dull, you'll probably have to use a rubbing compound to prepare the finish for waxing. If you're not sure which one to use, use the polishing compound, since you can easily ruin the finish by using too strong a compound.
4. Don't apply wax, polish or compound in direct sunlight, even if the directions on the can say you can. Most waxes will not cure properly in bright sunlight and you'll probably end up with a blotchy looking finish.
5. Don't rub the wax off too soon. The result will be a wet, dull looking finish. Let the wax dry thoroughly before buffing it off.
6. A constant debate among car enthusiasts is how wax should be applied. Some maintain pastes or liquids should be applied in a circular motion, but body shop experts have long thought that this approach results in barely detectable circular abrasions, especially on cars that are waxed frequently. They advise rubbing in straight lines, especially if any kind of cleaner is involved.
7. If an applicator is not supplied with the wax, use a piece of soft cheesecloth or very soft lint-free material. The same applies to buffing the surface.

SPECIAL SURFACES

One-step combination cleaner and wax formulas shouldn't be used on many of the special surfaces which abound on cars. The one-step materials contain abrasives to achieve a clean surface under the wax top coat. The abrasives are so mild that you could clean a car every week for a couple of years without fear of rubbing through the paint. But this same level of abrasiveness might, through repeated use, damage decals used for special trim effects. This includes wide stripes, wood-grain trim and other appliques.

Painted plastics must be cleaned with care. If a cleaner is too aggressive it will cut through the paint and expose the primer. If bright trim such as polished aluminum or chrome is painted, cleaning must be performed with even greater care. If rubbing compound is being used, it will cut faster than polish.

Abrasive cleaners will dull an acrylic finish. The best way to clean these newer finishes is with a non-abrasive liquid polish. Only dirt and oxidation, not paint, will be removed.

Taking a few minutes to read the instructions on the can of polish or wax will help prevent making serious mistakes. Not all preparations will work on all surfaces. And some are intended for power application while others will only work when applied by hand.

Don't get the idea that just pouring on some polish and then hitting it with a buffer will suffice. Power equipment speeds the operation. But it also adds a measure of risk. It's very easy to damage the finish if you use the wrong methods or materials.

Caring for Chrome

Read the label on the container. Many products are formulated specifically for chrome, but others contain abrasives that will scratch the chrome finish. If it isn't recommended for chrome, don't use it.

Never use steel wool or kitchen soap pads to clean chrome. Be careful not to get chrome cleaner on paint or interior vinyl surfaces. If you do, get it off immediately.

Troubleshooting 10

This section is designed to aid in the quick, accurate diagnosis of automotive problems. While automotive repairs can be made by many people, accurate troubleshooting is a rare skill for the amateur and professional alike.

In its simplest state, troubleshooting is an exercise in logic. It is essential to realize that an automobile is really composed of a series of systems. Some of these systems are interrelated; others are not. Automobiles operate within a framework of logical rules and physical laws, and the key to troubleshooting is a good understanding of all the automotive systems.

This section breaks the car or truck down into its component systems, allowing the problem to be isolated. The charts and diagnostic road maps list the most common problems and the most probable causes of trouble. Obviously it would be impossible to list every possible problem that could happen along with every possible cause, but it will locate MOST problems and eliminate a lot of unnecessary guesswork. The systematic format will locate problems within a given system, but, because many automotive systems are interrelated, the solution to your particular problem may be found in a number of systems on the car or truck.

USING THE TROUBLESHOOTING CHARTS

This book contains all of the specific information that the average do-it-yourself mechanic needs to repair and maintain his or her car or truck. The troubleshooting charts are designed to be used in conjunction with the specific procedures and information in the text. For instance, troubleshooting a point-type ignition system is fairly standard for all models, but you may be directed to the text to find procedures for troubleshooting an individual type of electronic ignition. You will also have to refer to the specification charts throughout the book for specifications applicable to your car or truck.

TOOLS AND EQUIPMENT

The tools illustrated in Chapter 1 (plus two more diagnostic pieces) will be adequate to troubleshoot most problems. The two other tools needed are a voltmeter and an ohmmeter. These can be purchased separately or in combination, known as a VOM meter.

In the event that other tools are required, they will be noted in the procedures.

TROUBLESHOOTING

Troubleshooting Engine Problems

See Chapters 2, 3, 4 for more information and service procedures.

Index to Systems

System	To Test	Group
Battery	Engine need not be running	1
Starting system	Engine need not be running	2
Primary electrical system	Engine need not be running	3
Secondary electrical system	Engine need not be running	4
Fuel system	Engine need not be running	5
Engine compression	Engine need not be running	6
Engine vacuum	Engine must be running	7
Secondary electrical system	Engine must be running	8
Valve train	Engine must be running	9
Exhaust system	Engine must be running	10
Cooling system	Engine must be running	11
Engine lubrication	Engine must be running	12

Index to Problems

Problem: Symptom	Begin at Specific Diagnosis, Number
Engine Won't Start:	
Starter doesn't turn	1.1, 2.1
Starter turns, engine doesn't	2.1
Starter turns engine very slowly	1.1, 2.4
Starter turns engine normally	3.1, 4.1
Starter turns engine very quickly	6.1
Engine fires intermittently	4.1
Engine fires consistently	5.1, 6.1
Engine Runs Poorly:	
Hard starting	3.1, 4.1, 5.1, 8.1
Rough idle	4.1, 5.1, 8.1
Stalling	3.1, 4.1, 5.1, 8.1
Engine dies at high speeds	4.1, 5.1
Hesitation (on acceleration from standing stop)	5.1, 8.1
Poor pickup	4.1, 5.1, 8.1
Lack of power	3.1, 4.1, 5.1, 8.1
Backfire through the carburetor	4.1, 8.1, 9.1
Backfire through the exhaust	4.1, 8.1, 9.1
Blue exhaust gases	6.1, 7.1
Black exhaust gases	5.1
Running on (after the ignition is shut off)	3.1, 8.1
Susceptible to moisture	4.1
Engine misfires under load	4.1, 7.1, 8.4, 9.1
Engine misfires at speed	4.1, 8.4
Engine misfires at idle	3.1, 4.1, 5.1, 7.1, 8.4

Sample Section

Test and Procedure	Results and Indications	Proceed to
4.1—Check for spark: Hold each spark plug wire approximately ¼" from ground with gloves or a heavy, dry rag. Crank the engine and observe the spark.	→ If no spark is evident:	→ 4.2
	→ If spark is good in some cases:	→ 4.3
	→ If spark is good in all cases:	→ 4.6

TROUBLESHOOTING 129

Specific Diagnosis

This section is arranged so that following each test, instructions are given to proceed to another, until a problem is diagnosed.

Section 1—Battery

Test and Procedure	Results and Indications	Proceed to
1.1—Inspect the battery visually for case condition (corrosion, cracks) and water level.	If case is cracked, replace battery:	1.4
	If the case is intact, remove corrosion with a solution of baking soda and water (**CAUTION**: *do not get the solution into the battery*), and fill with water:	1.2

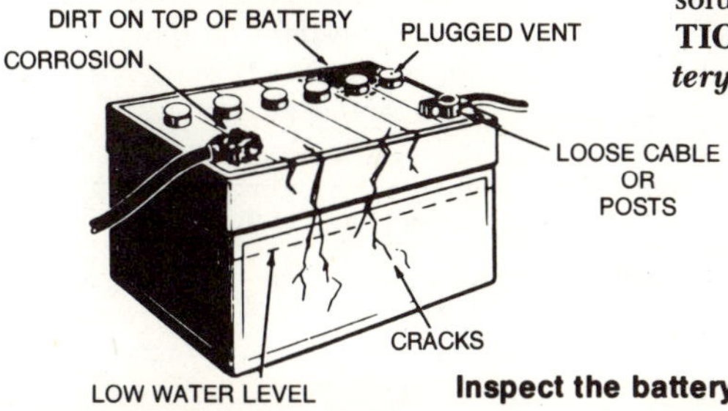

Inspect the battery case

1.2—Check the battery cable connections: Insert a screwdriver between the battery post and the cable clamp. Turn the headlights on high beam, and observe them as the screwdriver is gently twisted to ensure good metal to metal contact.	If the lights brighten, remove and clean the clamp and post; coat the post with petroleum jelly, install and tighten the clamp:	1.4
	If no improvement is noted:	1.3

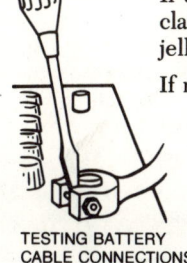

TESTING BATTERY CABLE CONNECTIONS USING A SCREWDRIVER

1.3—Test the state of charge of the battery using an individual cell tester or hydrometer.	If indicated, charge the battery. **NOTE**: *If no obvious reason exists for the low state of charge (i.e., battery age, prolonged storage)*, proceed to:	1.4

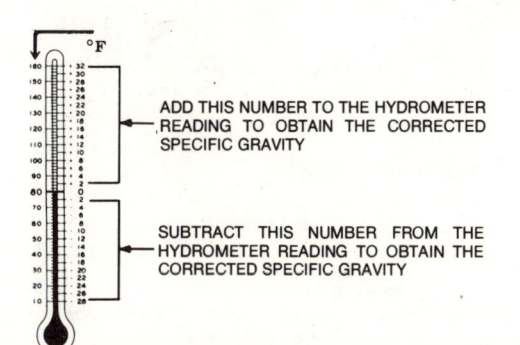

ADD THIS NUMBER TO THE HYDROMETER READING TO OBTAIN THE CORRECTED SPECIFIC GRAVITY

SUBTRACT THIS NUMBER FROM THE HYDROMETER READING TO OBTAIN THE CORRECTED SPECIFIC GRAVITY

Specific Gravity (@ 80° F.)

Minimum	Battery Charge
1.260	100% Charged
1.230	75% Charged
1.200	50% Charged
1.170	25% Charged
1.140	Very Little Power Left
1.110	Completely Discharged

The effects of temperature on battery specific gravity (left) and amount of battery charge in relation to specific gravity (right)

1.4—Visually inspect battery cables for cracking, bad connection to ground, or bad connection to starter.	If necessary, tighten connections or replace the cables:	2.1

TROUBLESHOOTING

Section 2—Starting System
See Chapter 3 for service procedures

Test and Procedure	Results and Indications	Proceed to
Note: Tests in Group 2 are performed with coil high tension lead disconnected to prevent accidental starting.		
2.1—Test the starter motor and solenoid: Connect a jumper from the battery post of the solenoid (or relay) to the starter post of the solenoid (or relay).	If starter turns the engine normally:	2.2
	If the starter buzzes, or turns the engine very slowly:	2.4
	If no response, replace the solenoid (or relay).	3.1
	If the starter turns, but the engine doesn't, ensure that the flywheel ring gear is intact. If the gear is undamaged, replace the starter drive.	3.1
2.2—Determine whether ignition override switches are functioning properly (clutch start switch, neutral safety switch), by connecting a jumper across the switch(es), and turning the ignition switch to "start".	If starter operates, adjust or replace switch:	3.1
	If the starter doesn't operate:	2.3
2.3—Check the ignition switch "start" position: Connect a 12V test lamp or voltmeter between the starter post of the solenoid (or relay) and ground. Turn the ignition switch to the "start" position, and jiggle the key.	If the lamp doesn't light or the meter needle doesn't move when the switch is turned, check the ignition switch for loose connections, cracked insulation, or broken wires. Repair or replace as necessary:	3.1
	If the lamp flickers or needle moves when the key is jiggled, replace the ignition switch.	3.3

Checking the ignition switch "start" position

STARTER RELAY (IF EQUIPPED)

2.4—Remove and bench test the starter, according to specifications in the engine electrical section.	If the starter does not meet specifications, repair or replace as needed:	3.1
	If the starter is operating properly:	2.5
2.5—Determine whether the engine can turn freely: Remove the spark plugs, and check for water in the cylinders. Check for water on the dipstick, or oil in the radiator. Attempt to turn the engine using an 18" flex drive and socket on the crankshaft pulley nut or bolt.	If the engine will turn freely only with the spark plugs out, and hydrostatic lock (water in the cylinders) is ruled out, check valve timing:	9.2
	If engine will not turn freely, and it is known that the clutch and transmission are free, the engine must be disassembled for further evaluation:	Chapter 3

Section 3—Primary Electrical System

Test and Procedure	Results and Indications	Proceed to
3.1—Check the ignition switch "on" position: Connect a jumper wire between the distributor side of the coil and ground, and a 12V test lamp between the switch side of the coil and ground. Remove the high tension lead from the coil. Turn the ignition switch on and jiggle the key.	If the lamp lights:	3.2
	If the lamp flickers when the key is jiggled, replace the ignition switch:	3.3
	If the lamp doesn't light, check for loose or open connections. If none are found, remove the ignition switch and check for continuity. If the switch is faulty, replace it:	3.3

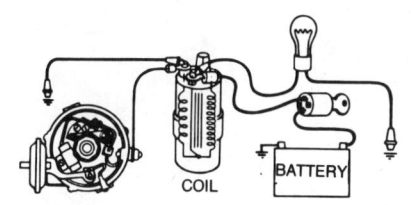

Checking the ignition switch "on" position

3.2—Check the ballast resistor or resistance wire for an open circuit, using an ohmmeter. See Chapter 3 for specific tests.	Replace the resistor or resistance wire if the resistance is zero. **NOTE:** *Some ignition systems have no ballast resistor.*	3.3

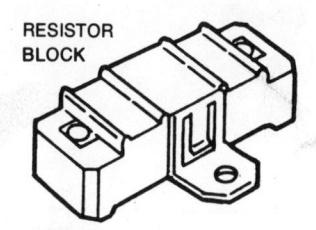

Two types of resistors

3.3—On point-type ignition systems, visually inspect the breaker points for burning, pitting or excessive wear. Gray coloring of the point contact surfaces is normal. Rotate the crankshaft until the contact heel rests on a high point of the distributor cam and adjust the point gap to specifications. On electronic ignition models, remove the distributor cap and visually inspect the armature. Ensure that the armature pin is in place, and that the armature is on tight and rotates when the engine is cranked. Make sure there are no cracks, chips or rounded edges on the armature.	If the breaker points are intact, clean the contact surfaces with fine emery cloth, and adjust the point gap to specifications. If the points are worn, replace them. On electronic systems, replace any parts which appear defective. If condition persists:	3.4

TROUBLESHOOTING

Test and Procedure	Results and Indications	Proceed to
3.4—On point-type ignition systems, connect a dwell-meter between the distributor primary lead and ground. Crank the engine and observe the point dwell angle. On electronic ignition systems, conduct a stator (magnetic pickup assembly) test. See Chapter 3.	On point-type systems, adjust the dwell angle if necessary. **NOTE:** *Increasing the point gap decreases the dwell angle and vice-versa.* If the dwell meter shows little or no reading; On electronic ignition systems, if the stator is bad, replace the stator. If the stator is good, proceed to the other tests in Chapter 3.	3.6 3.5

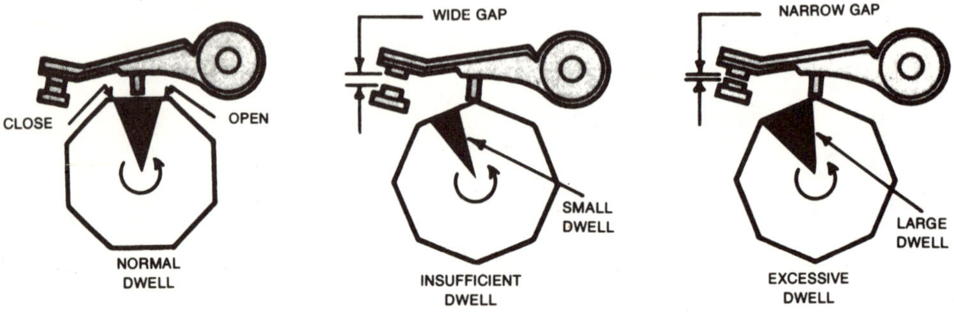

Dwell is a function of point gap

3.5—On the point-type ignition systems, check the condenser for short: connect an ohmeter across the condenser body and the pigtail lead.	If any reading other than infinite is noted, replace the condenser	3.6

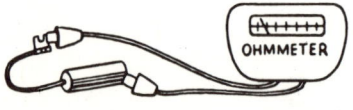

Checking the condenser for short

3.6—Test the coil primary resistance: On point-type ignition systems, connect an ohmmeter across the coil primary terminals, and read the resistance on the low scale. Note whether an external ballast resistor or resistance wire is used. On electronic ignition systems, test the coil primary resistance as in Chapter 3.	Point-type ignition coils utilizing ballast resistors or resistance wires should have approximately 1.0 ohms resistance. Coils with internal resistors should have approximately 4.0 ohms resistance. If values far from the above are noted, replace the coil.	4.1

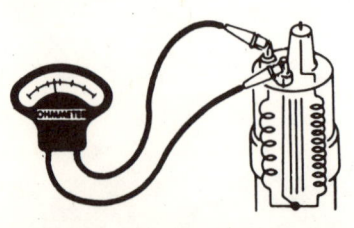

Check the coil primary resistance

TROUBLESHOOTING

Section 4—Secondary Electrical System
See Chapters 2–3 for service procedures

Test and Procedure	Results and Indications	Proceed to
4.1—Check for spark: Hold each spark plug wire approximately ¼" from ground with gloves or a heavy, dry rag. Crank the engine, and observe the spark.	If no spark is evident:	4.2
	If spark is good in some cylinders:	4.3
	If spark is good in all cylinders:	4.6

Check for spark at the plugs

4.2—Check for spark at the coil high tension lead: Remove the coil high tension lead from the distributor and position it approximately ¼" from ground. Crank the engine and observe spark. **CAUTION: *This test should not be performed on engines equipped with electronic ignition.***	If the spark is good and consistent:	4.3
	If the spark is good but intermittent, test the primary electrical system starting at 3.3:	3.3
	If the spark is weak or non-existent, replace the coil high tension lead, clean and tighten all connections and retest. If no improvement is noted:	4.4
4.3—Visually inspect the distributor cap and rotor for burned or corroded contacts, cracks, carbon tracks, or moisture. Also check the fit of the rotor on the distributor shaft (where applicable).	If moisture is present, dry thoroughly, and retest per 4.1:	4.1
	If burned or excessively corroded contacts, cracks, or carbon tracks are noted, replace the defective part(s) and retest per 4.1:	4.1
	If the rotor and cap appear intact, or are only slightly corroded, clean the contacts thoroughly (including the cap towers and spark plug wire ends) and retest per 4.1:	
	If the spark is good in all cases:	4.6
	If the spark is poor in all cases:	4.5

Inspect the distributor cap and rotor

134 TROUBLESHOOTING

Test and Procedure	Results and Indications	Proceed to
4.4—Check the coil secondary resistance: On point-type systems connect an ohmmeter across the distributor side of the coil and the coil tower. Read the resistance on the high scale of the ohmmeter. On electronic ignition systems, see Chapter 3 for specific tests.	The resistance of a satisfactory coil should be between 4,000 and 10,000 ohms. If resistance is considerably higher (i.e., 40,000 ohms) replace the coil and retest per 4.1. **NOTE:** *This does not apply to high performance coils.*	

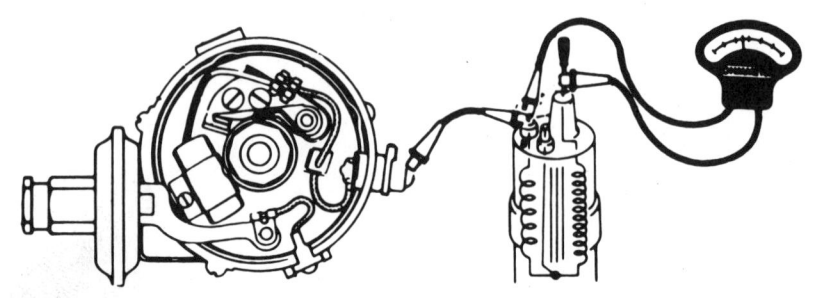

Testing the coil secondary resistance

4.5—Visually inspect the spark plug wires for cracking or brittleness. Ensure that no two wires are positioned so as to cause induction firing (adjacent and parallel). Remove each wire, one by one, and check resistance with an ohmmeter.	Replace any cracked or brittle wires. If any of the wires are defective, replace the entire set. Replace any wires with excessive resistance (over $8000\,\Omega$ per foot for suppression wire), and separate any wires that might cause induction firing.	4.6

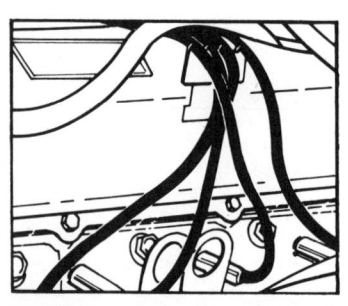

Misfiring can be the result of spark plug leads to adjacent, consecutively firing cylinders running parallel and too close together

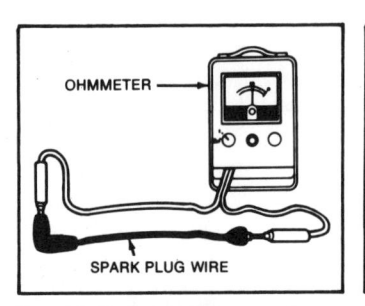

On point-type ignition systems, check the spark plug wires as shown. On electronic ignitions, do not remove the wire from the distributor cap terminal; instead, test through the cap

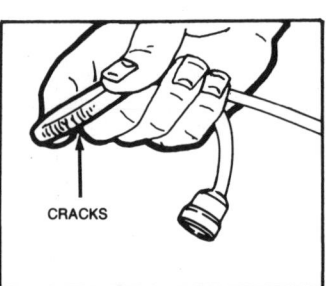

Spark plug wires can be checked visually by bending them in a loop over your finger. This will reveal any cracks, burned or broken insulation. Any wire with cracked insulation should be replaced

4.6—Remove the spark plugs, noting the cylinders from which they were removed, and evaluate according to the color photos in the middle of this book.	See following.	See following.

TROUBLESHOOTING 135

Test and Procedure	Results and Indications	Proceed to
4.7—Examine the location of all the plugs.	The following diagrams illustrate some of the conditions that the location of plugs will reveal.	4.8

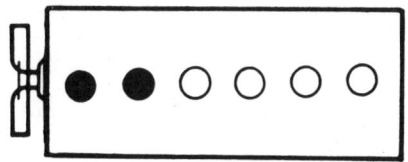

Two adjacent plugs are fouled in a 6-cylinder engine, 4-cylinder engine or either bank of a V-8. This is probably due to a blown head gasket between the two cylinders

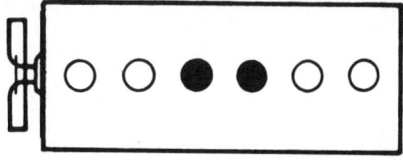

The two center plugs in a 6-cylinder engine are fouled. Raw fuel may be "boiled" out of the carburetor into the intake manifold after the engine is shut-off. Stop-start driving can also foul the center plugs, due to overly rich mixture. Proper float level, a new float needle and seat or use of an insulating spacer may help this problem

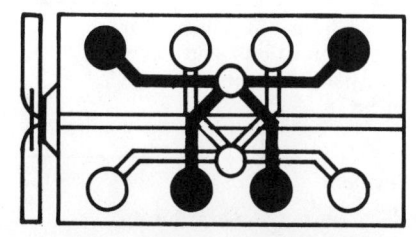

An unbalanced carburetor is indicated. Following the fuel flow on this particular design shows that the cylinders fed by the right-hand barrel are fouled from overly rich mixture, while the cylinders fed by the left-hand barrel are normal

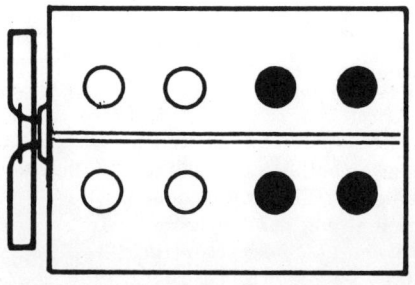

If the four rear plugs are overheated, a cooling system problem is suggested. A thorough cleaning of the cooling system may restore coolant circulation and cure the problem

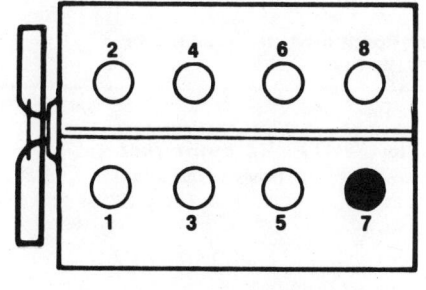

Finding one plug overheated may indicate an intake manifold leak near the affected cylinder. If the overheated plug is the second of two adjacent, consecutively firing plugs, it could be the result of ignition cross-firing. Separating the leads to these two plugs will eliminate cross-fire

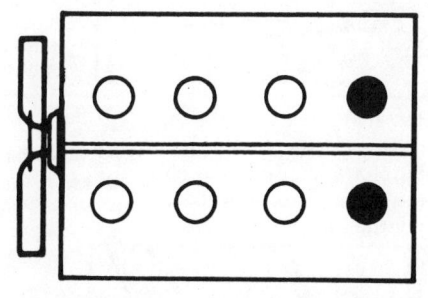

Occasionally, the two rear plugs in large, lightly used V-8's will become oil fouled. High oil consumption and smoky exhaust may also be noticed. It is probably due to plugged oil drain holes in the rear of the cylinder head, causing oil to be sucked in around the valve stems. This usually occurs in the rear cylinders first, because the engine slants that way

TROUBLESHOOTING

Test and Procedure	Results and Indications	Proceed to
4.8—Determine the static ignition timing. Using the crankshaft pulley timing marks as a guide, locate top dead center on the compression stroke of the number one cylinder.	The rotor should be pointing toward the No. 1 tower in the distributor cap, and, on electronic ignitions, the armature spoke for that cylinder should be lined up with the stator.	4.8
4.9—Check coil polarity: Connect a voltmeter negative lead to the coil high tension lead, and the positive lead to ground (**NOTE:** *Reverse the hook-up for positive ground systems*). Crank the engine momentarily. **Checking coil polarity**	If the voltmeter reads up-scale, the polarity is correct: If the voltmeter reads down-scale, reverse the coil polarity (switch the primary leads):	5.1 5.1

Section 5—Fuel System
See Chapter 4 for service procedures

Test and Procedure	Results and Indications	Proceed to
5.1—Determine that the air filter is functioning efficiently: Hold paper elements up to a strong light, and attempt to see light through the filter.	Clean permanent air filters in solvent (or manufacturer's recommendation), and allow to dry. Replace paper elements through which light cannot be seen:	5.2
5.2—Determine whether a flooding condition exists: Flooding is identified by a strong gasoline odor, and excessive gasoline present in the throttle bore(s) of the carburetor. *If the engine floods repeatedly, check the choke butterfly flap*	If flooding is not evident: If flooding is evident, permit the gasoline to dry for a few moments and restart. If flooding doesn't recur: If flooding is persistent:	5.3 5.7 5.5
5.3—Check that fuel is reaching the carburetor: Detach the fuel line at the carburetor inlet. Hold the end of the line in a cup (not styrofoam), and crank the engine. *Check the fuel pump by disconnecting the output line (fuel pump-to-carburetor) at the carburetor and operating the starter briefly*	If fuel flows smoothly: If fuel doesn't flow (**NOTE:** *Make sure that there is fuel in the tank*), or flows erratically:	5.7 5.4

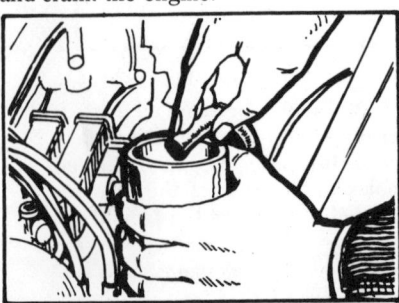

TROUBLESHOOTING

Test and Procedure	Results and Indications	Proceed to
5.4—Test the fuel pump: Disconnect all fuel lines from the fuel pump. Hold a finger over the input fitting, crank the engine (with electric pump, turn the ignition or pump on); and feel for suction.	If suction is evident, blow out the fuel line to the tank with low pressure compressed air until bubbling is heard from the fuel filler neck. Also blow out the carburetor fuel line (both ends disconnected):	5.7
	If no suction is evident, replace or repair the fuel pump: NOTE: *Repeated oil fouling of the spark plugs, or a no-start condition, could be the result of a ruptured vacuum booster pump diaphragm, through which oil or gasoline is being drawn into the intake manifold (where applicable).*	5.7
5.5—Occasionally, small specks of dirt will clog the small jets and orifices in the carburetor. With the engine cold, hold a flat piece of wood or similar material over the carburetor, where possible, and crank the engine.	If the engine starts, but runs roughly the engine is probably not run enough. If the engine won't start:	5.9
5.6—Check the needle and seat: Tap the carburetor in the area of the needle and seat.	If flooding stops, a gasoline additive (e.g., Gumout) will often cure the problem:	5.7
	If flooding continues, check the fuel pump for excessive pressure at the carburetor (according to specifications). If the pressure is normal, the needle and seat must be removed and checked, and/or the float level adjusted:	5.7
5.7—Test the accelerator pump by looking into the throttle bores while operating the throttle.	If the accelerator pump appears to be operating normally:	5.8
	If the accelerator pump is not operating, the pump must be reconditioned. Where possible, service the pump with the carburetor(s) installed on the engine. If necessary, remove the carburetor. Prior to removal:	5.8

Check for gas at the carburetor by looking down the carburetor throat while someone moves the accelerator

5.8—Determine whether the carburetor main fuel system is functioning: Spray a commercial starting fluid into the carburetor while attempting to start the engine.	If the engine starts, runs for a few seconds, and dies:	5.9
	If the engine doesn't start:	6.1

TROUBLESHOOTING

Test and Procedure	Results and Indications	Proceed to
5.9—Uncommon fuel system malfunctions: See below:	If the problem is solved:	6.1
	If the problem remains, remove and recondition the carburetor.	

Condition	Indication	Test	Prevailing Weather Conditions	Remedy
Vapor lock	Engine will not restart shortly after running.	Cool the components of the fuel system until the engine starts. Vapor lock can be cured faster by draping a wet cloth over a mechanical fuel pump.	Hot to very hot	Ensure that the exhaust manifold heat control valve is operating. Check with the vehicle manufacturer for the recommended solution to vapor lock on the model in question.
Carburetor icing	Engine will not idle, stalls at low speeds.	Visually inspect the throttle plate area of the throttle bores for frost.	High humidity, 32–40° F.	Ensure that the exhaust manifold heat control valve is operating, and that the intake manifold heat riser is not blocked.
Water in the fuel	Engine sputters and stalls; may not start.	Pump a small amount of fuel into a glass jar. Allow to stand, and inspect for droplets or a layer of water.	High humidity, extreme temperature changes.	For droplets, use one or two cans of commercial gas line anti-freeze. For a layer of water, the tank must be drained, and the fuel lines blown out with compressed air.

Section 6—Engine Compression
See Chapter 3 for service procedures

6.1—Test engine compression: Remove all spark plugs. Block the throttle wide open. Insert a compression gauge into a spark plug port, crank the engine to obtain the maximum reading, and record.	If compression is within limits on all cylinders:	7.1
	If gauge reading is extremely low on all cylinders:	6.2
	If gauge reading is low on one or two cylinders: (If gauge readings are identical and low on two or more adjacent cylinders, the head gasket must be replaced.)	6.2

Checking compression

6.2—Test engine compression (wet): Squirt approximately 30 cc. of engine oil into each cylinder, and retest per 6.1.	If the readings improve, worn or cracked rings or broken pistons are indicated:	See Chapter 3
	If the readings do not improve, burned or excessively carboned valves or a jumped timing chain are indicated: NOTE: *A jumped timing chain is often indicated by difficult cranking.*	7.1

TROUBLESHOOTING

Section 7—Engine Vacuum
See Chapter 3 for service procedures

Test and Procedure	Results and Indications	Proceed to
7.1—Attach a vacuum gauge to the intake manifold beyond the throttle plate. Start the engine, and observe the action of the needle over the range of engine speeds.	See below.	See below

INDICATION: normal engine in good condition

Proceed to: 8.1

Normal engine
Gauge reading: steady, from 17–22 in./Hg.

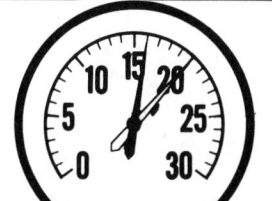

INDICATION: sticking valves or ignition miss

Proceed to: 9.1, 8.3

Sticking valves
Gauge reading: intermittent fluctuation at idle

INDICATION: late ignition or valve timing, low compression, stuck throttle valve, leaking carburetor or manifold gasket

Proceed to: 6.1

Incorrect valve timing
Gauge reading: low (10–15 in./Hg) but steady

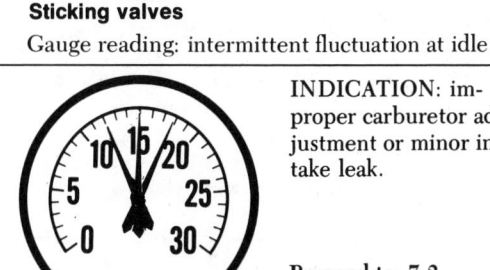

INDICATION: improper carburetor adjustment or minor intake leak.

Proceed to: 7.2

Carburetor requires adjustment
Gauge reading: drifting needle

INDICATION: ignition miss, blown cylinder head gasket, leaking valve or weak valve spring

Proceed to: 8.3, 6.1

Blown head gasket
Gauge reading: needle fluctuates as engine speed increases

INDICATION: burnt valve or faulty valve clearance. Needle will fall when defective valve operates

Proceed to: 9.1

Burnt or leaking valves
Gauge reading: steady needle, but drops regularly

INDICATION: choked muffler, excessive back pressure in system

Proceed to: 10.1

Clogged exhaust system
Gauge reading: gradual drop in reading at idle

INDICATION: worn valve guides

Proceed to: 9.1

Worn valve guides
Gauge reading: needle vibrates excessively at idle, but steadies as engine speed increases

White pointer = steady gauge hand   Black pointer = fluctuating gauge hand

Test and Procedure	Results and Indications	Proceed to
7.2—Attach a vacuum gauge per 7.1, and test for an intake manifold leak. Squirt a small amount of oil around the intake manifold gaskets, carburetor gaskets, plugs and fittings. Observe the action of the vacuum gauge.	If the reading improves, replace the indicated gasket, or seal the indicated fitting or plug: If the reading remains low:	8.1 7.3
7.3—Test all vacuum hoses and accessories for leaks as described in 7.2. Also check the carburetor body (dashpots, automatic choke mechanism, throttle shafts) for leaks in the same manner.	If the reading improves, service or replace the offending part(s): If the reading remains low:	8.1 6.1

Section 8—Secondary Electrical System
See Chapter 2 for service procedures

Test and Procedure	Results and Indications	Proceed to
8.1—Remove the distributor cap and check to make sure that the rotor turns when the engine is cranked. Visually inspect the distributor components.	Clean, tighten or replace any components which appear defective.	8.2
8.2—Connect a timing light (per manufacturer's recommendation) and check the dynamic ignition timing. Disconnect and plug the vacuum hose(s) to the distributor if specified, start the engine, and observe the timing marks at the specified engine speed.	If the timing is not correct, adjust to specifications by rotating the distributor in the engine: (Advance timing by rotating distributor opposite normal direction of rotor rotation, retard timing by rotating distributor in same direction as rotor rotation.)	8.3
8.3—Check the operation of the distributor advance mechanism(s): To test the mechanical advance, disconnect the vacuum lines from the distributor advance unit and observe the timing marks with a timing light as the engine speed is increased from idle. If the mark moves smoothly, without hesitation, it may be assumed that the mechanical advance is functioning properly. To test vacuum advance and/or retard systems, alternately crimp and release the vacuum line, and observe the timing mark for movement. If movement is noted, the system is operating.	If the systems are functioning: If the systems are not functioning, remove the distributor, and test on a distributor tester:	8.4 8.4
8.4—Locate an ignition miss: With the engine running, remove each spark plug wire, one at a time, until one is found that doesn't cause the engine to roughen and slow down.	When the missing cylinder is identified:	4.1

TROUBLESHOOTING

Section 9—Valve Train
See Chapter 3 for service procedures

Test and Procedure	Results and Indications	Proceed to
9.1—Evaluate the valve train: Remove the valve cover, and ensure that the valves are adjusted to specifications. A mechanic's stethoscope may be used to aid in the diagnosis of the valve train. By pushing the probe on or near push rods or rockers, valve noise often can be isolated. A timing light also may be used to diagnose valve problems. Connect the light according to manufacturer's recommendations, and start the engine. Vary the firing moment of the light by increasing the engine speed (and therefore the ignition advance), and moving the trigger from cylinder to cylinder. Observe the movement of each valve.	Sticking valves or erratic valve train motion can be observed with the timing light. The cylinder head must be disassembled for repairs.	See Chapter 3
9.2—Check the valve timing: Locate top dead center of the No. 1 piston, and install a degree wheel or tape on the crankshaft pulley or damper with zero corresponding to an index mark on the engine. Rotate the crankshaft in its direction of rotation, and observe the opening of the No. 1 cylinder intake valve. The opening should correspond with the correct mark on the degree wheel according to specifications.	If the timing is not correct, the timing cover must be removed for further investigation.	See Chapter 3

Section 10—Exhaust System

Test and Procedure	Results and Indications	Proceed to
10.1—Determine whether the exhaust manifold heat control valve is operating: Operate the valve by hand to determine whether it is free to move. If the valve is free, run the engine to operating temperature and observe the action of the valve, to ensure that it is opening.	If the valve sticks, spray it with a suitable solvent, open and close the valve to free it, and retest. If the valve functions properly: If the valve does not free, or does not operate, replace the valve:	10.2 10.2
10.2—Ensure that there are no exhaust restrictions: Visually inspect the exhaust system for kinks, dents, or crushing. Also note that gases are flowing freely from the tailpipe at all engine speeds, indicating no restriction in the muffler or resonator.	Replace any damaged portion of the system:	11.1

Section 11—Cooling System
See Chapter 3 for service procedures

Test and Procedure	Results and Indications	Proceed to
11.1—Visually inspect the fan belt for glazing, cracks, and fraying, and replace if necessary. Tighten the belt so that the longest span has approximately ½" play at its midpoint under thumb pressure (see Chapter 1).	Replace or tighten the fan belt as necessary: *Checking belt tension*	11.2
11.2—Check the fluid level of the cooling system.	If full or slightly low, fill as necessary:	11.5
	If extremely low:	11.3
11.3—Visually inspect the external portions of the cooling system (radiator, radiator hoses, thermostat elbow, water pump seals, heater hoses, etc.) for leaks. If none are found, pressurize the cooling system to 14–15 psi.	If cooling system holds the pressure:	11.5
	If cooling system loses pressure rapidly, reinspect external parts of the system for leaks under pressure. If none are found, check dipstick for coolant in crankcase. If no coolant is present, but pressure loss continues:	11.4
	If coolant is evident in crankcase, remove cylinder head(s), and check gasket(s). If gaskets are intact, block and cylinder head(s) should be checked for cracks or holes.	
	If the gasket(s) is blown, replace, and purge the crankcase of coolant:	12.6
	NOTE: *Occasionally, due to atmospheric and driving conditions, condensation of water can occur in the crankcase. This causes the oil to appear milky white. To remedy, run the engine until hot, and change the oil and oil filter.*	
11.4—Check for combustion leaks into the cooling system: Pressurize the cooling system as above. Start the engine, and observe the pressure gauge. If the needle fluctuates, remove each spark plug wire, one at a time, noting which cylinder(s) reduce or eliminate the fluctuation.	Cylinders which reduce or eliminate the fluctuation, when the spark plug wire is removed, are leaking into the cooling system. Replace the head gasket on the affected cylinder bank(s). *Pressurizing the cooling system*	

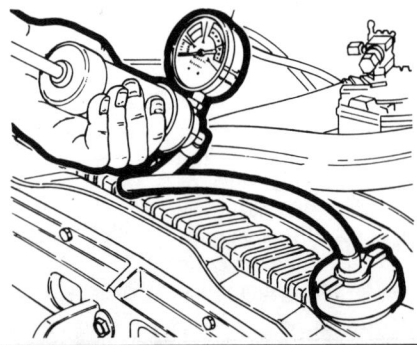

TROUBLESHOOTING 143

Test and Procedure	Results and Indications	Proceed to
11.5—Check the radiator pressure cap: Attach a radiator pressure tester to the radiator cap (wet the seal prior to installation). Quickly pump up the pressure, noting the point at which the cap releases.	If the cap releases within ± 1 psi of the specified rating, it is operating properly:	11.6
	If the cap releases at more than ± 1 psi of the specified rating, it should be replaced:	11.6
11.6—Test the thermostat: Start the engine cold, remove the radiator cap, and insert a thermometer into the radiator. Allow the engine to idle. After a short while, there will be a sudden, rapid increase in coolant temperature. The temperature at which this sharp rise stops is the thermostat opening temperature.	If the thermostat opens at or about the specified temperature:	11.7
	If the temperature doesn't increase: (If the temperature increases slowly and gradually, replace the thermostat.)	11.7
11.7—Check the water pump: Remove the thermostat elbow and the thermostat, disconnect the coil high tension lead (to prevent starting), and crank the engine momentarily.	If coolant flows, replace the thermostat and retest per 11.6:	11.6
	If coolant doesn't flow, reverse flush the cooling system to alleviate any blockage that might exist. If system is not blocked, and coolant will not flow, replace the water pump.	

Checking radiator pressure cap

Section 12—Lubrication
See Chapter 3 for service procedures

Test and Procedure	Results and Indications	Proceed to
12.1—Check the oil pressure gauge or warning light: If the gauge shows low pressure, or the light is on for no obvious reason, remove the oil pressure sender. Install an accurate oil pressure gauge and run the engine momentarily.	If oil pressure builds normally, run engine for a few moments to determine that it is functioning normally, and replace the sender.	—
	If the pressure remains low:	12.2
	If the pressure surges:	12.3
	If the oil pressure is zero:	12.3
12.2—Visually inspect the oil: If the oil is watery or very thin, milky, or foamy, replace the oil and oil filter.	If the oil is normal:	12.3
	If after replacing oil the pressure remains low:	12.3
	If after replacing oil the pressure becomes normal:	—

TROUBLESHOOTING

Test and Procedure	Results and Indications	Proceed to
12.3—Inspect the oil pressure relief valve and spring, to ensure that it is not sticking or stuck. Remove and thoroughly clean the valve, spring, and the valve body.	If the oil pressure improves: If no improvement is noted:	— 12.4
12.4—Check to ensure that the oil pump is not cavitating (sucking air instead of oil): See that the crankcase is neither over nor underfull, and that the pickup in the sump is in the proper position and free from sludge.	Fill or drain the crankcase to the proper capacity, and clean the pickup screen in solvent if necessary. If no improvement is noted:	12.5
12.5—Inspect the oil pump drive and the oil pump:	If the pump drive or the oil pump appear to be defective, service as necessary and retest per 12.1: If the pump drive and pump appear to be operating normally, the engine should be disassembled to determine where blockage exists:	12.1 See Chapter 3
12.6—Purge the engine of ethylene glycol coolant: Completely drain the crankcase and the oil filter. Obtain a commercial butyl cellosolve base solvent, designated for this purpose, and follow the instructions precisely. Following this, install a new oil filter and refill the crankcase with the proper weight oil. The next oil and filter change should follow shortly thereafter (1000 miles).		

TROUBLESHOOTING EMISSION CONTROL SYSTEMS

See Chapter 4 for procedures applicable to individual emission control systems used on specific combinations of engine/transmission/model.

TROUBLESHOOTING THE CARBURETOR
See Chapter 4 for service procedures

Carburetor problems cannot be effectively isolated unless all other engine systems (particularly ignition and emission) are functioning properly and the engine is properly tuned.

TROUBLESHOOTING

Condition	Possible Cause
Engine cranks, but does not start	1. Improper starting procedure 2. No fuel in tank 3. Clogged fuel line or filter 4. Defective fuel pump 5. Choke valve not closing properly 6. Engine flooded 7. Choke valve not unloading 8. Throttle linkage not making full travel 9. Stuck needle or float 10. Leaking float needle or seat 11. Improper float adjustment
Engine stalls	1. Improperly adjusted idle speed or mixture **Engine hot** 2. Improperly adjusted dashpot 3. Defective or improperly adjusted solenoid 4. Incorrect fuel level in fuel bowl 5. Fuel pump pressure too high 6. Leaking float needle seat 7. Secondary throttle valve stuck open 8. Air or fuel leaks 9. Idle air bleeds plugged or missing 10. Idle passages plugged **Engine Cold** 11. Incorrectly adjusted choke 12. Improperly adjusted fast idle speed 13. Air leaks 14. Plugged idle or idle air passages 15. Stuck choke valve or binding linkage 16. Stuck secondary throttle valves 17. Engine flooding—high fuel level 18. Leaking or misaligned float
Engine hesitates on acceleration	1. Clogged fuel filter 2. Leaking fuel pump diaphragm 3. Low fuel pump pressure 4. Secondary throttle valves stuck, bent or misadjusted 5. Sticking or binding air valve 6. Defective accelerator pump 7. Vacuum leaks 8. Clogged air filter 9. Incorrect choke adjustment (engine cold)
Engine feels sluggish or flat on acceleration	1. Improperly adjusted idle speed or mixture 2. Clogged fuel filter 3. Defective accelerator pump 4. Dirty, plugged or incorrect main metering jets 5. Bent or sticking main metering rods 6. Sticking throttle valves 7. Stuck heat riser 8. Binding or stuck air valve 9. Dirty, plugged or incorrect secondary jets 10. Bent or sticking secondary metering rods. 11. Throttle body or manifold heat passages plugged 12. Improperly adjusted choke or choke vacuum break.
Carburetor floods	1. Defective fuel pump. Pressure too high. 2. Stuck choke valve 3. Dirty, worn or damaged float or needle valve/seat 4. Incorrect float/fuel level 5. Leaking float bowl

TROUBLESHOOTING

Condition	Possible Cause
Engine idles roughly and stalls	1. Incorrect idle speed 2. Clogged fuel filter 3. Dirt in fuel system or carburetor 4. Loose carburetor screws or attaching bolts 5. Broken carburetor gaskets 6. Air leaks 7. Dirty carburetor 8. Worn idle mixture needles 9. Throttle valves stuck open 10. Incorrectly adjusted float or fuel level 11. Clogged air filter
Engine runs unevenly or surges	1. Defective fuel pump 2. Dirty or clogged fuel filter 3. Plugged, loose or incorrect main metering jets or rods 4. Air leaks 5. Bent or sticking main metering rods 6. Stuck power piston 7. Incorrect float adjustment 8. Incorrect idle speed or mixture 9. Dirty or plugged idle system passages 10. Hard, brittle or broken gaskets 11. Loose attaching or mounting screws 12. Stuck or misaligned secondary throttle valves
Poor fuel economy	1. Poor driving habits 2. Stuck choke valve 3. Binding choke linkage 4. Stuck heat riser 5. Incorrect idle mixture 6. Defective accelerator pump 7. Air leaks 8. Plugged, loose or incorrect main metering jets 9. Improperly adjusted float or fuel level 10. Bent, misaligned or fuel-clogged float 11. Leaking float needle seat 12. Fuel leak 13. Accelerator pump discharge ball not seating properly 14. Incorrect main jets
Engine lacks high speed performance or power	1. Incorrect throttle linkage adjustment 2. Stuck or binding power piston 3. Defective accelerator pump 4. Air leaks 5. Incorrect float setting or fuel level 6. Dirty, plugged, worn or incorrect main metering jets or rods 7. Binding or sticking air valve 8. Brittle or cracked gaskets 9. Bent, incorrect or improperly adjusted secondary metering rods 10. Clogged fuel filter 11. Clogged air filter 12. Defective fuel pump

TROUBLESHOOTING FUEL INJECTION PROBLEMS

Each fuel injection system has its own unique components and test procedures, for which it is impossible to generalize. Refer to Chapter 4 of this Repair & Tune-Up Guide for specific test and repair procedures, if the vehicle is equipped with fuel injection.

TROUBLESHOOTING ELECTRICAL PROBLEMS

See Chapter 5 for service procedures

For any electrical system to operate, it must make a complete circuit. This simply means that the power flow from the battery must make a complete circle. When an electrical component is operating, power flows from the battery to the component, passes through the component causing it to perform its function (lighting a light bulb), and then returns to the battery through the ground of the circuit. This ground is usually (but not always) the metal part of the car or truck on which the electrical component is mounted.

Perhaps the easiest way to visualize this is to think of connecting a light bulb with two wires attached to it to the battery. If one of the two wires attached to the light bulb were attached to the negative post of the battery and the other were attached to the positive post of the battery, you would have a complete circuit. Current from the battery would flow to the light bulb, causing it to light, and return to the negative post of the battery.

The normal automotive circuit differs from this simple example in two ways. First, instead of having a return wire from the bulb to the battery, the light bulb returns the current to the battery through the chassis of the vehicle. Since the negative battery cable is attached to the chassis and the chassis is made of electrically conductive metal, the chassis of the vehicle can serve as a ground wire to complete the circuit. Secondly, most automotive circuits contain switches to turn components on and off as required.

Every complete circuit from a power source must include a component which is using the power from the power source. If you were to disconnect the light bulb from the wires and touch the two wires together (don't do this) the power supply wire to the component would be grounded before the normal ground connection for the circuit.

Because grounding a wire from a power source makes a complete circuit—less the required component to use the power—this phenomenon is called a short circuit. Common causes are: broken insulation (exposing the metal wire to a metal part of the car or truck), or a shorted switch.

Some electrical components which require a large amount of current to operate also have a relay in their circuit. Since these circuits carry a large amount of current, the thickness of the wire in the circuit (gauge size) is also greater. If this large wire were connected from the component to the control switch on the instrument panel, and then back to the component, a voltage drop would occur in the circuit. To prevent this potential drop in voltage, an electromagnetic switch (relay) is used. The large wires in the circuit are connected from the battery to one side of the relay, and from the opposite side of the relay to the component. The relay is normally open, preventing current from passing through the circuit. An additional, smaller, wire is connected from the relay to the control switch for the circuit. When the control switch is turned on, it grounds the smaller wire from the relay and completes the circuit. This closes the relay and allows current to flow from the battery to the component. The horn, headlight, and starter circuits are three which use relays.

It is possible for larger surges of current to pass through the electrical system of your car or truck. If this surge of current were to reach an electrical component, it could burn it out. To prevent this, fuses, circuit breakers or fusible links are connected into the current supply wires of most of the major electrical systems. When an electrical current of excessive power passes through the component's fuse, the fuse blows out and breaks the circuit, saving the component from destruction.

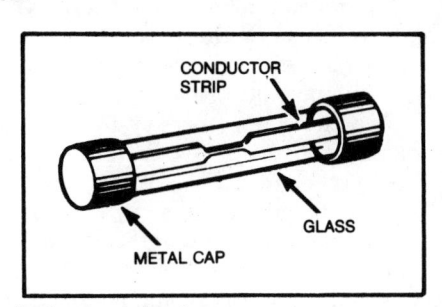

Typical automotive fuse

A circuit breaker is basically a self-repairing fuse. The circuit breaker opens the circuit the same way a fuse does. However, when either the short is removed from the circuit or the surge subsides, the circuit breaker resets itself and does not have to be replaced as a fuse does.

A fuse link is a wire that acts as a fuse. It is normally connected between the starter relay and the main wiring harness. This connection is usually under the hood. The fuse link (if installed) protects all the

TROUBLESHOOTING

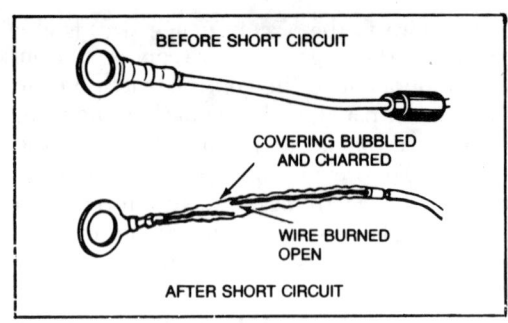

Most fusible links show a charred, melted insulation when they burn out

chassis electrical components, and is the probable cause of trouble when none of the electrical components function, unless the battery is disconnected or dead.

Electrical problems generally fall into one of three areas:
1. The component that is not functioning is not receiving current.
2. The component itself is not functioning.
3. The component is not properly grounded.

The electrical system can be checked with a test light and a jumper wire. A test light is a device that looks like a pointed screwdriver with a wire attached to it and has a light bulb in its handle. A jumper wire is a piece of insulated wire with an alligator clip attached to each end.

If a component is not working, you must follow a systematic plan to determine which of the three causes is the villain.
1. Turn on the switch that controls the inoperable component.
2. Disconnect the power supply wire from the component.
3. Attach the ground wire on the test light to a good metal ground.
4. Touch the probe end of the test light to the end of the power supply wire that was disconnected from the component. If the component is receiving current, the test light will go on.

NOTE: *Some components work only when the ignition switch is turned on.*

If the test light does not go on, then the problem is in the circuit between the battery and the component. This includes all the switches, fuses, and relays in the system. Follow the wire that runs back to the battery. The problem is an open circuit between the

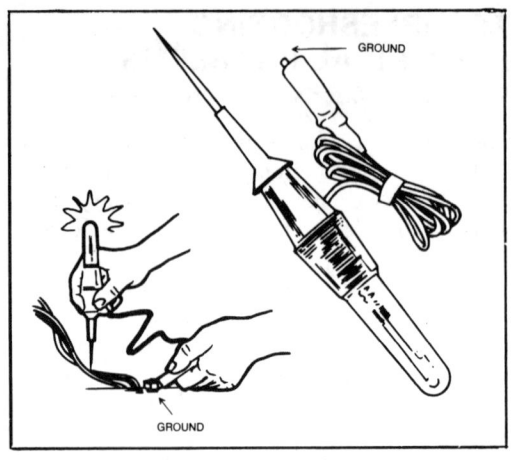

The test light will show the presence of current when touched to a hot wire and grounded at the other end

battery and the component. If the fuse is blown and, when replaced, immediately blows again, there is a short circuit in the system which must be located and repaired. If there is a switch in the system, bypass it with a jumper wire. This is done by connecting one end of the jumper wire to the power supply wire into the switch and the other end of the jumper wire to the wire coming out of the switch. If the test light lights with the jumper wire installed, the switch or whatever was bypassed is defective.

NOTE: *Never substitute the jumper wire for the component, since it is required to use the power from the power source.*

5. If the bulb in the test light goes on, then the current is getting to the component that is not working. This eliminates the first of the three possible causes. Connect the power supply wire and connect a jumper wire from the component to a good metal ground. Do this with the switch which controls the component turned on, and also the ignition switch turned on if it is required for the component to work. If the component works with the jumper wire installed, then it has a bad ground. This is usually caused by the metal area on which the component mounts to the chassis being coated with some type of foreign matter.

6. If neither test located the source of the trouble, then the component itself is defective. Remember that for any electrical system to work, all connections must be clean and tight.

TROUBLESHOOTING 149

Troubleshooting Basic Turn Signal and Flasher Problems
See Chapter 5 for service procedures

Most problems in the turn signals or flasher system can be reduced to defective flashers or bulbs, which are easily replaced. Occasionally, the turn signal switch will prove defective.

F = Front   R = Rear   ● = Lights off   ○ = Lights on

Condition	Possible Cause
Turn signals light, but do not flash	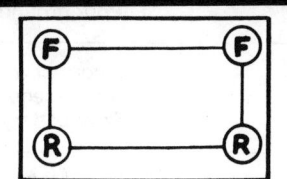 Defective flasher
No turn signals light on either side	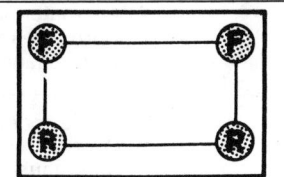 Blown fuse. Replace if defective. Defective flasher. Check by substitution. Open circuit, short circuit or poor ground.
Both turn signals on one side don't work	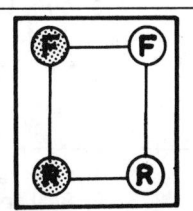 Bad bulbs. Bad ground in both (or either) housings.
One turn signal light on one side doesn't work	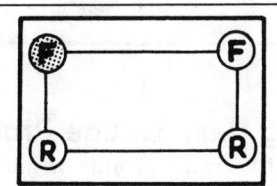 Defective bulb. Corrosion in socket. Clean contacts. Poor ground at socket.
Turn signal flashes too fast or too slowly	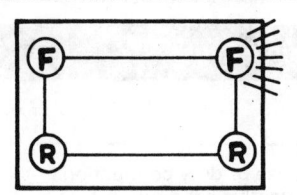 Check any bulb on the side flashing too fast. A heavy-duty bulb is probably installed in place of a regular bulb. Check the bulb flashing too slowly. A standard bulb was probably installed in place of a heavy-duty bulb. Loose connections or corrosion at the bulb socket.
Indicator lights don't work in either direction	 Check if the turn signals are working. Check the dash indicator lights. Check the flasher by substitution.
One indicator light doesn't light	 On systems with one dash indicator: See if the lights work on the same side. Often the filaments have been reversed in systems combining stoplights with taillights and turn signals. Check the flasher by substitution. On systems with two indicators: Check the bulbs on the same side. Check the indicator light bulb. Check the flasher by substitution.

TROUBLESHOOTING

Troubleshooting Lighting Problems
See Chapter 5 for service procedures

Condition	Possible Cause
One or more lights don't work, but others do	1. Defective bulb(s) 2. Blown fuse(s) 3. Dirty fuse clips or light sockets 4. Poor ground circuit
Lights burn out quickly	1. Incorrect voltage regulator setting or defective regulator 2. Poor battery/alternator connections
Lights go dim	1. Low/discharged battery 2. Alternator not charging 3. Corroded sockets or connections 4. Low voltage output
Lights flicker	1. Loose connection 2. Poor ground. (Run ground wire from light housing to frame) 3. Circuit breaker operating (short circuit)
Lights "flare"—Some flare is normal on acceleration—If excessive, see "Lights Burn Out Quickly"	High voltage setting
Lights glare—approaching drivers are blinded	1. Lights adjusted too high 2. Rear springs or shocks sagging 3. Rear tires soft

Troubleshooting Dash Gauge Problems

Most problems can be traced to a defective sending unit or faulty wiring. Occasionally, the gauge itself is at fault. See Chapter 5 for service procedures.

Condition	Possible Cause
COOLANT TEMPERATURE GAUGE	
Gauge reads erratically or not at all	1. Loose or dirty connections 2. Defective sending unit. 3. Defective gauge. To test a bi-metal gauge, remove the wire from the sending unit. Ground the wire for an instant. If the gauge registers, replace the sending unit. To test a magnetic gauge, disconnect the wire at the sending unit. With ignition ON gauge should register COLD. Ground the wire; gauge should register HOT.
AMMETER GAUGE—TURN HEADLIGHTS ON (DO NOT START ENGINE). NOTE REACTION	
Ammeter shows charge Ammeter shows discharge Ammeter does not move	1. Connections reversed on gauge 2. Ammeter is OK 3. Loose connections or faulty wiring 4. Defective gauge

TROUBLESHOOTING

Condition	Possible Cause

OIL PRESSURE GAUGE

Gauge does not register or is inaccurate	1. On mechanical gauge, Bourdon tube may be bent or kinked. 2. Low oil pressure. Remove sending unit. Idle the engine briefly. If no oil flows from sending unit hole, problem is in engine. 3. Defective gauge. Remove the wire from the sending unit and ground it for an instant with the ignition ON. A good gauge will go to the top of the scale. 4. Defective wiring. Check the wiring to the gauge. If it's OK and the gauge doesn't register when grounded, replace the gauge. 5. Defective sending unit.

ALL GAUGES

All gauges do not operate All gauges read low or erratically All gauges pegged	1. Blown fuse 2. Defective instrument regulator 3. Defective or dirty instrument voltage regulator 4. Loss of ground between instrument voltage regulator and frame 5. Defective instrument regulator

WARNING LIGHTS

Light(s) do not come on when ignition is ON, but engine is not started Light comes on with engine running	1. Defective bulb 2. Defective wire 3. Defective sending unit. Disconnect the wire from the sending unit and ground it. Replace the sending unit if the light comes on with the ignition ON. 4. Problem in individual system 5. Defective sending unit

Troubleshooting Clutch Problems

It is false economy to replace individual clutch components. The pressure plate, clutch plate and throwout bearing should be replaced as a set, and the flywheel face inspected, whenever the clutch is overhauled. See Chapter 6 for service procedures.

Condition	Possible Cause
Clutch chatter	1. Grease on driven plate (disc) facing 2. Binding clutch linkage or cable 3. Loose, damaged facings on driven plate (disc) 4. Engine mounts loose 5. Incorrect height adjustment of pressure plate release levers 6. Clutch housing or housing to transmission adapter misalignment 7. Loose driven plate hub
Clutch grabbing	1. Oil, grease on driven plate (disc) facing 2. Broken pressure plate 3. Warped or binding driven plate. Driven plate binding on clutch shaft
Clutch slips	1. Lack of lubrication in clutch linkage or cable (linkage or cable binds, causes incomplete engagement) 2. Incorrect pedal, or linkage adjustment 3. Broken pressure plate springs 4. Weak pressure plate springs 5. Grease on driven plate facings (disc)

TROUBLESHOOTING

Troubleshooting Clutch Problems (cont.)

Condition	Possible Cause
Incomplete clutch release	1. Incorrect pedal or linkage adjustment or linkage or cable binding 2. Incorrect height adjustment on pressure plate release levers 3. Loose, broken facings on driven plate (disc) 4. Bent, dished, warped driven plate caused by overheating
Grinding, whirring grating noise when pedal is depressed	1. Worn or defective throwout bearing 2. Starter drive teeth contacting flywheel ring gear teeth. Look for milled or polished teeth on ring gear.
Squeal, howl, trumpeting noise when pedal is being released (occurs during first inch to inch and one-half of pedal travel)	Pilot bushing worn or lack of lubricant. If bushing appears OK, polish bushing with emery cloth, soak lube wick in oil, lube bushing with oil, apply film of chassis grease to clutch shaft pilot hub, reassemble. NOTE: Bushing wear may be due to misalignment of clutch housing or housing to transmission adapter
Vibration or clutch pedal pulsation with clutch disengaged (pedal fully depressed)	1. Worn or defective engine transmission mounts 2. Flywheel run out. (Flywheel run out at face not to exceed 0.005") 3. Damaged or defective clutch components

Troubleshooting Manual Transmission Problems
See Chapter 6 for service procedures

Condition	Possible Cause
Transmission jumps out of gear	1. Misalignment of transmission case or clutch housing. 2. Worn pilot bearing in crankshaft. 3. Bent transmission shaft. 4. Worn high speed sliding gear. 5. Worn teeth or end-play in clutch shaft. 6. Insufficient spring tension on shifter rail plunger. 7. Bent or loose shifter fork. 8. Gears not engaging completely. 9. Loose or worn bearings on clutch shaft or mainshaft. 10. Worn gear teeth. 11. Worn or damaged detent balls.
Transmission sticks in gear	1. Clutch not releasing fully. 2. Burred or battered teeth on clutch shaft, or sliding sleeve. 3. Burred or battered transmission mainshaft. 4. Frozen synchronizing clutch. 5. Stuck shifter rail plunger. 6. Gearshift lever twisting and binding shifter rail. 7. Battered teeth on high speed sliding gear or on sleeve. 8. Improper lubrication, or lack of lubrication. 9. Corroded transmission parts. 10. Defective mainshaft pilot bearing. 11. Locked gear bearings will give same effect as stuck in gear.
Transmission gears will not synchronize	1. Binding pilot bearing on mainshaft, will synchronize in high gear only. 2. Clutch not releasing fully. 3. Detent spring weak or broken. 4. Weak or broken springs under balls in sliding gear sleeve. 5. Binding bearing on clutch shaft, or binding countershaft. 6. Binding pilot bearing in crankshaft. 7. Badly worn gear teeth. 8. Improper lubrication. 9. Constant mesh gear not turning freely on transmission mainshaft. Will synchronize in that gear only.

TROUBLESHOOTING 153

Condition	Possible Cause
Gears spinning when shifting into gear from neutral	1. Clutch not releasing fully. 2. In some cases an extremely light lubricant in transmission will cause gears to continue to spin for a short time after clutch is released. 3. Binding pilot bearing in crankshaft.
Transmission noisy in all gears	1. Insufficient lubricant, or improper lubricant. 2. Worn countergear bearings. 3. Worn or damaged main drive gear or countergear. 4. Damaged main drive gear or mainshaft bearings. 5. Worn or damaged countergear anti-lash plate.
Transmission noisy in neutral only	1. Damaged main drive gear bearing. 2. Damaged or loose mainshaft pilot bearing. 3. Worn or damaged countergear anti-lash plate. 4. Worn countergear bearings.
Transmission noisy in one gear only	1. Damaged or worn constant mesh gears. 2. Worn or damaged countergear bearings. 3. Damaged or worn synchronizer.
Transmission noisy in reverse only	1. Worn or damaged reverse idler gear or idler bushing. 2. Worn or damaged mainshaft reverse gear. 3. Worn or damaged reverse countergear. 4. Damaged shift mechanism.

TROUBLESHOOTING AUTOMATIC TRANSMISSION PROBLEMS

Keeping alert to changes in the operating characteristics of the transmission (changing shift points, noises, etc.) can prevent small problems from becoming large ones. If the problem cannot be traced to loose bolts, fluid level, misadjusted linkage, clogged filters or similar problems, you should probably seek professional service.

Transmission Fluid Indications

The appearance and odor of the transmission fluid can give valuable clues to the overall condition of the transmission. Always note the appearance of the fluid when you check the fluid level or change the fluid. Rub a small amount of fluid between your fingers to feel for grit and smell the fluid on the dipstick.

If the fluid appears:	It indicates:
Clear and red colored	Normal operation
Discolored (extremely dark red or brownish) or smells burned	Band or clutch pack failure, usually caused by an overheated transmission. Hauling very heavy loads with insufficient power or failure to change the fluid often result in overheating. Do not confuse this appearance with newer fluids that have a darker red color and a strong odor (though not a burned odor).
Foamy or aerated (light in color and full of bubbles)	1. The level is too high (gear train is churning oil) 2. An internal air leak (air is mixing with the fluid). Have the transmission checked professionally.
Solid residue in the fluid	Defective bands, clutch pack or bearings. Bits of band material or metal abrasives are clinging to the dipstick. Have the transmission checked professionally.
Varnish coating on the dipstick	The transmission fluid is overheating

TROUBLESHOOTING DRIVE AXLE PROBLEMS

First, determine when the noise is most noticeable.

Drive Noise: Produced under vehicle acceleration.

Coast Noise: Produced while coasting with a closed throttle.

Float Noise: Occurs while maintaining constant speed (just enough to keep speed constant) on a level road.

External Noise Elimination

It is advisable to make a thorough road test to determine whether the noise originates in the rear axle or whether it originates from the tires, engine, transmission, wheel bearings or road surface. Noise originating from other places cannot be corrected by servicing the rear axle.

ROAD NOISE

Brick or rough surfaced concrete roads produce noises that seem to come from the rear axle. Road noise is usually identical in Drive or Coast and driving on a different type of road will tell whether the road is the problem.

TIRE NOISE

Tire noise can be mistaken as rear axle noise, even though the tires on the front are at fault. Snow tread and mud tread tires or tires worn unevenly will frequently cause vibrations which seem to originate elsewhere; *temporarily, and for test purposes only,* inflate the tires to 40–50 lbs. This will significantly alter the noise produced by the tires, but will not alter noise from the rear axle. Noises from the rear axle will normally cease at speeds below 30 mph on coast, while tire noise will continue at lower tone as speed is decreased. The rear axle noise will usually change from drive conditions to coast conditions, while tire noise will not. Do not forget to lower the tire pressure to normal after the test is complete.

ENGINE/TRANSMISSION NOISE

Determine at what speed the noise is most pronounced, then stop in a quiet place. With the transmission in Neutral, run the engine through speeds corresponding to road speeds where the noise was noticed. Noises produced with the vehicle standing still are coming from the engine or transmission.

FRONT WHEEL BEARINGS

Front wheel bearing noises, sometimes confused with rear axle noises, will not change when comparing drive and coast conditions. While holding the speed steady, lightly apply the footbrake. This will often cause wheel bearing noise to lessen, as some of the weight is taken off the bearing. Front wheel bearings are easily checked by jacking up the wheels and spinning the wheels. Shaking the wheels will also determine if the wheel bearings are excessively loose.

REAR AXLE NOISES

Eliminating other possible sources can narrow the cause to the rear axle, which normally produces noise from worn gears or bearings. Gear noises tend to peak in a narrow speed range, while bearing noises will usually vary in pitch with engine speeds.

Noise Diagnosis

The Noise Is:	Most Probably Produced By:
1. Identical under Drive or Coast	Road surface, tires or front wheel bearings
2. Different depending on road surface	Road surface or tires
3. Lower as speed is lowered	Tires
4. Similar when standing or moving	Engine or transmission
5. A vibration	Unbalanced tires, rear wheel bearing, unbalanced driveshaft or worn U-joint
6. A knock or click about every two tire revolutions	Rear wheel bearing
7. Most pronounced on turns	Damaged differential gears
8. A steady low-pitched whirring or scraping, starting at low speeds	Damaged or worn pinion bearing
9. A chattering vibration on turns	Wrong differential lubricant or worn clutch plates (limited slip rear axle)
10. Noticed only in Drive, Coast or Float conditions	Worn ring gear and/or pinion gear

TROUBLESHOOTING

Troubleshooting Steering & Suspension Problems

Condition	Possible Cause
Hard steering (wheel is hard to turn)	1. Improper tire pressure 2. Loose or glazed pump drive belt 3. Low or incorrect fluid 4. Loose, bent or poorly lubricated front end parts 5. Improper front end alignment (excessive caster) 6. Bind in steering column or linkage 7. Kinked hydraulic hose 8. Air in hydraulic system 9. Low pump output or leaks in system 10. Obstruction in lines 11. Pump valves sticking or out of adjustment 12. Incorrect wheel alignment
Loose steering (too much play in steering wheel)	1. Loose wheel bearings 2. Faulty shocks 3. Worn linkage or suspension components 4. Loose steering gear mounting or linkage points 5. Steering mechanism worn or improperly adjusted 6. Valve spool improperly adjusted 7. Worn ball joints, tie-rod ends, etc.
Veers or wanders (pulls to one side with hands off steering wheel)	1. Improper tire pressure 2. Improper front end alignment 3. Dragging or improperly adjusted brakes 4. Bent frame 5. Improper rear end alignment 6. Faulty shocks or springs 7. Loose or bent front end components 8. Play in Pitman arm 9. Steering gear mountings loose 10. Loose wheel bearings 11. Binding Pitman arm 12. Spool valve sticking or improperly adjusted 13. Worn ball joints
Wheel oscillation or vibration transmitted through steering wheel	1. Low or uneven tire pressure 2. Loose wheel bearings 3. Improper front end alignment 4. Bent spindle 5. Worn, bent or broken front end components 6. Tires out of round or out of balance 7. Excessive lateral runout in disc brake rotor 8. Loose or bent shock absorber or strut
Noises (see also "Troubleshooting Drive Axle Problems")	1. Loose belts 2. Low fluid, air in system 3. Foreign matter in system 4. Improper lubrication 5. Interference or chafing in linkage 6. Steering gear mountings loose 7. Incorrect adjustment or wear in gear box 8. Faulty valves or wear in pump 9. Kinked hydraulic lines 10. Worn wheel bearings
Poor return of steering	1. Over-inflated tires 2. Improperly aligned front end (excessive caster) 3. Binding in steering column 4. No lubrication in front end 5. Steering gear adjusted too tight
Uneven tire wear (see "How To Read Tire Wear")	1. Incorrect tire pressure 2. Improperly aligned front end 3. Tires out-of-balance 4. Bent or worn suspension parts

TROUBLESHOOTING

HOW TO READ TIRE WEAR

The way your tires wear is a good indicator of other parts of the suspension. Abnormal wear patterns are often caused by the need for simple tire maintenance, or for front end alignment.

Excessive wear at the center of the tread indicates that the air pressure in the tire is consistently too high. The tire is riding on the center of the tread and wearing it prematurely. Occasionally, this wear pattern can result from outrageously wide tires on narrow rims. The cure for this is to replace either the tires or the wheels.

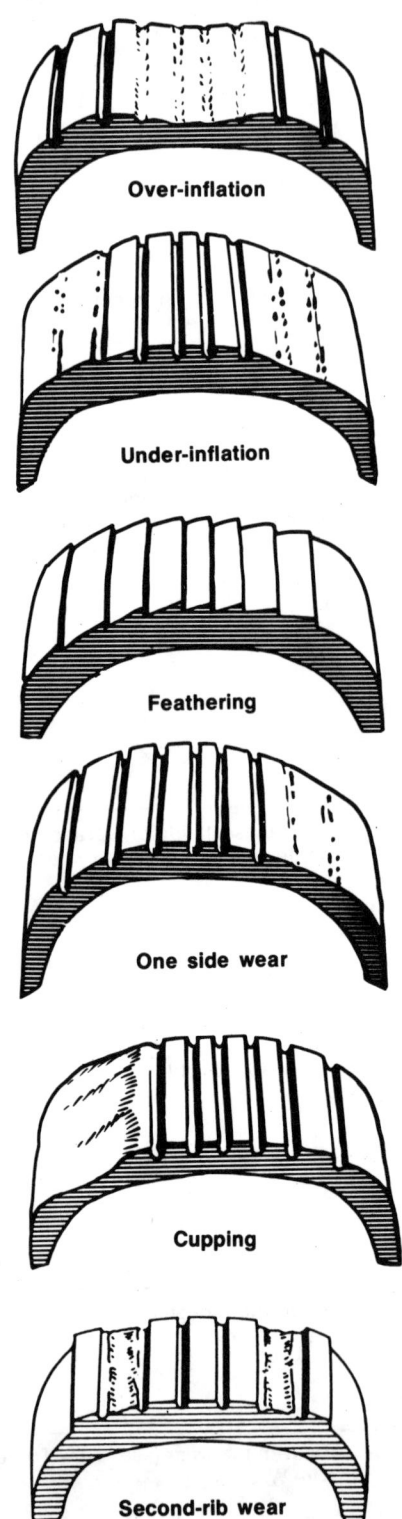

Over-inflation

This type of wear usually results from consistent under-inflation. When a tire is under-inflated, there is too much contact with the road by the outer treads, which wear prematurely. When this type of wear occurs, and the tire pressure is known to be consistently correct, a bent or worn steering component or the need for wheel alignment could be indicated.

Under-inflation

Feathering is a condition when the edge of each tread rib develops a slightly rounded edge on one side and a sharp edge on the other. By running your hand over the tire, you can usually feel the sharper edges before you'll be able to see them. The most common causes of feathering are incorrect toe-in setting or deteriorated bushings in the front suspension.

Feathering

When an inner or outer rib wears faster than the rest of the tire, the need for wheel alignment is indicated. There is excessive camber in the front suspension, causing the wheel to lean too much putting excessive load on one side of the tire. Misalignment could also be due to sagging springs, worn ball joints, or worn control arm bushings. Be sure the vehicle is loaded the way it's normally driven when you have the wheels aligned.

One side wear

Cups or scalloped dips appearing around the edge of the tread almost always indicate worn (sometimes bent) suspension parts. Adjustment of wheel alignment alone will seldom cure the problem. Any worn component that connects the wheel to the suspension can cause this type of wear. Occasionally, wheels that are out of balance will wear like this, but wheel imbalance usually shows up as bald spots between the outside edges and center of the tread.

Cupping

Second-rib wear is usually found only in radial tires, and appears where the steel belts end in relation to the tread. It can be kept to a minimum by paying careful attention to tire pressure and frequently rotating the tires. This is often considered normal wear but excessive amounts indicate that the tires are too wide for the wheels.

Second-rib wear

TROUBLESHOOTING

Troubleshooting Disc Brake Problems

Condition	Possible Cause
Noise—groan—brake noise emanating when slowly releasing brakes (creep-groan)	Not detrimental to function of disc brakes—no corrective action required. (This noise may be eliminated by slightly increasing or decreasing brake pedal efforts.)
Rattle—brake noise or rattle emanating at low speeds on rough roads, (front wheels only).	1. Shoe anti-rattle spring missing or not properly positioned. 2. Excessive clearance between shoe and caliper. 3. Soft or broken caliper seals. 4. Deformed or misaligned disc. 5. Loose caliper.
Scraping	1. Mounting bolts too long. 2. Loose wheel bearings. 3. Bent, loose, or misaligned splash shield.
Front brakes heat up during driving and fail to release	1. Operator riding brake pedal. 2. Stop light switch improperly adjusted. 3. Sticking pedal linkage. 4. Frozen or seized piston. 5. Residual pressure valve in master cylinder. 6. Power brake malfunction. 7. Proportioning valve malfunction.
Leaky brake caliper	1. Damaged or worn caliper piston seal. 2. Scores or corrosion on surface of cylinder bore.
Grabbing or uneven brake action—Brakes pull to one side	1. Causes listed under "Brakes Pull". 2. Power brake malfunction. 3. Low fluid level in master cylinder. 4. Air in hydraulic system. 5. Brake fluid, oil or grease on linings. 6. Unmatched linings. 7. Distorted brake pads. 8. Frozen or seized pistons. 9. Incorrect tire pressure. 10. Front end out of alignment. 11. Broken rear spring. 12. Brake caliper pistons sticking. 13. Restricted hose or line. 14. Caliper not in proper alignment to braking disc. 15. Stuck or malfunctioning metering valve. 16. Soft or broken caliper seals. 17. Loose caliper.
Brake pedal can be depressed without braking effect	1. Air in hydraulic system or improper bleeding procedure. 2. Leak past primary cup in master cylinder. 3. Leak in system. 4. Rear brakes out of adjustment. 5. Bleeder screw open.
Excessive pedal travel	1. Air, leak, or insufficient fluid in system or caliper. 2. Warped or excessively tapered shoe and lining assembly. 3. Excessive disc runout. 4. Rear brake adjustment required. 5. Loose wheel bearing adjustment. 6. Damaged caliper piston seal. 7. Improper brake fluid (boil). 8. Power brake malfunction. 9. Weak or soft hoses.

Troubleshooting Disc Brake Problems (cont.)

Condition	Possible Cause
Brake roughness or chatter (pedal pumping)	1. Excessive thickness variation of braking disc. 2. Excessive lateral runout of braking disc. 3. Rear brake drums out-of-round. 4. Excessive front bearing clearance.
Excessive pedal effort	1. Brake fluid, oil or grease on linings. 2. Incorrect lining. 3. Frozen or seized pistons. 4. Power brake malfunction. 5. Kinked or collapsed hose or line. 6. Stuck metering valve. 7. Scored caliper or master cylinder bore. 8. Seized caliper pistons.
Brake pedal fades (pedal travel increases with foot on brake)	1. Rough master cylinder or caliper bore. 2. Loose or broken hydraulic lines/connections. 3. Air in hydraulic system. 4. Fluid level low. 5. Weak or soft hoses. 6. Inferior quality brake shoes or fluid. 7. Worn master cylinder piston cups or seals.

Troubleshooting Drum Brakes

Condition	Possible Cause
Pedal goes to floor	1. Fluid low in reservoir. 2. Air in hydraulic system. 3. Improperly adjusted brake. 4. Leaking wheel cylinders. 5. Loose or broken brake lines. 6. Leaking or worn master cylinder. 7. Excessively worn brake lining.
Spongy brake pedal	1. Air in hydraulic system. 2. Improper brake fluid (low boiling point). 3. Excessively worn or cracked brake drums. 4. Broken pedal pivot bushing.
Brakes pulling	1. Contaminated lining. 2. Front end out of alignment. 3. Incorrect brake adjustment. 4. Unmatched brake lining. 5. Brake drums out of round. 6. Brake shoes distorted. 7. Restricted brake hose or line. 8. Broken rear spring. 9. Worn brake linings. 10. Uneven lining wear. 11. Glazed brake lining. 12. Excessive brake lining dust. 13. Heat spotted brake drums. 14. Weak brake return springs. 15. Faulty automatic adjusters. 16. Low or incorrect tire pressure.

TROUBLESHOOTING

Condition	Possible Cause
Squealing brakes	1. Glazed brake lining. 2. Saturated brake lining. 3. Weak or broken brake shoe retaining spring. 4. Broken or weak brake shoe return spring. 5. Incorrect brake lining. 6. Distorted brake shoes. 7. Bent support plate. 8. Dust in brakes or scored brake drums. 9. Linings worn below limit. 10. Uneven brake lining wear. 11. Heat spotted brake drums.
Chirping brakes	1. Out of round drum or eccentric axle flange pilot.
Dragging brakes	1. Incorrect wheel or parking brake adjustment. 2. Parking brakes engaged or improperly adjusted. 3. Weak or broken brake shoe return spring. 4. Brake pedal binding. 5. Master cylinder cup sticking. 6. Obstructed master cylinder relief port. 7. Saturated brake lining. 8. Bent or out of round brake drum. 9. Contaminated or improper brake fluid. 10. Sticking wheel cylinder pistons. 11. Driver riding brake pedal. 12. Defective proportioning valve. 13. Insufficient brake shoe lubricant.
Hard pedal	1. Brake booster inoperative. 2. Incorrect brake lining. 3. Restricted brake line or hose. 4. Frozen brake pedal linkage. 5. Stuck wheel cylinder. 6. Binding pedal linkage. 7. Faulty proportioning valve.
Wheel locks	1. Contaminated brake lining. 2. Loose or torn brake lining. 3. Wheel cylinder cups sticking. 4. Incorrect wheel bearing adjustment. 5. Faulty proportioning valve.
Brakes fade (high speed)	1. Incorrect lining. 2. Overheated brake drums. 3. Incorrect brake fluid (low boiling temperature). 4. Saturated brake lining. 5. Leak in hydraulic system. 6. Faulty automatic adjusters.
Pedal pulsates	1. Bent or out of round brake drum.
Brake chatter and shoe knock	1. Out of round brake drum. 2. Loose support plate. 3. Bent support plate. 4. Distorted brake shoes. 5. Machine grooves in contact face of brake drum (Shoe Knock). 6. Contaminated brake lining. 7. Missing or loose components. 8. Incorrect lining material. 9. Out-of-round brake drums. 10. Heat spotted or scored brake drums. 11. Out-of-balance wheels.

Troubleshooting Drum Brakes (cont.)

Condition	Possible Cause
Brakes do not self adjust	1. Adjuster screw frozen in thread. 2. Adjuster screw corroded at thrust washer. 3. Adjuster lever does not engage star wheel. 4. Adjuster installed on wrong wheel.
Brake light glows	1. Leak in the hydraulic system. 2. Air in the system. 3. Improperly adjusted master cylinder pushrod. 4. Uneven lining wear. 5. Failure to center combination valve or proportioning valve.

Appendix

General Conversion Table

Multiply by	To convert	To		
2.54	Inches	Centimeters		.3937
30.48	Feet	Centimeters		.0328
.914	Yards	Meters		1.094
1.609	Miles	Kilometers		.621
6.45	Square inches	Square cm.		.155
.836	Square yards	Square meters		1.196
16.39	Cubic inches	Cubic cm.		.061
28.3	Cubic feet	Liters		.0353
.4536	Pounds	Kilograms		2.2045
3.785	Gallons	Liters		.264
.068	Lbs./sq. in. (psi)	Atmospheres		14.7
.138	Foot pounds	Kg. m.		7.23
1.014	H.P. (DIN)	H.P. (SAE)		.9861
—	To obtain	From		Multiply by

Note: 1 cm. equals 10 mm.; 1 mm. equals .0394".

Conversion—Common Fractions to Decimals and Millimeters

Common Fractions	Decimal Fractions	Millimeters (approx.)	Common Fractions	Decimal Fractions	Millimeters (approx.)	Common Fractions	Decimal Fractions	Millimeters (approx.)
1/128	.008	0.20	11/32	.344	8.73	43/64	.672	17.07
1/64	.016	0.40	23/64	.359	9.13	11/16	.688	17.46
1/32	.031	0.79	3/8	.375	9.53	45/64	.703	17.86
3/64	.047	1.19	25/64	.391	9.92	23/32	.719	18.26
1/16	.063	1.59	13/32	.406	10.32	47/64	.734	18.65
5/64	.078	1.98	27/64	.422	10.72	3/4	.750	19.05
3/32	.094	2.38	7/16	.438	11.11	49/64	.766	19.45
7/64	.109	2.78	29/64	.453	11.51	25/32	.781	19.84
1/8	.125	3.18	15/32	.469	11.91	51/64	.797	20.24
9/64	.141	3.57	31/64	.484	12.30	13/16	.813	20.64
5/32	.156	3.97	1/2	.500	12.70	53/64	.828	21.03
11/64	.172	4.37	33/64	.516	13.10	27/32	.844	21.43
3/16	.188	4.76	17/32	.531	13.49	55/64	.859	21.83
13/64	.203	5.16	35/64	.547	13.89	7/8	.875	22.23
7/32	.219	5.56	9/16	.563	14.29	57/64	.891	22.62
15/64	.234	5.95	37/64	.578	14.68	29/32	.906	23.02
1/4	.250	6.35	19/32	.594	15.08	59/64	.922	23.42
17/64	.266	6.75	39/64	.609	15.48	15/16	.938	23.81
9/32	.281	7.14	5/8	.625	15.88	61/64	.953	24.21
19/64	.297	7.54	41/64	.641	16.27	31/32	.969	24.61
5/16	.313	7.94	21/32	.656	16.67	63/64	.984	25.00
21/64	.328	8.33						

Conversion—Millimeters to Decimal Inches

mm	*inches*	*mm*	*inches*	*mm*	*inches*	*mm*	*inches*	*mm*	*inches*
1	.039 370	31	1.220 470	61	2.401 570	91	3.582 670	210	8.267 700
2	.078 740	32	1.259 840	62	2.440 940	92	3.622 040	220	8.661 400
3	.118 110	33	1.299 210	63	2.480 310	93	3.661 410	230	9.055 100
4	.157 480	34	1.338 580	64	2.519 680	94	3.700 780	240	9.448 800
5	.196 850	35	1.377 949	65	2.559 050	95	3.740 150	250	9.842 500
6	.236 220	36	1.417 319	66	2.598 420	96	3.779 520	260	10.236 200
7	.275 590	37	1.456 689	67	2.637 790	97	3.818 890	270	10.629 900
8	.314 960	38	1.496 050	68	2.677 160	98	3.858 260	280	11.032 600
9	.354 330	39	1.535 430	69	2.716 530	99	3.897 630	290	11.417 300
10	.393 700	40	1.574 800	70	2.755 900	100	3.937 000	300	11.811 000
11	.433 070	41	1.614 170	71	2.795 270	105	4.133 848	310	12.204 700
12	.472 440	42	1.653 540	72	2.834 640	110	4.330 700	320	12.598 400
13	.511 810	43	1.692 910	73	2.874 010	115	4.527 550	330	12.992 100
14	.551 180	44	1.732 280	74	2.913 380	120	4.724 400	340	13.385 800
15	.590 550	45	1.771 650	75	2.952 750	125	4.921 250	350	13.779 500
16	.629 920	46	1.811 020	76	2.992 120	130	5.118 100	360	14.173 200
17	.669 290	47	1.850 390	77	3.031 490	135	5.314 950	370	14.566 900
18	.708 660	48	1.889 760	78	3.070 860	140	5.511 800	380	14.960 600
19	.748 030	49	1.929 130	79	3.110 230	145	5.708 650	390	15.354 300
20	.787 400	50	1.968 500	80	3.149 600	150	5.905 500	400	15.748 000
21	.826 770	51	2.007 870	81	3.188 970	155	6.102 350	500	19.685 000
22	.866 140	52	2.047 240	82	3.228 340	160	6.299 200	600	23.622 000
23	.905 510	53	2.086 610	83	3.267 710	165	6.496 050	700	27.559 000
24	.944 880	54	2.125 980	84	3.307 080	170	6.692 900	800	31.496 000
25	.984 250	55	2.165 350	85	3.346 450	175	6.889 750	900	35.433 000
26	1.023 620	56	2.204 720	86	3.385 820	180	7.086 600	1000	39.370 000
27	1.062 990	57	2.244 090	87	3.425 190	185	7.283 450	2000	78.740 000
28	1.102 360	58	2.283 460	88	3.464 560	190	7.480 300	3000	118.110 000
29	1.141 730	59	2.322 830	89	3.503 903	195	7.677 150	4000	157.480 000
30	1.181 100	60	2.362 200	90	3.543 300	200	7.874 000	5000	196.850 000

To change decimal millimeters to decimal inches, position the decimal point where desired on either side of the millimeter measurement shown and reset the inches decimal by the same number of digits in the same direction. For example, to convert 0.001 mm to decimal inches, reset the decimal behind the 1 mm (shown on the chart) to 0.001; change the decimal inch equivalent (0.039″ shown) to 0.000039″.

Tap Drill Sizes

National Fine or S.A.E.

Screw & Tap Size	*Threads Per Inch*	*Use Drill Number*
No. 5	44	37
No. 6	40	33
No. 8	36	29
No. 10	32	21
No. 12	28	15
¼	28	3
5/16	24	1
⅜	24	Q
7/16	20	W
½	20	29/64
9/16	18	33/64
⅝	18	37/64
¾	16	11/16
⅞	14	13/16
1⅛	12	1 3/64
1¼	12	1 11/64
1½	12	1 27/64

Tap Drill Sizes

National Coarse or U.S.S.

Screw & Tap Size	*Threads Per Inch*	*Use Drill Number*
No. 5	40	39
No. 6	32	36
No. 8	32	29
No. 10	24	25
No. 12	24	17
¼	20	8
5/16	18	F
⅜	16	5/16
7/16	14	U
½	13	27/64
9/16	12	31/64
⅝	11	17/32
¾	10	21/32
⅞	9	49/64
1	8	⅞
1⅛	7	63/64
1¼	7	1 7/64
1½	6	1 11/32

APPENDIX 163

Decimal Equivalent Size of the Number Drills

Drill No.	Decimal Equivalent	Drill No.	Decimal Equivalent	Drill No.	Decimal Equivalent
80	.0135	53	.0595	26	.1470
79	.0145	52	.0635	25	.1495
78	.0160	51	.0670	24	.1520
77	.0180	50	.0700	23	.1540
76	.0200	49	.0730	22	.1570
75	.0210	48	.0760	21	.1590
74	.0225	47	.0785	20	.1610
73	.0240	46	.0810	19	.1660
72	.0250	45	.0820	18	.1695
71	.0260	44	.0860	17	.1730
70	.0280	43	.0890	16	.1770
69	.0292	42	.0935	15	.1800
68	.0310	41	.0960	14	.1820
67	.0320	40	.0980	13	.1850
66	.0330	39	.0995	12	.1890
65	.0350	38	.1015	11	.1910
64	.0360	37	.1040	10	.1935
63	.0370	36	.1065	9	.1960
62	.0380	35	.1100	8	.1990
61	.0390	34	.1110	7	.2010
60	.0400	33	.1130	6	.2040
59	.0410	32	.1160	5	.2055
58	.0420	31	.1200	4	.2090
57	.0430	30	.1285	3	.2130
56	.0465	29	.1360	2	.2210
55	.0520	28	.1405	1	.2280
54	.0550	27	.1440		

Decimal Equivalent Size of the Letter Drills

Letter Drill	Decimal Equivalent	Letter Drill	Decimal Equivalent	Letter Drill	Decimal Equivalent
A	.234	J	.277	S	.348
B	.238	K	.281	T	.358
C	.242	L	.290	U	.368
D	.246	M	.295	V	.377
E	.250	N	.302	W	.386
F	.257	O	.316	X	.397
G	.261	P	.323	Y	.404
H	.266	Q	.332	Z	.413
I	.272	R	.339		

Anti-Freeze Chart

Temperatures Shown in Degrees Fahrenheit +32 is Freezing

Cooling System Capacity Quarts	\multicolumn{14}{c}{Quarts of ETHYLENE GLYCOL Needed for Protection to Temperatures Shown Below}
	1	2	3	4	5	6	7	8	9	10	11	12	13	14
10	+24°	+16°	+ 4°	−12°	−34°	−62°								
11	+25	+18	+ 8	− 6	−23	−47								
12	+26	+19	+10	0	−15	−34	−57°							
13	+27	+21	+13	+ 3	− 9	−25	−45							
14			+15	+ 6	− 5	−18	−34							
15			+16	+ 8	0	−12	−26							
16			+17	+10	+ 2	− 8	−19	−34	−52°					
17			+18	+12	+ 5	− 4	−14	−27	−42					
18			+19	+14	+ 7	0	−10	−21	−34	−50°				
19			+20	+15	+ 9	+ 2	− 7	−16	−28	−42				
20				+16	+10	+ 4	− 3	−12	−22	−34	−48°			
21				+17	+12	+ 6	0	− 9	−17	−28	−41			
22				+18	+13	+ 8	+ 2	− 6	−14	−23	−34	−47°		
23				+19	+14	+ 9	+ 4	− 3	−10	−19	−29	−40		
24				+19	+15	+10	+ 5	0	− 8	−15	−23	−34	−46°	
25				+20	+16	+12	+ 7	+ 1	− 5	−12	−20	−29	−40	−50°
26					+17	+13	+ 8	+ 3	− 3	− 9	−16	−25	−34	−44
27					+18	+14	+ 9	+ 5	− 1	− 7	−13	−21	−29	−39
28					+18	+15	+10	+ 6	+ 1	− 5	−11	−18	−25	−34
29					+19	+16	+12	+ 7	+ 2	− 3	− 8	−15	−22	−29
30					+20	+17	+13	+ 8	+ 4	− 1	− 6	−12	−18	−25

For capacities over 30 quarts divide true capacity by 3. Find quarts Anti-Freeze for the ⅓ and multiply by 3 for quarts to add.

For capacities under 10 quarts multiply true capacity by 3. Find quarts Anti-Freeze for the tripled volume and divide by 3 for quarts to add.

To Increase the Freezing Protection of Anti-Freeze Solutions Already Installed

Cooling System Capacity Quarts	\multicolumn{14}{c}{Number of Quarts of ETHYLENE GLYCOL Anti-Freeze Required to Increase Protection}
	\multicolumn{5}{c	}{From +20° F. to}	\multicolumn{5}{c	}{From +10° F. to}	\multicolumn{4}{c}{From 0° F. to}
	0°	−10°	−20°	−30°	−40°	0°	−10°	−20°	−30°	−40°	−10°	−20°	−30°	−40°
10	1¾	2¼	3	3½	3¾	¾	1½	2¼	2¾	3¼	¾	1½	2	2½
12	2	2¾	3½	4	4½	1	1¾	2½	3¼	3¾	1	1¾	2½	3¼
14	2¼	3¼	4	4¾	5½	1¼	2	3	3¾	4½	1	2	3	3½
16	2½	3½	4½	5¼	6	1¼	2½	3½	4¼	5¼	1¼	2¼	3¼	4
18	3	4	5	6	7	1½	2¾	4	5	5¾	1½	2½	3¾	4¾
20	3¼	4½	5¾	6¾	7½	1¾	3	4¼	5½	6½	1½	2¾	4¼	5¼
22	3½	5	6¼	7¼	8¼	1¾	3¼	4¾	6	7¼	1¾	3¼	4½	5½
24	4	5½	7	8	9	2	3½	5	6½	7½	1¾	3½	5	6
26	4¼	6	7½	8¾	10	2	4	5½	7	8¼	2	3¾	5½	6¾
28	4½	6¼	8	9½	10½	2¼	4¼	6	7½	9	2	4	5¾	7¼
30	5	6¾	8½	10	11½	2½	4½	6½	8	9½	2¼	4¼	6¼	7¾

Test radiator solution with proper hydrometer. Determine from the table the number of quarts of solution to be drawn off from a full cooling system and replace with undiluted anti-freeze, to give the desired increased protection. For example, to increase protection of a 22-quart cooling system containing Ethylene Glycol (permanent type) anti-freeze, from +20° F. to −20° F. will require the replacement of 6¼ quarts of solution with undiluted anti-freeze.

Index

A
Air cleaner, 4
Air conditioning, 8
Alternator, 29
Antifreeze, 164
Automatic transaxle
　Adjustment, 86
　Filter change, 86
　Removal and installation, 80
Axle
　Fluid recommendations, 10
　Lubricant level, 10
Axle shaft, 80

B
Ball joints, 89
Battery
　Jump starting, 15
　Maintenance, 29
Belt tension adjustment, 5
Body, 110
Brakes
　Bleeding, 100
　Caliper, 102
　Fluid level, 9
　Fluid recommendations, 9
　Front brakes, 102
　Master cylinder, 98
　Parking brake, 107
　Power booster, 100
　Rear brakes, 104
Bulbs, 79

C
Camber, 92
Camshaft and bearings, 38, 51
Capacities, 11
Carburetor
　Adjustment, 27, 68
　Overhaul, 69
　Replacement, 67
Caster, 92
Catalytic converter, 61
Charging system, 29
Clutch
　Adjustment, 85
　Replacement, 84
Control arm, 92
Cooling system, 40
Crankcase ventilation (PCV), 4
Crankshaft, 51
Cylinder head
　Reconditioning, 45
　Removal and installation, 33
　Torque sequence, 33

D
Dents and scratches, 114
Differential
　Fluid change, 10
Distributor, 28
Door panels, 111

E
Electrical
　Chassis, 72
　Engine, 28
Electronic ignition, 22
Emission controls, 61
Engine
　Camshaft, 38
　Cylinder head torque sequence, 33
　Design, 32
　Exhaust manifold, 35
　Front cover, 35
　Identification, 4
　Intake manifold, 34
　Oil recommendations, 12
　Pistons and rings, 38
　Rebuilding, 42
　Removal and installation, 32
　Rocker arm (or shaft), 34
　Specifications, 30
　Timing belt, 35
　Timing gears, 37
　Tune-up, 20
Evaporative canister, 4, 64
Exhaust manifold, 35

F
Fan belt adjustment, 5
Firing order, 28
Fluid level checks
　Battery, 10
　Coolant, 9
　Engine oil, 8
　Master cylinder, 9
　Differential, 10
　Steering gear, 10
　Transmission, 8
Front suspension
　Ball joints, 89
　Lower control arm, 92
　Springs, 91
　Struts, 89
　Wheel alignment, 92
Fuel filter, 12
Fuel pump, 66
Fuel system, 66
Fuel tank, 71
Fusible links, 79

INDEX

G
Gearshift linkage adjustment
    Automatic, 86
    Manual, 83, 84

H
Halfshaft, 80
Hand brake, 107
Headlights, 77, 78
Heater, 72
Hoses, 5
How to buy a used car, 17

I
Identification
    Vehicle, 3
    Engine, 4
    Transmission, 4
Idle speed and mixture, 27
Ignition switch, 96
Ignition timing, 24
Instrument cluster, 77
Intake manifold, 34

J
Jacking points, 14
Jump starting, 15

L
Light bulb specifications, 79
Lower control arm, 92
Lubrication
    Chassis, 12
    Differential, 10
    Engine, 39

M
Manifolds
    Intake, 34
    Exhaust, 35
Manual transaxle, 80
Master cylinder, 98
Model identification, 3

N
Neutral safety switch, 86

O
Oil and fuel recommendations, 12
Oil change, 13
Oil filter (engine), 13
Oil pan, 39
Oil pump, 39

P
Parking brake, 107
Pistons and rings
    Installation, 38, 52
    Positioning, 38, 52
PCV valve, 4
Power brakes, 100

R
Radiator, 41
Radio, 75
Rear axle, 94
Rear suspension, 93
Regulator, 29
Rear main oil seal, 39
Rings, 56
Rocker arm (or shaft), 34
Rust spots, 118

S
Safety notice, ii
Scratches and dents, 114
Serial number location, 3
Shock absorbers, 93
Spark plugs, 20
Specifications
    Brakes, 108
    Capacities, 11
    Crankshaft and connecting rod, 31
    General engine, 30
    Light bulb, 79
    Piston and ring, 30, 31
    Torque, 31
    Tune-up, 23
    Valve, 30
    Wheel alignment, 92
Speedometer cable, 78
Springs
    Front, 91
    Rear, 93
Starter, 29
Steering
    Linkage, 97
    Wheel, 95
Stripped threads, 43
Struts, 89

T
Thermostat, 41
Tie-rod, 97
Timing (ignition), 24
Tires, 11
Tools, 1
Towing, 14
Transaxle
    Automatic, 80
    Manual, 80
Troubleshooting, 127

Tune-up
    Procedures, 20
    Specifications, 23
Turn signal switch, 95

V

Valves
    Adjustment, 25
    Service, 34, 45
    Specifications, 30
Vehicle identification, 3

W

Water pump, 41
Wheel alignment, 92
Wheel bearings, 14
Wheel cylinders, 106
Windshield wipers
    Arm, 77
    Blade, 76
    Linkage, 77
    Motor, 76

Chilton's Repair & Tune-Up Guides

The complete line covers domestic cars, imports, trucks, vans, RV's and 4-wheel drive vehicles.

BOOK CODE	TITLE	BOOK CODE	TITLE
# 7163	Aries 81-82	# 5821	GTX 68-73
# 7032	Arrow Pick-Up 79-81	# 6980	Honda 73-80
# 6637	Aspen 76-78	# 6845	Horizon 78-80
# 5902	Audi 70-73	# 5912	International Scout 67-73
# 7028	Audi 4000/5000 77-81	# 5998	Jaguar 69-74
# 6337	Audi Fox 73-75	# 7136	Jeep CJ 1945-81
# 5807	Barracuda 65-72	# 6739	Jeep Wagoneer, Commando, Cherokee 66-79
# 6931	Blazer 69-80	# 6962	Jetta 1980
# 5576	BMW 59-70	# 6931	Jimmy 69-81
# 6844	BMW 70-79	# 7059	J-2000 1982
# 5821	Belvedere 68-73	# 5905	Le Mans 68-73
# 7027	Bobcat	# 7055	Lynx 81-82 inc. EXP & LN-7
# 7045	Camaro 67-81	# 6634	Maverick 70-77
# 6695	Capri 70-77	# 6981	Mazda 71-80
# 6963	Capri 79-80	# 7031	Mazda RX-7 79-81
# 7059	Cavalier 1982	# 6065	Mercedes-Benz 59-70
# 5807	Challenger 65-72	# 5907	Mercedes-Benz 68-73
# 7037	Challenger (Import) 71-81	# 6809	Mercedes-Benz 74-79
# 7041	Champ 78-81	# 7128	Mercury 68-71 all full sized models
# 6316	Charger 71-75	# 6696	Mercury Mid-Size 71-78 inc. T-Bird, Montego & Cougar
# 7162	Chevette 76-82 inc. diesel	# 6780	MG 61-81
# 7135	Chevrolet 68-81 all full size models	# 6973	Monarch 75-80
# 6936	Chevrolet/GMC Pick-Ups 70-80	# 6542	Mustang 65-73
# 6930	Chevrolet/GMC Vans 67-80	# 6812	Mustang II 74-78
# 7051	Chevy Luv 72-81 inc. 4wd	# 6963	Mustang 79-80
# 7056	Chevy Mid-Size 64-82 inc. El Camino, Chevelle, Laguna, Malibu & Monte Carlo	# 6841	Nova 69-79
# 6841	Chevy II 62-68	# 7049	Omega 81-82
# 7059	Cimarron 1982	# 6845	Omni 78-80
# 7049	Citation 80-81	# 5792	Opel 64-70
# 7037	Colt 71-81	# 6575	Opel 71-75
# 6634	Comet 70-77	# 6473	Pacer 75-76
# 6316	Coronet 71-75	# 5982	Peugeot 70-74
# 6691	Corvair 60-69 inc. Turbo	# 7049	Phoenix 81-82
# 6576	Corvette 53-62	# 7027	Pinto 71-80
# 6843	Corvette 63-79	# 6552	Plymouth 68-76 all full sized models
# 6933	Cutlass 70-80	# 6934	Plymouth Vans 67-80
# 6324	Dart 68-76	# 5822	Porche 69-73
# 6962	Dasher 74-80	# 7048	Porche 924 & 928 76-81 inc. Turbo
# 5790	Datsun 61-72	# 6962	Rabbit 75-80
# 6960	Datsun 73-80	# 6331	Ramcharger/Trail Duster 74-75
# 6932	Datsun Z & ZX 70-80	# 7163	Reliant 81-82
# 7050	Datsun Pick-Ups 70-81 inc. 4wd	# 5821	Roadrunner 68-73
# 6324	Demon 68-76	# 5988	Saab 69-75
# 6554	Dodge 68-77 all full sized models	# 7041	Sapporo 78-81
# 6486	Dodge Charger 67-70	# 5821	Satellite 68-73
# 6934	Dodge Vans 67-80	# 6962	Scirocco 75-80
# 6326	Duster 68-76	# 7049	Skylark 80-81
# 7055	Escort 81-82 inc. EXP & LN-7	# 6982	Subaru 70-80
# 6320	Fairlane 62-75	# 5905	Tempest 68-73
# 6965	Fairmont 78-80	# 6320	Torino 62-75
# 6485	Fiat 64-70	# 5795	Toyota 66-70
# 7042	Fiat 69-81	# 7043	Toyota Celica & Supra 71-81
# 6846	Fiesta 78-80	# 7036	Toyota Corolla, Carina, Tercel, Starlet 70-81
# 7046	Firebird 67-81	# 7044	Toyota Corona, Cressida, Crown, Mark II 70-81
# 7128	Ford 68-81 all full sized models	# 7035	Toyota Pick-Ups 70-81
# 7140	Ford Bronco 66-81	# 5910	Triumph 69-73
# 6983	Ford Courier 72-80	# 7162	T-1000 1982
# 6696	Ford Mid-Size 71-78 inc. Torino, Gran Torino, Ranchero, Elite & LTD II	# 6326	Valiant 68-76
# 6913	Ford Pick-Ups 65-80 inc. 4wd	# 5796	Volkswagen 49-71
# 6849	Ford Vans 61-82	# 6837	Volkswagen 70-81
# 6935	GM Sub-compact 71-81 inc. Vega, Monza, Astre, Sunbird, Starfire & Skyhawk	# 6637	Volare 76-78
		# 6529	Volvo 56-69
# 6937	Granada 75-80	# 7040	Volvo 70-80
# 5905	GTO 68-73	# 6965	Zephyr 78-80

Chilton's Repair & Tune-Up Guides are available at your local retailer or by mailing a check or money order for **$9.95** plus **$1.00** to cover postage and handling to:

Chilton Book Company
Dept. DM
Radnor, PA 19089

NOTE: When ordering be sure to include your name & address, book code & title.